Robin Miller
Quick Fix Meals

Robin Miller
Quick Fix Meals

200 simple, delicious recipes
to make mealtime easy

The Taunton Press

 The Taunton Press

The Taunton Press, Inc., 63 South Main Street, PO Box 5506, Newtown, CT 06470-5506
email: tp@taunton.com

Editor: Pamela Hoenig
Cover design: Chris Thompson, Archie Morterro
Interior design: Silverfish Design
Layout: Susan Fazekas, Lynne Phillips
Photographers: Jeremy Frechette, Mark Ferri

Library of Congress Cataloging-in-Publication Data
Miller, Robin, 1964-
  Quick fix meals : 200 simple, delicious recipes to make mealtime easy / Robin Miller.
       p. cm.
  Includes bibliographical references and index.
  ISBN-13: 978-1-56158-947-0 (alk. paper)
  ISBN-10: 1-56158-947-0 (alk. paper)
  1. Quick and easy cookery. I. Title.

TX833.5.M545 2007
641.5'55--dc22

                                            2006038782

Printed in the United States of America
10 9 8 7 6 5 4 3 2 1

This book is dedicated to my best buddies,
Darrin, Kyle, and Luke. You're my partners in the kitchen
and the light that shines over my cook-top
(and everywhere else)!

ACKNOWLEDGMENTS

Although it was eons ago, I'd like to thank *Family Circle* magazine for giving me my first "real" recipe writing and recipe testing experience. A simple part-time opportunity blossomed into a full-time job and I truly believe those *Family Circle* days provided the groundwork for all my magazine writing in the years that followed. Plus, it was *Family Circle* that first put me on the air—I appeared in a "Countdown to Thanksgiving" segment on the ABC evening news (local New York edition). Shortly thereafter (like one week!), I made Christmas cookies with Al Roker on the NBC *Today Show* and pancakes with Harry Smith on the CBS *Early Show.* Thanks for trusting me to pull it off.

A heartfelt thank you goes to Robyn Mait Levine for hunting me down when I lived in Princeton in the hopes of making me contributing editor and television spokesperson for *Health* magazine. We've worked together for over a decade, and, thanks to your efforts, I became a regular guest on the *Today Show, Early Show, The View,* CNN, and others. Aside from that, the friendship that grew has been more valuable than any media opportunity you created. I'd also like to thank Doug Crichton, Frances Largeman, and Lisa Delaney at *Health* for their continued interest in my writing and contributions to the magazine.

I'd like to thank the editors of *Cooking Light* magazine, the great folks at *Shape,* and Leslie Fink at weightwatchers.com, for all their years of continued support.

Food Network, where do I start? Bob Tuschman, your creative vision has made the show what it is, and I can't thank you enough for giving me a chance. You've got brilliant ideas and you consistently find new ways to make the show (and me) better. I'd also like to thank Brian Hatchett and Pat Guy for dotting all the i's, crossing all the t's, and putting everything together on paper. Lynn Brindell, thanks for your brilliant ideas for getting this book in front of the people who will find it helpful! It was a complete joy to work with you. Brooke Johnson, it's no wonder Food Network is a huge success with you at the helm. I'm proud to be working with you and Food Network on this book.

On to the amazing people who work on my show. If I took as much space as I wanted with these folks, we'd never get to the recipes! Natalie Gustafson, executive producer, director, and owner of Silver Plume Productions, thank you for being not only an amazing director, but a true friend and caring soul. You have the ability to get the most from people while making them feel warm and wonderful inside. And, to your loving husband, Matt Shapiro, thanks for your support and for sharing Natalie! Adrienne Hammel (senior producer) and Kirstin Moburg (associate producer), you both treat me like gold and I'm always overwhelmed by your generosity. Thanks for being my friends *and* the folks who keep me revved when I'm ready to collapse. Leslie Orlandini (culinary producer), I couldn't possibly do the show without you—you not only get all the food and utensils ready and in perfect order before each segment, you make my food come to life. I'm still not sure how you live without a microwave—maybe someday you'll teach me your secrets. Rebecca Flaste, you rock the prop world. You create the most beautiful settings and you always have a smile—both of which make the set shine. Kim Burns, thanks for getting those blonde highlights where everyone wants them and for making me look more presentable in my show kitchen than I've *ever* looked in my own kitchen! You've also become an amazing friend and confidant. Dan Anderson, Ron McCain, and Greg Peterson, you make me laugh all day long and, although you've got 50-pound cameras on your shoulders for 12 hours at a time, you never waver or wince. Plus, you like my cooking! Thanks for keeping me upbeat every minute of the day. Kate Rohmann (production manager), although I don't see you on the set every day, I realize you're working tirelessly in the office making sure everything runs smoothly. Your presence is always felt on set.

In the Food Network Kitchens, thank you Susan Stockton, vice president of culinary production. We've known each other forever and I'm thankful that this new venture has put us closer together. You've given me enormous support and encouragement and you've been my go-to person for culinary advice. I slept soundly at night knowing you had my back when dealing with the recipes in this book. Thank you Jill Novatt (senior culinary producer) and Lissa Wood (culinary producer) for working on all the recipes, including those that are making their debut in "still life" on the pages of this book. Thank you Jay Brooks, Bob Hoebee, and Rob Bleifer for styling the food so beautifully my mouth waters with every shot. And, speaking of those gorgeous food pictures, thank you, Mark Ferri, for your skill behind the camera.

Lauren Mueller, you're a PR dynamo. Thanks for showing up at the crack of dawn (or earlier) to keep me company in the Green Room. Who needs coffee when you've got that brilliant smile waiting for me? I look forward to many more mornings with you.

I want to thank my agent, Debra Goldstein, for her tireless efforts and stamina. For someone who must sleep as little as I do, you always present undeniable energy and a bright, positive face. Thanks for holding my hand through every step of this process. I look forward to learning more from you as we continue to push forward.

To my editor, Pam Hoenig, you've made this book a shining star. I truly enjoyed your input and ideas and I know that you worked diligently on every syllable on every page. It shows and the readers will notice it, too. Also at Taunton, I'd like to thank marketing director, Melissa Possick, for her marketing and publicity efforts and publisher, Jim Childs, for making this book come to life. Thank you, Wendi Mijal, for managing the photography; Chris Thompson, for your amazing art direction; Carol Singer, for managing the design of the book; and Lynne Phillips, for making sure it all got done. Jeremy Frechette, thanks for a fun day of picture-taking in the kitchen! You kept me smiling in an effort to get the "best shot" for the cover. Katie Benoit, thanks for getting me to and from the places I needed to be and for handling all those other behind-the-scenes jobs that make this "machine" run so smoothly. Thank you, Kevin Hamric at Taunton, and Rose Marie Morse, Katy Keiffer, and Kate Morgan at Morse Partners, for getting this book into the homes of people starving for Quick Fix solutions to everyday meals.

To my parents, Dollie and Frank, thanks for always watching my show (even the reruns, then pretending you haven't seen them before) and for getting everyone within a 2,000-mile radius do the same. Dad, how do you get those guys in the locker room to put my show on instead of ESPN—on *Saturday* mornings? You must have some serious pull.

To my in-laws, June and Frank, thank you for your endless support and encouragement. In the early days of shooting, I was able to film my show knowing that the best caregivers in the world were watching my two little boys. I worked with a clear head, confident that Kyle and Luke were in good hands, and every night when I called you told me to stay focused and do my best because "the boys are fine." Thanks to you, I was able to give it my all.

Now a very special thanks to my three main men. Of course, I couldn't do any of this without the support of my husband, Darrin. Our life is crazy and, although we love the chaos, it's nice to hunker down for some sane time and there's no other person I'd rather do that with. You're a pillar of strength yet amazingly calm. Thankfully, some of that is rubbing off on me. Kyle and Luke, my two remarkable sons, thanks for being the best little boys on the planet. You add a burst of sunshine to every waking moment. You light up my days and, truth is, my work life pales in comparison to a day at the zoo with you.

CONTENTS

THE QUICK FIX way

Got an hour on the weekend? If you're like me, that's about all you have. But get this—spend that hour in the kitchen having fun and prepping meals and you can enjoy weeknight meals in a flash. What's "a flash" in "Robin-speak"? How does 15 to 20 minutes grab you? I bet that sounds pretty good after a long, hard day. Plus, since you're only spending an hour in the kitchen, the rest of the weekend is wide open! I'm thinking zoo, bike riding, playground, reading, shopping, maybe a little laundry.

Like you, I've got a crazy life, so I make cooking my outlet, the UNcrazy part of my routine. Have you ever thought this: "I want my family to enjoy a healthy, home-cooked meal, but today was so hectic I can't imagine pulling it all together"? I know I have. Here's the good news. I've developed a host of ways to take the stress out of making dinner. The icing on the cake? Dinner is fast *and* delicious *and* nutritious. Follow my simple strategies for meal-planning and healthful, mouthwatering weeknight meals will be a breeze (as for the rest of your crazy life, you're on your own!). Here's the deal: spend an hour on the weekend (or less in some cases) and you can enjoy scrumptious weeknight meals in a fraction of the time it would take to start from scratch. Some recipes take under 20 minutes, thanks to a little advance planning. But there are also recipes with somewhat longer cooking times (I'll always keep your prep time to the bare minimum), simmering on the stove-top or baking in the oven, which will allow you to get a few errands done, put in a load of laundry, or just kick back and take a breath for the first time that day.

Until now, quick and healthful were mutually exclusive mealtime goals. Not anymore. I'm a nutritionist, so I always include a healthy spin in my cooking. If you follow my recipes, you'll not only enjoy fantastic meals fast, you can savor them without guilt. When cooking and writing recipes, I try to stick to whole grains, lean meats, skinless turkey and chicken, fish and shellfish, and beans and legumes, and try to include vegetables, fruits, nuts, and seeds whenever I can. As well, I like my meals to have a healthy balance of complex carbohydrates, lean protein, and healthy fats, while keeping saturated fat and sodium in check. Throughout the book, I give you the choice to use low-fat or non-fat ingredients so you can keep calories and fat within reason. As far as I'm concerned, your palate, not your arteries, should be doing backflips when you eat. Follow my lead and I'll make it easy for you to get delicious, nutritious meals on the weeknight table, from family classics to new creations inspired by a world of mouthwatering flavors.

I've also written these recipes to help you in your meal planning. Each recipe tells you the total cooking time, prep time, active cooking time, and walk-away time. When appropriate, you'll also find a "resting" time (for some meats, casseroles, and desserts that need to settle a bit before being cut into). That way, when planning your meals, side dishes, and desserts, you won't be confronted with any unexpected delays! The total cooking time is the time from kitchen arrival to fork-in-mouth. That time is broken out into prep time, the time it takes to get your ingredients ready (shortened by stocking your Quick Fix Pantry and Freezer!) and active cooking time, or the amount of time you'll actually be needed in the kitchen for hands-on things like stirring, flipping, and seasoning. In many cases, I've also provided walk-away time, which is your ticket to freedom. For example, if a dish gets baked for 20 minutes, that's your chance to go read a magazine, throw a ball to your kids, or take a shower! Armed with all this information, you can make mealtime decisions with ease.

THE QUICK FIX KITCHEN

I'm no magician. My trick for getting weeknight meals on the table in a flash is my strategically stocked pantry, refrigerator, and freezer. Notice I didn't say "well-stocked." In the Quick Fix Kitchen it's not the quantity but the quality that matters. In this chapter you'll find my list of ten pantry items I can't live without, as well as other ingredients that help.

Your freezer is an important tool in the Quick Fix Kitchen and the section Freezer Magic is filled with useful tips and suggestions for using it to the max. For example, when roasting vegetables, roast a bunch of them, then freeze the leftovers in separate plastic bags or resealable containers. Do the same thing when you're grilling—if you're going to the effort to grill pork or steak, why not throw extras on the barbie? Then you can enjoy steak fajitas or pulled pork sandwiches later that week or month! I'll also give you five quick-simmer sauces that freeze beautifully and can be defrosted at a moment's notice and paired with your choice of meat, chicken, fish, vegetables, rice, or pasta.

IN THE BAG: MEAL KITS FOR MEALS IN MOMENTS

My number one strategy? Prepping meals in advance. I'm the queen of prepping. When I've got time on the weekend, I grab a bunch of ingredients and get them ready for weeknight meals. Come dinnertime on a hectic weekday, I'm able to assemble a complete meal in minutes. I chop vegetables; precook chicken, turkey, and beef; wash and chop herbs; and precook pasta and rice so I don't have to do it at 5 PM on Wednesday. I even prep my sons' preschool lunches so I'm not crazed on school mornings (until that first cup of coffee, I'm a little slow around the stove!). Let's face it, at the end of a long day, who feels like slaving over a cutting board? Knowing you've prepped ingredients in advance takes the pressure off dinner and, trust me, you'll have fun putting everything together with ease.

Once the prep work is done, I make meals "In the Bag," meaning I prepare ingredients for complete meals, then place them in separate plastic bags. For example, when making Seafood Pomodoro with Linguine (page 26), I put the marinara sauce in one bag and the cooked linguine in another, then I refrigerate the bags until later in the week. Just before dinner, I simply unzip the bags and reheat the linguine in the sauce. Dinner is served in less than 10 minutes! Some nights dinner's ready so fast, I hardly have time to change into "comfy" clothes! I call these "Meal Kits" because, since all the prep work is done in advance, weeknights' meals just need assembly. Add a simple side dish and dinner is "In the Bag."

MORPH IT: ONE RECIPE, MANY MEALS

My "morph" strategy means to take one ingredient and turn it into several different dishes during the week. I don't mean a roasted chicken that turns into chicken soup and chicken salad (OK, I do mean that and I'll give you a recipe for the best darn roasted chicken you've ever tasted). But I explore beyond your basic chicken with delicious dishes that transform into completely different meals the second (or third) time around. For example, my Grilled Chicken with Tangy Tomato Ragout and Melted Swiss on the weekend turns into Turkey Bolognese over Rigatoni one night, Shrimp Fra Diavolo over Linguine another night, then Pan-Seared Pork Chops with Tomato Chutney at the end of the week. Thanks to a little time spent on the weekend, your weeknight meals will be ready in just minutes.

DINNER EXPRESS

OK, Jeff Gordon, if the previous chapters weren't fast enough to inspire you, read on. This chapter promises meals on the table in about 20 minutes with no cheating involved. It *is* possible to create homemade meals during the week in just minutes. I rely heavily on my Quick Fix Kitchen to pull ingredients from the pantry at will. You might want to make sure you've got your pantry stocked and ready to race to the finish line during the week.

SIMPLE SIDES

Thanks to convenience items at the grocery store, side dishes can be ready in less time than it takes to preheat the oven. Prechopped and shredded fresh vegetables, frozen vegetable combinations (beyond peas and carrots), bagged lettuce mixes, sliced and chopped fruits, and prepared salsas, sauces, chutneys, and marinades are a Quick Fix cook's best friend. If you think I don't regularly purchase these convenience products because I'm a "food writer," think again. I guarantee you'd find at least ten convenience items in my fridge or pantry right now.

If you're thinking, "Some nights, I'm lucky to get the main course on the table, now you want me to make a side dish?" read on. I take vegetables, fruits, grains, and other ingredients and create unique combinations of flavors and colors that will jazz up any weeknight meal. Since the ingredients are widely available and super convenient, these recipes will make it to the dinner table with ease.

SWEETS IN A HURRY

Everyone who knows me knows I have a sweet tooth. Just because it's Tuesday doesn't mean I don't want cake! That's why my dessert strategy is two-fold: either it comes together fast using a few simple ingredients, or I prep ingredients in advance so I can put everything together quickly during the week. For example, to make my super-moist Banana-Raspberry Bread, I mix the dry ingredients and wet ingredients separately, bag them, and then just mix and bake during the week. It's a wonderful strategy for all kinds of cakes, muffins, quick breads, and cookies. While you're enjoying dinner, you know something sweet and wonderful is just around the corner!

MIX AND MATCH

Now that you know my strategies, take advantage of the information and mix and match them to fit your lifestyle. For example, make a big batch of chili or your favorite tomato sauce and save leftovers to use in the Dinner Express chapter. This gives you a head start on meals that are already a snap to prepare. Turn Simple Sides into complete meals by adding a protein (chicken, turkey, fish, shellfish, pork tenderloin, lean steak, or tofu). Freeze leftover Morph It ingredients in separate plastic bags and containers and use them as Meal Kits down the road. Double your favorite Dinner Express recipes and freeze leftovers for super-fast dinners months away. Or create dessert Meal Kits by prepping the ingredients and refrigerating or freezing them until you're ready to assemble the sweet treat.

All these strategies work incredibly well together and once you've got the whole system down, your meal planning will become a fine-tuned, delicious machine.

What's left to do now? Get cooking!

1

The
QUICK FIX
KITCHEN
fabulous meals fast

"A STRATEGICALLY-STOCKED KITCHEN CAN GUARANTEE IT—
Who needs TAKEOUT?"

Think of your Quick Fix Kitchen as your mealtime buddy, your wingman. A strategically stocked kitchen (pantry, refrigerator, and freezer) is the key to putting together fast, fabulous meals. It can almost guarantee pain-free meal prep. With a friend like that, who needs take-out?

STOCKING THE QUICK FIX KITCHEN

Let's start with the pantry. Your Quick Fix shelves should be overflowing with items you use on a regular basis: pasta, rice, seasonings, sauces (that don't need refrigeration), condiments, oils and cooking sprays, vinegars, spices and spice blends, and replacements for often-used ingredients that need to go into the refrigerator once they're opened. Handy pantry items put you just minutes away from feasting on dinner.

On to the fridge. No surprise, the concept is the same as the pantry—load up your shelves and drawers with necessary items. Choose items such as fresh meats, fish, and poultry; cheeses; fresh vegetables; bottled sauces, pestos, and condiments; chopped produce and salad bar items that can streamline meal preparation. Store the most frequently used items up front and tuck other items in back. Every other week or so, switch things around so the food in the back of the fridge gets remembered and used (remember that hoisin sauce?). This will also help ensure variety on the table!

FREEZER MAGIC

Your freezer is your ally for weeknight meals; it's not just for leftovers. Sure, leftover meals can be quickly thawed and reheated in the microwave for home-cooked dinners in a snap but the freezer's value goes beyond that.

PREP IT AND FORGET IT (UNTIL YOU NEED IT)

When you freeze chopped onions, carrots, bell peppers, celery, leeks, and florets of broccoli and cauliflower in 1- to 2-cup measurements, you can pull them out any night of the week and add them to a meal or side dish. It's as basic as this—when you're chopping onions for a recipe, simply chop extra and freeze in single-meal portions you're likely to use. Do the same with other vegetables and fruits. When you're ready to make a sauce, roasted dish, stir-fry, or side dish, pull the prepped ingredients straight from the freezer and get cracking on dinner! There's no need to thaw chopped vegetables and fruits before cooking.

When roasting and grilling, plan ahead and cook more than you need. Once foods like steak, chicken, pork, and vegetables are cooked, let them come to room temperature, then freeze in plastic containers or freezer bags. You can also slice meats, poultry, and vegetables into thin slices or cubes and freeze them in 1- to 2-cup measurements for future meals. Thaw overnight in the refrigerator or in the microwave for a few minutes on LOW before reheating or adding to new meals.

PRECOOK LIKE THE PROS DO FOR FAST ASSEMBLY

I also cook large batches of rice and pasta so I can freeze leftovers. The truth is, some nights waiting for a pot of water to boil isn't an option because it simply takes too long. To freeze rice and pasta, store in freezer bags or plastic containers in amounts that make sense for your family. There's no need to thaw rice or pasta before using—simply add to hot sauces or reheat in the microwave.

REHEAT AND EAT

Casseroles are a friendly addition to any freezer because they simply need baking or reheating—no additional prep is required. The best casseroles for freezing are things like baked ziti, lasagna, shepherd's pie, and macaroni and cheese. Make more than you need the next time you're preparing a casserole and freeze the leftovers in convenient serving portions for next-to-instant meals. When you're ready to reheat, simply thaw leftovers in the refrigerator or microwave and then reheat in a preheated 350°F oven until warm (15 to 20 minutes). You can also reheat portions in the microwave for a few minutes on HIGH.

10 PANTRY ITEMS I LIKE TO HAVE AROUND

1. **Low-fat sour cream, yogurt, and/or cream cheese**

2. **Shredded reduced-fat cheese (cheddar, Monterey Jack)**

3. **Herb seasoning blends (such as garlic-and-herb, lemon-and-herb, Old Bay, mesquite)**

4. **Flavored oils (such as garlic, roasted red pepper, basil)**

5. **Roasted nuts and soy nuts**

6. **Canned soup (tomato, chicken, clam chowder make excellent bases for sauces)**

7. **Prepared Asian sauces (black bean, hoisin, plum, oyster, ponzu)**

8. **Canned beans (white, red, pink, black, navy, chickpeas)**

9. **Quick-cooking oats**

10. **Dried mushrooms (porcini, shiitake, or any combination of wild mushrooms)**

SENSIBLE AND SAFE FREEZER STORAGE

When freezing leftovers, be sure to portion the food so you don't have to thaw more than you plan to use or eat. For example, freeze meats, fish, and chicken in 1- to 1¼-pound portions that are common for many four-serving recipes. Freeze sauces in 1- to 2-cup measurements. Freeze leftover casseroles and baked dishes in individual portions so you can just pop them in the microwave for a quick, single-serving lunch, dinner, or snack for a hungry teenager!

To avoid freezer burn, make sure you press all the air from the freezer bags and tightly seal the lids on plastic containers. When freezing meats and poultry in plastic wrap (instead of freezer bags), cover the plastic with aluminum foil for extra protection. My favorite storage items are plastic freezer bags (true space-savers) and resealable plastic containers. Most foods, from fruits and vegetables to meats and poultry, will last from three to six months in the freezer without suffering in quality or flavor. I like to stick to a three-month maximum to ensure that's the case. Make sure you label and date all freezer items so you know what you have. I like to keep a "freezer diary" taped to the outside of the freezer; it helps me plan meals. Once I pull an item out, I simply cross it off the list.

USE THAT MICROWAVE

The microwave has an important role in the Quick Fix Kitchen. Use it to reheat leftovers and precooked rice and pasta, thaw meats and poultry, melt butter for recipes, steam vegetables, and soften hardened brown sugar. But think outside the microwave box. I like to give firm vegetables such as sweet potatoes, regular potatoes, and winter squash a head start in the microwave to soften them a bit before roasting in the oven—this truly cuts cooking time (about 20 minutes) and you still get a deep roasted flavor. Whole white and sweet potatoes, and halved and seeded winter squashes (such as butternut, acorn, and spaghetti) take just 5 minutes on HIGH to start to soften. Wrap all vegetables in plastic wrap or place in plastic containers before microwaving.

10 PANTRY ITEMS I AM NEVER WITHOUT

1. Olives (especially stuffed olives and Greek olives, such as kalamata)

2. Jarred roasted red peppers

3. Toasted sesame oil

4. Flour tortillas and/or corn tortillas (store in the freezer)

5. Canned diced tomatoes

6. Cooking spray (olive oil and butter flavor)

7. Reduced-sodium broth (chicken, beef, vegetable)

8. Dried herbs and spices (thyme, oregano, bay leaves, chili powder, ground cumin, curry powder, cinnamon, nutmeg)

9. Elbow and other small-shaped macaroni (they cook fast!)

10. Quick-cooking brown, white, and jasmine rice and couscous (they cook even faster than elbow macaroni!)

It's best to chop fresh herbs just before using

them in a dish. So, for example, if a recipe calls for chopped fresh parsley or cilantro (typically added at the end of the cooking time), chop them while the dish is cooking. The way to shave time off the meal prep is to wash fresh herbs when you get home from the grocery store. Simply rinse them, wrap in paper towels, and refrigerate until ready to use. You can also store cleaned fresh herbs standing up in 1 to 2 inches of water in a small vase or jar in the refrigerator. At mealtime, you can just grab the leaves and get chopping (or snipping with scissors).

What about those nights when I realize I've forgotten to take the ground turkey breast out of the freezer to thaw? No big deal—the microwave thaws like magic. It typically takes 1¼ pounds of frozen meat 4 to 5 minutes on LOW to thaw. If it's not thawed at that point, I continue to cook on LOW, checking every minute or so, to make sure the meat is thawed but not cooked.

I can't envision a Morph It or Meal Kit recipe that could exist without taking advantage of the microwave for thawing and reheating—either the individual ingredients or the whole meal. Simply thaw for a few minutes on LOW and then reheat for a few minutes on HIGH. The recipes in this book give you the option for cooking, thawing, and reheating all types of main dishes, leftovers, prepped ingredients, and side dishes in the microwave.

The microwave helps in other ways, too. Need a quick grilled cheese for a hungry toddler? Toast the bread in the toaster before slamming cheese between the slices and melting it in the microwave (my babysitter May taught me that). Do the same thing for quesadillas, enchiladas, and egg rolls. Simply assemble all your ingredients inside tortillas, wonton skins, or egg roll wrappers, roll up, wrap in plastic or paper towels, and microwave for about 1 minute, until the cheese melts. You can also melt cheese and salsa together to pour over tortilla chips—instant nachos!

When I'm in a mad rush at the end of the day, I often get my pasta water hot in the microwave before transferring it to a large saucepan. Just 3 to 4 minutes on HIGH usually does the trick; it cuts several minutes off the time it takes to bring the water to a boil. Depending on how fast your stove is, this could be a time saver.

COOKWARE COUNTS

Believe it or not, your cookware can help make mealtime easier. I love stove-top grill pans and griddles. The grill pans cook with very little fat, preheat lightning fast, provide grill marks, and there's no coal to light or outdoor grill to tend to. Because they get super hot, meals are ready in a flash. Stove-top griddles are awesome because they afford lots of space, so you can cook big batches of food at one time (2 pounds of chicken, 8 quesadillas, 6 sandwiches, etc.).

SHOP SMART

I can sum up my grocery-shopping strategy in two words: be efficient. Write a shopping list and stick to it. Start your list early in the week and keep adding to it as you think of items. That way, you won't get home to find out you have two drops of milk or a half a spoonful of peanut butter left. Regarding supermarket layout, most stores put the fresh produce, meats, fish, poultry, and dairy products around the perimeter of the store. The "dry goods" fill up the center aisles. Hit the core aisles first and save the perishable, refrigerated, and frozen items for last (so they stay cold).

Look for prepped ingredients at the supermarket. I often buy shredded carrots, coleslaw mix, chopped garlic, bagged washed lettuce, shredded or grated cheese, frozen mixed vegetables (such as peeled pearl onions, sliced green peppers, and chopped onions), pestos and salsas, halved melons, peeled and cored pineapple, and so on. I welcome any help I can get and you should, too. Plan your weekly meals in advance, follow your list, and you can enjoy Quick Fix Shopping before devouring your Quick Fix Meals.

FIVE SIMPLE SAUCES THAT WILL SAVE YOUR LIFE

Bottled sauces are available in many markets from the little bodega on the corner to the supercenter grocery. That's great because prepared sauces are the quintessential time savers of meal prep. The problem is, when you relegate dinner to a mass-produced (or even semimass-produced) sauce, you have little control over what goes into it. More often than not, that means there's more salt than you need and fewer vegetables than you want! When I take the time to make sauces from scratch (about once every two weeks), I make big batches and freeze the leftovers in 1- to 2-cup measurements. When I open the freezer, the homemade sauces are ready for me. Once thawed (in the fridge or microwave), rich homemade sauces jazz up all kinds of meat, fish, poultry, vegetable, pasta, and rice dishes in just minutes. Do the work *once* and reap the rewards several times over.

On pages 12–15, you'll find my five favorite and most versatile sauces. They don't yield enormous amounts because you simply may not need that much, even if you're freezing portions, and you can give the recipe a trial run without waste. If you do find yourself using these sauces regularly, just double or triple the ingredients to suit your needs.

GET IN THE QUICK FIX FRAME OF MIND

The next time you prep a dinner, remember this: The pasta pot is already out and the cutting board and knives are dirty, so take a few minutes to make extra ingredients to store in the freezer for even quicker Quick Fix Meals down the road.

SIMPLE SAUCES
YOU SHOULD HAVE
IN YOUR REFRIGERATOR
OR FREEZER

1. TOMATO-BASIL SAUCE

This is excellent over pasta, as a sauce for meatballs or sausage, or as a base for ground meat sauces. For a richer sauce, add one vegetable or chicken bouillon cube when you add the tomatoes. This recipe yields enough to sauce 1 pound of cooked pasta or 1 pound of meatballs. Two cups is perfect as the base for a meat sauce and you can refrigerate or freeze the remaining cup for another use.

MAKES 3 CUPS; 6 SERVINGS

One 28-ounce can diced tomatoes

One 6-ounce can tomato paste

1 teaspoon dried oregano

1 teaspoon dried basil

¼ cup chopped fresh basil

Salt and freshly ground black pepper (or crushed red pepper for added "heat")

In a medium saucepan over medium heat, combine the diced tomatoes, tomato paste, oregano, and dried basil. Bring to a simmer and let simmer for at least 10 minutes and up to 30 minutes. Remove from the heat and stir in fresh basil. Season to taste with salt and pepper. Let cool to room temperature, then store in a plastic container in the refrigerator for up to 1 week or in the freezer for up to 3 months.

2. GARLICKY MUSHROOM SAUCE

This is super over mashed potatoes, couscous, and grilled or roasted chicken, turkey, pork, beef, and fish. For added flavor, add ¼ cup dry sherry when you add the broth.

MAKES 2 CUPS; 4 SERVINGS

2 teaspoons olive oil

2 cloves garlic, minced

4 cups sliced mushrooms (any combination, any variety)

1 teaspoon dried thyme

2½ cups reduced-sodium vegetable, chicken, or beef broth

Salt and freshly ground black pepper

Heat the oil in a large skillet over medium heat. Add the garlic and cook, stirring, for 1 minute. Add the mushrooms and cook 3 to 5 minutes, until the mushrooms are soft and releasing natural juices. Add the thyme and cook 1 minute, until fragrant. Add the broth and bring to a simmer. Partially cover the pan and simmer 10 minutes. Season to taste with salt and pepper. Let cool to room temperature, then store in a plastic container in the refrigerator for up to 1 week or in the freezer for up to 3 months.

3. SPICY (OR MILD) PEANUT SAUCE

You can't beat this sauce over grilled or roasted chicken, stir-fried vegetables, rice dishes, and skewered shrimp.

MAKES 1 CUP; 4 SERVINGS

1 cup reduced-sodium chicken broth

3 tablespoons creamy peanut butter

2 tablespoons reduced-sodium soy sauce

1 teaspoon toasted sesame oil

1 teaspoon hot chili oil, or more to taste (leave this out for a mild sauce)

2 tablespoons chopped fresh cilantro

In a small saucepan, whisk together the broth, peanut butter, soy sauce, sesame oil, and chili oil. Set the pan over medium heat, bring to a simmer, and let simmer for 5 minutes. Remove from the heat and stir in the cilantro. Let cool to room temperature, then store in a plastic container in the refrigerator for up to 1 week or in the freezer for up to 3 months.

4. ROASTED RED PEPPER SAUCE

This sauce is perfect over seafood, grilled or roasted chicken and turkey, broiled flank steak, and roasted vegetables; it's also amazing with pasta. Try substituting an equal amount of oil-packed sun-dried tomatoes for the roasted red peppers.

MAKES 2 CUPS; 4 SERVINGS

1 cup roasted red peppers (from water-packed jar)

1 cup reduced-sodium vegetable or chicken broth

1 tablespoon balsamic vinegar

1 tablespoon olive oil

¼ cup chopped fresh basil

Salt and freshly ground black pepper

In a blender, combine the red peppers, broth, vinegar, oil, and basil and process until smooth. Transfer mixture to a small saucepan and set over medium heat. Bring to a simmer, partially cover, and simmer for 10 minutes. Remove from the heat. Season to taste with salt and pepper. Let come to room temperature and store in a plastic container in the refrigerator for up to 1 week or in the freezer up to 3 months.

5. SWEET-N-SOUR SAUCE

Warm or chilled, this sauce is sensational with pork tenderloin, chicken, turkey, shrimp, and crab.

MAKES 2 CUPS; 4 SERVINGS

2 cups chopped or crushed pineapple (canned in juice; two 11-ounce cans)

3 tablespoons hoisin sauce

1 tablespoon light brown sugar

Combine the undrained pineapple, hoisin sauce, and brown sugar in a blender and process until smooth. Transfer mixture to a medium saucepan and set over medium heat. Bring to a simmer, partially cover, and simmer for 10 minutes. Let come to room temperature, then store in a plastic container in the refrigerator for up to 1 week or in the freezer for up to 3 months.

2

Meal kits
IN THE BAG:
for meals in moments

> **"THE TRUTH IS, I'D RATHER BE GOING DOWN THE SLIDE AT THE PLAYGROUND,** not sautéing onions and chopping chicken."

WHAT'S A MEAL KIT?

In my world, it's a combination of ingredients prepared in advance, placed in separate plastic bags or plastic containers, ready for reheating later in the week. I developed Meal Kits for one simple reason: After a long, crazy, hectic day, I cherish the thought of a quickly assembled meal. In the past, that meant frozen entrées, family-friendly restaurants, or take-out. But since I love to eat at home with my family, I created the Meal Kit strategy to take the pressure off weeknight meals. The truth is, I'd rather be going down the slide at the playground (with both boys on my lap!) until the sun sets, not sautéing onions and chopping chicken. Late afternoons are much more fun when you can relax and enjoy your family. If you're like me, once you create a Meal Kit or two, you'll become obsessed with it. You'll move beyond dinner and start creating "Kits" for all types of occasions: birthday parties, dinner parties, picnics, breakfast, and even dishes to take along to a friend's house.

This strategy of prepping can be found in every chapter in this book. If you have time on the weekend, use it to get meals ready for the week ahead. Don't worry, I'm not taking away any of your precious family, friend, and fun time. I'm not willing to give that up and I don't expect you to! If you can set aside one hour on the weekend, that's all you'll need. Make it *your* hour. Throw on some comfy clothes, crank up the music, and get out your ingredients for the week. If you're planning to serve vegetables, chop them in advance and store them in plastic bags. Precook rice or pasta and store it in plastic bags or plastic containers. You can do the same with meats and vegetables, too. Cook, roast, or bake chicken, turkey, pork, beef, fish, and vegetables so that during the week you just need to reheat, assemble, and serve. Think of it this way: The little bit of work you do now will keep meals moving along on autopilot all week long. It's not a chore, it's a strategy and this strategy can be a blast!

ROASTED VEGETABLE SOUP OVER BROWN RICE

Prep day:
PREP TIME: 10 MINUTES
ACTIVE COOKING TIME: 5 MINUTES
WALK-AWAY TIME: 20 MINUTES

To finish the meal:
ACTIVE COOKING TIME: 3–5 MINUTES

SERVES 4

Looking for a way to get your kids (and yourself) to eat more vegetables? Roasting them first may be the answer. My kids love roasted vegetables, probably because the roasting process caramelizes the outside and brings out the natural sweetness of the vegetable (kids love sugary things, right?). This is also a fantastic vegetarian meal when you're tired of chicken and fish! I like to serve the stew with brown rice because the grain is fast, fun, and yummy. Feel free to substitute couscous for the rice.

This dish has a substantial walk-away time, so use it to make the rice and then sit back and relax (or walk the dog!).

● ●

Preheat the oven to 450°F. Coat a large baking sheet with cooking spray.

In a large bowl, combine the zucchini, bell pepper, carrots, and asparagus. Add the olive oil, salt, and black pepper and toss to coat. Transfer the vegetables to the prepared baking sheet and roast until tender and golden brown, about 20 minutes.

In a large saucepan, combine the broth, tomatoes, thyme, and bay leaves and bring to a boil. Stir in the roasted vegetables, reduce the heat to medium, and simmer for 5 minutes.

Cook the rice according to the package directions.

Cooking spray

2 medium zucchini, cut into 1-inch pieces

1 large red bell pepper, seeded and chopped

2 medium carrots, cut diagonally into ½-inch-thick slices

1 bunch asparagus, bottoms snapped off and stalks cut into 1-inch pieces

2 tablespoons olive oil

½ teaspoon salt

½ teaspoon freshly ground black pepper

4 cups reduced-sodium vegetable or chicken broth

One 28-ounce can diced tomatoes

1 teaspoon dried thyme

2 bay leaves

1 cup quick-cooking brown rice

¼ cup chopped fresh basil

This soup is also amazing when you puree it. After simmering, remove the bay leaves and, working in batches, puree the soup in a blender (or use a handheld blender and puree it right in the pot) until smooth. Stir in basil and season with salt and black pepper as directed.

●●IF YOU'RE STOPPING HERE:

Let the soup and rice cool to room temperature. Transfer the soup and rice to separate large plastic containers and refrigerate up to 3 days or freeze up to 3 months (no need to thaw before reheating).

●●WHEN YOU'RE READY TO EAT:

Reheat the soup in a large saucepan over medium-high heat for 10 minutes (or slightly longer if you start with frozen soup) or reheat in the microwave on HIGH for 3 to 5 minutes, until hot. Remove the bay leaves, and stir in basil. Season to taste with salt and pepper. Reheat the rice in the microwave for 1 to 2 minutes on HIGH. Spoon the rice into shallow dinner bowls, ladle the soup over the top, and serve.

PREP POINTER:

If you don't have a microwave, reheat the rice in a bowl set over a saucepan of simmering water. Even though I have a microwave, sometimes I don't reheat my rice at all. I let the hot soup do all the work when it's ladled over the fluffy grain!

ONION SOUP WITH GOOEY SWISS AND MOZZARELLA CROSTINI

Prep day:
PREP TIME: 10 MINUTES
ACTIVE COOKING TIME: 10 MINUTES
WALK-AWAY TIME: 10 MINUTES

To finish the meal:
ACTIVE COOKING TIME: 5 MINUTES

SERVES 4

I grew up on onion soup. I ordered it at every restaurant that served it. In fact, I still do—when I go out. But since I have two toddlers, we tend to eat home more often (trust me, the restaurants appreciate that). I decided that until my kids can sit at the dinner table for longer than 3 minutes, I'd have to come up with an onion soup recipe that tastes as good as the best restaurants' version. Behold my creation: a mouthwatering combination of three onion varieties simmered in broth and jazzed up with a golden brown and gooey cheese-smothered wedge of bread.

When I want to add a salad, I whip up White Bean–Green Pepper Salad with Mandarin Oranges and Chives (page 199) because it's ready in the time it takes to reheat the soup and melt the cheese on the crostini. You might actually get your kids to sit down for this one!

• •

Heat the oil in a large saucepan or Dutch oven over medium heat. Add the onions, leeks, and garlic and cook, stirring, until onions are soft, about 10 minutes. Add the broth, bay leaves, thyme, salt, and pepper, increase the heat to high, and bring to a boil.

Reduce the heat to medium, partially cover the pan, and simmer for 10 minutes. Remove the bay leaves and season to taste with salt and pepper.

2 teaspoons olive oil

1 cup sliced yellow onion

1 cup sliced red onion

2 leeks (white part only), rinsed well (see Prep Pointer on page 222) and chopped

2 cloves garlic, minced

4 cups reduced-sodium beef broth

2 bay leaves

1 teaspoon dried thyme

½ teaspoon salt

¼ teaspoon freshly ground black pepper

Four 1-inch-thick slices baguette

½ cup shredded Swiss cheese

½ cup shredded part-skim mozzarella cheese

● ● IF YOU'RE STOPPING HERE:

Let the soup come to room temperature, then transfer to a large plastic container (or two) and refrigerate up to 3 days or freeze up to 3 months (no need to thaw before continuing).

● ● WHEN YOU'RE READY TO EAT:

Preheat the broiler. Reheat the soup in the microwave for 3 to 4 minutes on HIGH or in a large saucepan over medium heat. Top each baguette slice with an equal amount of both of the shredded cheeses. Ladle the soup into individual heatproof bowls and place a cheese-topped bread in the center of the soup. Place the bowls on a baking sheet and broil until the cheese melts, 1 to 2 minutes. Serve immediately.

TIME SAVER tip:

Buy frozen sliced onions instead of slicing them yourself.

GOOD HEALTH note:

Thanks to the cheese on the crostini, this soup boasts 935 mg of bone-strengthening calcium, or 234 mg per serving. Onions are also a rich source of sulfur compounds, powerful anticancer agents.

CURRIED BUTTERNUT SQUASH SOUP WITH GARLIC-SCENTED PITA CHIPS

Prep day:
PREP TIME: 10 MINUTES
ACTIVE COOKING TIME: 6 MINUTES
WALK-AWAY TIME: 10 MINUTES

To finish the meal:
ACTIVE COOKING TIME: 5–7 MINUTES

SERVES 4

Whenever I make this soup, or write recipes for butternut squash soup, I get rave reviews. Maybe it's the incredible orange color. Perhaps it's the super creamy texture. Or, it could be that the flavor is unbelievable: sweet butternut squash, simmered in vegetable broth with hints of onion, garlic, and curry. My guess is it's all those things! Crunchy, garlicky pita chips on the side are the perfect partner. If you want to add a salad, make Warm Spinach Salad with Pancetta and Gorgonzola (page 196) while the soup reheats and the chips bake.

● ●

Heat the oil in a large saucepan or Dutch oven over medium heat. Add the onion and garlic and cook, stirring, until softened, about 5 minutes. Stir in the curry powder and cumin until well combined and the spices are fragrant. Add the broth, squash, salt, and pepper, increase the heat to high, and bring to a boil. Reduce the heat to medium, partially cover the pan, and simmer until the squash is fork-tender, about 10 minutes. Working in batches, puree the soup in a blender or food processor until smooth or use a handheld blender and puree it directly in the pot.

CURRIED BUTTERNUT SQUASH SOUP:

1 tablespoon olive oil

½ cup chopped onion

2 cloves garlic, minced

1 teaspoon curry powder

½ teaspoon ground cumin

6 cups reduced-sodium vegetable broth

4 cups peeled, cubed butternut squash (about 2 medium or 1 large squash)

½ teaspoon salt

¼ teaspoon freshly ground black pepper

GARLIC-SCENTED PITA CHIPS:

Olive oil cooking spray

4 pita pockets, cut into 4 to 6 wedges each

1 teaspoon garlic powder

Salt

●●IF YOU'RE STOPPING HERE:

Let cool to room temperature, then transfer the soup to a large plastic container (or two) and refrigerate up to 3 days or freeze up to 3 months. No need to thaw before continuing.

●●WHEN YOU'RE READY TO EAT:

Preheat the oven to 400°F. Coat a large baking sheet with cooking spray. Arrange the pita wedges on the prepared baking sheet and spray the top of them with cooking spray. Sprinkle the garlic powder evenly over the wedges, then season to taste with salt. Bake until golden brown, 5 to 7 minutes.

Reheat the soup in a large saucepan over medium heat or in the microwave for 3 to 4 minutes on HIGH until hot. Season to taste with salt and pepper and serve with the pita wedges on the side.

GOOD HEALTH note:

Orange-fleshed butternut squash is brimming with beta–carotene, a powerful antioxidant.

BOW TIES WITH WARM BLUE CHEESE SAUCE

Prep day:
PREP TIME: 10-15 MINUTES
ACTIVE COOKING TIME: 6 MINUTES

To finish the meal:
ACTIVE COOKING TIME: 5 MINUTES

SERVES 4

My son Kyle and I *love* blue cheese—on salads, crackers, sprinkled over rice, you name it. We both love pasta, too. To combine our loves, I created a creamy blue cheese sauce that's served over fun-shaped bow-tie pasta (also called farfalle). I toss in bright green peas for color and nutrients. The sweet peas pair beautifully with the pungent blue cheese. Feel free to substitute any pasta shape, but I recommend using one with nooks and crannies to give the heavenly sauce a place to hang out.

• •

Cook the pasta according to the package directions. Drain and transfer to a large bowl.

Meanwhile, heat the oil in a large skillet over medium heat. Add the shallots and cook, stirring, until tender, about 5 minutes. Stir in the thyme, salt, and pepper until well combined and the thyme is fragrant. Add this mixture to the cooked pasta and toss to combine (I typically keep pasta and sauce separate when refrigerating so the pasta doesn't absorb all the sauce, but this isn't a true sauce, so throw them together).

•• IF YOU'RE STOPPING HERE:

Let come to room temperature, then transfer the pasta to a large zip-top plastic bag or container and refrigerate up to 3 days.

•• WHEN YOU'RE READY TO EAT:

Heat the milk in a large skillet over medium heat. When tiny bubbles appear around the edges of the pan, reduce the heat to low and stir in the sour cream and blue cheese. Stir until the cheese melts. Add the peas and cooked pasta and simmer for 1 minute to heat through. Meanwhile, chop the parsley. Remove from the heat, stir in the parsley, and serve.

12 ounces bowtie (farfalle) pasta

2 teaspoons olive oil

¼ cup chopped shallots

1 teaspoon dried thyme

½ teaspoon salt

¼ teaspoon freshly ground black pepper

2 cups low-fat milk

½ cup low-fat sour cream

1 cup crumbled blue cheese

1 cup frozen green peas (no need to thaw)

1 tablespoon chopped fresh parsley

SPINACH FETTUCCINE WITH SAUTÉED VEGETABLES, ARTICHOKE HEARTS, AND SHREDDED MOZZARELLA

SERVES 4

Think of this as a pasta dish/stir-fry combination. Colorful pasta is tossed with sautéed asparagus, carrots, mushrooms, artichoke hearts, and tomatoes and then smothered with mozzarella cheese. What a delicious way to sneak veggies past the finicky eaters in the family! Feel free to vary the vegetables and use whatever you have in the fridge.

● ●

Cook the pasta according to the package directions, then drain.

Meanwhile, heat the oil in a large skillet over medium heat. Add the onion and garlic and cook, stirring, for 1 minute. Add the asparagus, carrot, mushrooms, and artichoke hearts and cook, stirring a few times, until the vegetables are crisp-tender and the mushrooms release their juices, about 5 minutes. Add the salt and pepper and stir to coat.

● ● IF YOU'RE STOPPING HERE:

Let the pasta and vegetables cool to room temperature. Transfer them separately to large zip-top plastic bags or containers and refrigerate for up to 3 days or freeze up to 3 months. There's no need to thaw before continuing.

● ● WHEN YOU'RE READY TO EAT:

Transfer the vegetables to a large saucepan and stir in the tomatoes. Set the pan over medium-high heat and bring to a simmer (or reheat both together in the microwave for about 3 minutes on HIGH). Add the fettuccine and simmer for 2 minutes to heat through (or microwave for an additional 2 minutes). Serve topped with the mozzarella.

Prep day:
PREP TIME: 10 MINUTES
ACTIVE COOKING TIME: 6 MINUTES

To finish the meal:
ACTIVE COOKING TIME: 3–5 MINUTES

12 ounces spinach fettuccine

1 tablespoon olive oil

½ cup sliced red onion

2 cloves garlic, minced

2 cups asparagus cut into 1-inch pieces

1 medium carrot, cut diagonally into ¼-inch-thick slices

1 cup sliced button or cremini mushrooms

One 14-ounce can artichoke hearts, drained and cut in half

½ teaspoon salt

½ teaspoon freshly ground black pepper

One 28-ounce can diced tomatoes

1 cup shredded part-skim mozzarella cheese

SEAFOOD POMODORO WITH LINGUINE

Prep day:
PREP TIME: 10 MINUTES
ACTIVE COOKING TIME: 2 MINUTES
WALK-AWAY TIME: 10 MINUTES

To finish the meal:
ACTIVE COOKING TIME: 5 MINUTES

SERVES 4

Shrimp and I are *one.* I adore shrimp. In fact, I love it so much that (as a surprise) at my wedding, I was served the world's *largest* shrimp cocktail. There must have been 30 shrimp hanging over the side of the cocktail glass. Suffice to say, I ate them all. In this dish, I partner my beloved with some of his friends from the sea: clams and crabmeat. It's a seafood party on the plate and in your mouth!

• •

Cook the linguine according to the package directions, then drain.

Meanwhile, heat the oil in a large skillet over medium-high heat. Add the onion and garlic and cook, stirring, for 1 minute. Add the oregano, basil, and red pepper and stir to coat. Add the tomatoes and tomato sauce and bring the mixture to a boil. Reduce the heat to medium, partially cover, and simmer for 10 minutes.

• • IF YOU'RE STOPPING HERE:

Let the sauce and linguine cool to room temperature and refrigerate separately in large zip-top plastic bags or containers up to 6 days or freeze up to 3 months. Another option is to cook the seafood (see the next step) and refrigerate for 3 days.

12 ounces linguine

2 teaspoons olive oil

½ cup finely chopped red onion

4 cloves garlic, minced

1 teaspoon dried oregano

1 teaspoon dried basil

½ teaspoon crushed red pepper

One 15-ounce can diced tomatoes

One 15-ounce can tomato sauce

½ pound medium shrimp, peeled and deveined

1 pound fresh littleneck clams, scrubbed well to remove debris and sand (discard any whose shells won't shut)

½ pound lump crabmeat (fresh, canned, or frozen and thawed), picked over for shells and cartilage

¼ cup chopped fresh parsley

GOOD HEALTH note:

Canned tomatoes are crammed with vitamin C and cancer-fighting lycopene.

●●WHEN YOU'RE READY TO EAT:

Thaw if necessary, then transfer the sauce to a large skillet and set over medium heat. Bring to a simmer, add the shrimp and clams, cover, and simmer until the clam shells have opened and the shrimp are bright pink and cooked through, 3 to 5 minutes. Discard any clams that won't open. Remove from the heat and stir in the crab. (At this point, you could let everything cool, then transfer the mixture to a large plastic bag or plastic container and refrigerate up to 3 days.)

Stir the pasta into the sauce and simmer 5 minutes to heat through. Meanwhile, chop the parsley, stir it into the sauce, and serve.

DOLLAR SAVER tip:

This dish is incredibly flavorful thanks to the onion, garlic, herbs, tomatoes, and mixed seafood. Given that, you can eliminate the crabmeat if desired and the dish won't suffer one bit!

"I PARTNER SHRIMP WITH CLAMS AND MUSSELS. IT'S A SEAFOOD PARTY on the plate and IN YOUR MOUTH!"

ANGEL HAIR WITH CREAMY TURKEY SAUSAGE AND WILD MUSHROOM SAUCE

Prep day:
PREP TIME: 10 MINUTES
ACTIVE COOKING TIME: 10–12 MINUTES
WALK-AWAY TIME: 10 MINUTES

To finish the meal:
ACTIVE COOKING TIME: 5 MINUTES

SERVES 4

Some dishes are so downright delicious they scream, "I'm the new family favorite!" If tetrazzini isn't already a part of your dinner repertoire, this recipe may change that. I use turkey sausage in this recipe, but if you don't have any (and don't feel like running out to get it), use chicken or turkey breast cut into cubes. This dish is the perfect way to incorporate (aka "sneak") vegetables into a main dish. If you've got finicky diners at the table, try this winner—my guess is, you won't be throwing away vegetables after dinner.

• •

Cook the pasta according to the package directions, then drain.

Meanwhile, heat the oil in a large skillet over medium-high heat. Add the shallots and garlic and cook, stirring, for 1 minute. Add the mushrooms and cook, stirring a few times, until they are tender and releasing juice, 3 to 5 minutes. Add the sausage and brown on all sides, about 5 minutes. Add the thyme, oregano, salt, and pepper and stir until well combined and the herbs are fragrant, about 1 minute. Add the broth and bring to a simmer. Reduce the heat to medium-low, partially cover the pan, and simmer until the sausage is cooked through, about 10 minutes.

12 ounces angel hair pasta

1 tablespoon olive oil

½ cup chopped shallots

3 cloves garlic, minced

2 cups sliced mushrooms (button, cremini, portobello, or any type of wild mushroom)

1 pound sweet or hot turkey or chicken sausage, cut into ½-inch pieces

1 teaspoon dried thyme

1 teaspoon dried oregano

½ teaspoon salt

½ teaspoon freshly ground black pepper

2 cups reduced-sodium chicken broth

½ cup frozen green peas

1½ cups low-fat sour cream

¼ cup grated Parmesan cheese, preferably freshly grated

2 tablespoons chopped fresh parsley

••IF YOU'RE STOPPING HERE:

Let the sauce cool for 10 minutes, then transfer to a large plastic zip-top bag or container (or two) and refrigerate up to 3 days or freeze up to 3 months (no need to thaw before continuing). Let the pasta cool to room temperature and refrigerate up to 3 days.

••WHEN YOU'RE READY TO EAT:

Reheat the turkey mixture in a large skillet over medium heat until simmering. Add the peas and simmer 1 minute more. Stir in the sour cream and Parmesan and simmer 1 minute to heat through. Remove from the heat, season with salt and pepper to taste, and stir in the parsley.

Reheat the angel hair in the microwave for 1 to 2 minutes on HIGH. Transfer the angel hair to individual shallow bowls, spoon the turkey mixture over the top, and serve.

QUICK FIX IT YOUR WAY:

To reheat in the microwave, place the pasta in a large, microwave-safe dish, pour the turkey mixture over it, and cover with plastic wrap. Microwave on HIGH for 3 minutes until hot. Add the peas, cover, and cook 1 more minute. Remove the plastic wrap, season with salt and pepper to taste, and stir in the parsley.

"SOME DISHES ARE SO DOWNRIGHT DELICIOUS THEY SCREAM, 'I'M THE NEW FAMILY FAVORITE!' If you've got finicky diners at the table, TRY THIS WINNER!"

LINGUINE CARBONARA

Prep day:
PREP TIME: 10 MINUTES
ACTIVE COOKING TIME: 12–14 MINUTES

To finish the meal:
ACTIVE COOKING TIME: 5 MINUTES

SERVES 4

Traditional carbonara sauce is made with loads of bacon, eggs, and Parmesan cheese. Since I want to live long enough to enjoy this dish for years to come, I've cut the fat and calories significantly (½ cup of regular sour cream has 246 calories and 24 grams of fat versus ½ cup of low-fat sour cream with 157 calories and 12 grams of fat). Turkey bacon makes the perfect substitute for regular (vegetarians can use soy bacon) and the sauce is rich and creamy thanks to low-fat sour cream, used in place of the cream and eggs. I serve this rich and sinful-tasting meal with a chopped romaine or baby lettuce salad with reduced-fat dressing.

• •

Cook the linguine according to the package directions, then drain.

Meanwhile, cook the bacon in a large skillet over medium-high heat, stirring a few times, until golden brown, 3 to 5 minutes. Add the onion and garlic and cook, stirring, until the onion is soft, about 3 minutes. Stir in the oregano and basil and cook for 1 minute. Add the flour and stir to coat. Reduce heat to medium, add the milk, stir to combine, and bring to a simmer. Let simmer until the sauce thickens, about 5 minutes, stirring frequently. Remove from the heat and whisk in the sour cream and Parmesan.

12 ounces linguine

1 cup chopped turkey bacon, soy bacon, or regular bacon

½ cup chopped red onion

3 cloves garlic, minced

1 teaspoon dried oregano

1 teaspoon dried basil

2 tablespoons all-purpose flour

1½ cups low-fat milk

½ cup low-fat sour cream

¼ cup grated Parmesan cheese, preferably freshly grated

¼ cup chopped fresh parsley

Salt and freshly ground black pepper

TIME SAVER tip:

Rinse and chop vegetables and fresh herbs on the weekend and freeze small batches in plastic bags or plastic containers; pull them from the freezer when you're ready to cook (no need to thaw first).

●●IF YOU'RE STOPPING HERE:

Let the pasta and sauce cool to room temperature, then transfer to separate large zip-top plastic bags or containers and refrigerate up to 3 days.

●●WHEN YOU'RE READY TO EAT:

Pour the sauce into a large saucepan and set over medium heat. When sauce just begins to simmer, add the linguine and toss to combine. Cook for 1 minute to heat through. Or, to reheat the whole dish in the microwave, combine the sauce and linguine in a large, microwave-safe dish, cover with plastic wrap, and microwave on HIGH for 3 to 5 minutes, until hot. Meanwhile, chop the parsley. Remove from the heat, stir in the parsley, season to taste with salt and pepper, and serve.

STORAGE SAVVY:

When storing food in freezer bags, push all the air out before zipping the top. This will ensure no oxygen gets to the food (oxygen will shorten its life).

When using plastic containers, once the lid is on, lift one corner to allow steam to escape before tightly closing the top. The top will be almost concave once all the air is out (and that's a good thing!).

SWEET TURKEY SAUSAGE MEATBALLS IN MARINARA SAUCE

Prep day:
PREP TIME: 10 MINUTES
ACTIVE COOKING TIME: 15 MINUTES

To finish the meal:
ACTIVE COOKING TIME: 3–5 MINUTES

SERVES 4

A Quick Fix cook's best friend is one ingredient that boasts loads of flavor. Sweet Italian sausage (I like to use turkey sausage but you can use pork) is crammed with the bold taste of garlic, herbs, and spices—lots of flavor, one ingredient. Add sausage to any dish and send flavors soaring without rummaging through your spice rack! I like to serve this with Baby Spinach, Fennel, and Grapefruit Salad with Shallot Vinaigrette (page 197) because I can throw it together while the meatballs reheat.

• •

12 ounces capellini or angel hair pasta

1 pound sweet Italian turkey or chicken sausage

4 teaspoons olive oil

½ cup finely chopped onion

2 cloves garlic, minced

1 teaspoon dried oregano

One 28-ounce can diced tomatoes

One 8-ounce can tomato sauce

¼ cup chopped fresh basil

¼ cup grated Parmesan cheese, preferably freshly grated

Cook the pasta according to the package directions, then drain.

Meanwhile, remove the casings from sausage and shape the sausage into 16 meatballs. Heat 2 teaspoons of the oil in a large skillet over medium heat. Add the meatballs and cook until browned on all sides, 5 to 7 minutes.

Meanwhile, heat the remaining 2 teaspoons oil in a large saucepan over medium heat. Add the onion and garlic and cook, stirring, until softened, about 3 minutes. Add the oregano and cook 1 minute, until fragrant. Add the tomatoes and tomato sauce and bring to a simmer. Transfer the meatballs to the simmering sauce and cook until the meatballs are cooked through, about 10 minutes.

● ●IF YOU'RE STOPPING HERE:

Let the pasta and sauce cool to room temperature, then transfer to separate large zip-top plastic bags or containers and refrigerate up to 3 days or freeze up to 3 months. There's no need to thaw the meatballs and sauce before continuing. Thaw the pasta in the microwave for 3 to 4 minutes on LOW.

● ●WHEN YOU'RE READY TO EAT:

Transfer the meatballs and sauce to a large saucepan, set over medium heat, bring to a simmer, and let simmer for 5 minutes to heat through or longer if meatballs are frozen. Remove from the heat and stir in the basil. Spoon the meatballs and sauce over the pasta, sprinkle the Parmesan over the top, and serve. Or, reheat the whole dish in the microwave—reheat the pasta for 3 minutes on HIGH, the meatballs for 3 to 4 minutes on HIGH, then spoon the meatballs over the pasta before topping with basil and Parmesan.

"ADD SAUSAGE TO ANY DISH AND SEND FLAVORS SOARING without rummaging through your spice rack!"

BAKED ZITI WITH TURKEY SAUSAGE

SERVES 4 TO 6

Baked ziti is a crowd-pleaser in any family. I like to think of it as a complete meal in one dish since it boasts carbohydrates, protein (from the turkey sausage), vegetables (tomatoes), and dairy! That's not stretching the truth, it's a fact!

Since you've got 45 minutes of walk-away time, you have time to whip up Wilted Baby Spinach with Honey-Maple Vinaigrette (page 198) and get a manicure.

• •

Cook the pasta according to the package directions, then drain.

Meanwhile, heat the oil in a large saucepan over medium-high heat. Add the sausage and cook until browned, about 5 minutes, breaking up the meat as it cooks. Add the diced tomatoes, tomato sauce, oregano, and basil and bring to a simmer. Partially cover the pan, reduce heat to medium-low and continue to simmer for 10 minutes. Remove from the heat.

In a medium bowl, combine the ricotta, half the mozzarella, and the garlic powder until well combined.

Spoon 1 cup of the tomato sauce in the bottom of a 4-quart casserole dish. Top with half the cooked ziti. Top with half the cheese mixture, spreading it evenly with the back of a spoon or a rubber spatula. Top with another cup of the tomato sauce. Repeat the layers using the remaining ziti and ricotta mixture, then top with the remaining sauce. Sprinkle the remaining mozzarella and the Parmesan evenly over the top.

Prep day:
PREP TIME: 20 MINUTES
ACTIVE COOKING TIME: 6 MINUTES
WALK-AWAY TIME: 10 MINUTES

To finish the meal:
WALK-AWAY TIME: 45 MINUTES

1 pound ziti noodles

2 teaspoons olive oil

8 ounces turkey or chicken sausage (sweet or hot), casing removed

One 28-ounce can diced tomatoes

One 8-ounce can tomato sauce

1 teaspoon dried oregano

1 teaspoon dried basil

One 15-ounce container part-skim ricotta cheese

8 ounces shredded part-skim mozzarella cheese

½ teaspoon garlic powder

¼ cup grated Parmesan cheese, preferably freshly grated

• • IF YOU'RE STOPPING HERE:

Cover the dish with plastic wrap and refrigerate up to 3 days or freeze up to 3 months. Thaw completely in the refrigerator or microwave for 4 to 6 minutes on LOW before baking.

• • WHEN YOU'RE READY TO EAT:

Preheat the oven to 350°F. Remove the plastic wrap from the baking dish and cover with aluminum foil. Bake for 30 minutes, then uncover and bake until the cheese is golden and bubbly, about 15 more minutes.

STOVE-TOP JAMBALAYA WITH ANDOUILLE SAUSAGE, CHICKEN, AND SHRIMP

Prep day:
PREP TIME: 10 MINUTES
ACTIVE COOKING TIME: 13 MINUTES

To finish the meal:
ACTIVE COOKING TIME: 5 MINUTES

SERVES 4

What a fun combination of flavors and colors! This whole concoction boasts an amazing array of ingredients—garlic, peppers (sweet and hot), tomatoes, herbs, spices, and Cajun-seasoned chicken, shrimp, and sausage. A party for your palate!

● ●

Cook the rice according to the package directions.

Heat the oil in a large saucepan or Dutch oven over medium heat. Add the onion, bell pepper, garlic, and jalapeños and cook, stirring, until softened, about 3 minutes. Add the chicken and cook until browned on all sides, about 5 minutes. Add the Cajun seasoning and oregano and stir to coat the chicken and vegetables. Add the sausage and shrimp and cook, stirring, for 2 minutes. Add the tomatoes and bay leaves, bring to a simmer, and let simmer until the chicken and shrimp are cooked through (the shrimp will be bright pink), about 3 minutes.

1 cup quick-cooking brown or white rice

2 teaspoons olive oil

½ cup chopped onion

1 large green bell pepper, seeded and chopped

2 cloves garlic, minced

¼ cup diced pickled jalapeños

½ pound boneless, skinless chicken breasts or tenders, cut into 1-inch chunks

1 teaspoon Cajun or Creole seasoning

1 teaspoon dried oregano

½ pound andouille sausage, chorizo sausage, or kielbasa, cut into 1-inch-thick rounds

½ pound medium shrimp, peeled and deveined

One 28-ounce can diced tomatoes

2 bay leaves

¼ cup chopped fresh parsley

Salt and freshly ground black pepper

●●IF YOU'RE STOPPING HERE:

Let the rice and simmered mixture cool to room temperature, then transfer to separate large zip-top plastic bags or containers and refrigerate up to 3 days. The jambalaya mixture will also keep in the freezer up to 3 months. There's no need to thaw before continuing.

●●WHEN YOU'RE READY TO EAT:

Transfer the jambalaya to a large saucepan and set over medium heat. Bring to a simmer and let simmer for 5 minutes to heat through. Or, place the mixture in a large microwave-safe dish, cover it with plastic wrap, and microwave on HIGH for 3 to 5 minutes, until hot. Remove the bay leaves and stir in the cooked rice and parsley. Season to taste with salt and pepper and serve.

WILD MUSHROOM TART WITH BROCCOLI RABE AND GOAT CHEESE

Prep day:
PREP TIME: 10 MINUTES
ACTIVE COOKING TIME: 9–11 MINUTES

To finish the meal:
PREP TIME: 5 MINUTES
WALK-AWAY TIME: 25–30 MINUTES
RESTING TIME: 10 MINUTES

SERVES 4

If you think a *real* tart is beyond your reach on a weeknight, take note. Prepare this simple filling when you've got a little extra time and you can enjoy a fresh-baked, wild mushroom tart any busy night (while amazing your family and friends). If you're not a fan of goat cheese, substitute shredded cheddar or Monterey Jack. If you can't find broccoli rabe, substitute a 10-ounce bag of spinach, and, if necessary, drain away any excess water in the pan before adding the egg-and-milk mixture (spinach gives off more water than broccoli rabe when heated).

I like to serve this with Creamed Spinach My Way (page 216) on the side. Since you've got 25 to 30 minutes of walk-away time, you can make the spinach and still have time to get a few things done around the house.

● ●

Press the pie crust into the bottom and up the sides of a 9-inch removable-bottom tart pan. Set aside.

Heat the oil in large skillet over medium heat. Add the garlic and cook, stirring, for 1 minute. Add the mushrooms and cook, stirring a few times, until they release their juices, about 5 minutes. Add the broccoli rabe and cook, stirring a few times, until tender, 3 to 5 minutes. Remove from the heat and pour into the pie crust.

One 9-inch refrigerated pie crust

2 teaspoons olive oil

2 cloves garlic, minced

4 cups sliced wild mushrooms (any combination of cremini, portobello, shiitake, oyster, button, and porcini)

4 cups chopped broccoli rabe

2/3 cup low-fat milk

2 large eggs

1 teaspoon dried sage

1/2 teaspoon salt

1/4 teaspoon freshly ground black pepper

1/2 cup crumbled goat cheese

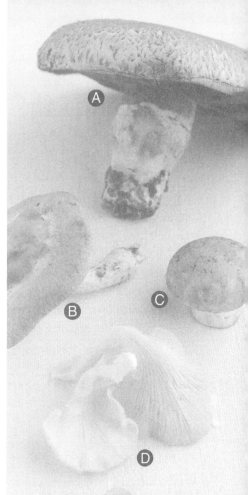

●●IF YOU'RE STOPPING HERE:

After the filling has cooled, cover the tart pan with plastic wrap and refrigerate up to 3 days or freeze up to 3 months. Thaw completely in the refrigerator before cooking.

●●WHEN YOU'RE READY TO EAT:

Preheat the oven to 400°F. In a large bowl, whisk together the milk, eggs, sage, salt, and pepper. Pour into the tart pan. Sprinkle the goat cheese evenly over the top, then bake until a knife inserted into the center comes out clean, 25 to 30 minutes. Let cool 10 minutes before slicing into wedges. At this point, you can refrigerate the tart up to 3 days or freeze up to 4 months. Reheat the thawed tart in a preheated 350°F oven for 20 minutes or thaw and reheat in the microwave (thaw for 3 minutes on LOW, then reheat for 3 minutes on HIGH). If it suits you, you can slice the tart into pieces and freeze them individually so you can just grab a piece for lunch or a snack.

GOOD HEALTH note:

Mushrooms are rich in selenium (an essential mineral that creates antioxidants that neutralize cell-damaging free radicals), potassium (which helps maintain normal heart rhythm, fluid balance, muscle, and nerve function), and copper (which helps iron make red blood cells and deliver oxygen to every part of the body).

A Portobello **B** Shiitake
C Cremini **D** Oyster

NEW ORLEANS FLANK STEAK

Prep day:
PREP TIME: 10 MINUTES

To finish the meal:
WALK-AWAY TIME: 10–14 MINUTES
RESTING TIME: 10 MINUTES

SERVES 4

Even though I'm not a huge red meat–eater, I love flank steak because it's lean and nutritious, and boasting high-quality protein and iron. It's also incredibly easy to prepare. This dish was inspired by my family's intense love of Cajun/Creole seasoning. We dump the stuff on everything, from chicken and fish to roasted potatoes and vegetables. I also use it in bold marinades like this one—Creole seasoning spruced up with vinegar, salty soy sauce, and cracked black pepper. A hint of sugar adds a little sweetness and helps caramelize the steak during cooking, creating a nice, sweet crunch.

For a complete meal, while the flank steak cooks, make Swiss Chard with Garlic and Pine Nuts (page 213) and quick-cooking rice (you can whip up both in the time it takes for the steak to cook).

• •

In a large zip-top plastic bag or shallow plastic container, combine the vinegar, sugar, Creole seasoning, teriyaki sauce, oregano, salt, and pepper. Seal the bag or container and shake to combine the ingredients. Add the flank steak, seal, and shake again to coat.

••IF YOU'RE STOPPING HERE:

Refrigerate up to 3 days or freeze (in the marinade) up to 3 months. Thaw completely in the refrigerator or microwave before cooking (if using the microwave, keep a close eye on the steak and stop thawing before the meat starts cooking).

••WHEN YOU'RE READY TO EAT:

Preheat the broiler, a stove-top grill pan, or outdoor grill, then broil or grill the steak 5 to 7 minutes per side for medium or to your desired degree of doneness. Let the steak stand 10 minutes on a serving platter before slicing crosswise into ½-inch-thick slices.

2 tablespoons red wine vinegar

2 teaspoons light brown sugar

2 teaspoons Creole or Cajun seasoning

2 teaspoons reduced-sodium teriyaki sauce

1 teaspoon dried oregano

¼ teaspoon salt

¼ teaspoon cracked black pepper

One 1¼-pound flank steak

TIME SAVER tip:

Containing oodles of ingredients in one little bottle, spice blends like Creole seasoning eliminate the need for measuring and adding several different spices and herbs. The perfect Quick Fix ingredients!

SESAME-GINGER PORK
WITH SOBA NOODLES

SERVES 4

I love lo mein noodle–based meals, but when you order them at restaurants, they're typically loaded with grease. My lightened version still boasts the distinct flavors of sesame, soy, ginger, and cilantro, but it's much more healthful. No need to loosen the belt on this one, or spend the next day repenting on the treadmill.

• •

Cook the soba noodles according to the package directions. Drain and transfer to a large zip-top plastic bag. Add 2 teaspoons of the oil, seal the bag, and shake to coat the noodles.

Meanwhile, heat the remaining 2 teaspoons oil in a large skillet over medium heat. Add the ginger and cook, stirring, for 1 minute. Increase the heat to medium-high, add the pork, and cook, stirring, until browned on all sides, about 5 minutes total. Add the salt and pepper and stir to coat the pork. Add the scallions and sesame seeds and cook, stirring, for 1 minute. Add the broth and soy sauce, reduce heat to medium, and simmer until the pork is cooked through, about 5 minutes. Remove from the heat and stir in the water chestnuts.

• • IF YOU'RE STOPPING HERE:

Let cool to room temperature, then transfer the mixture to a large zip-top plastic bag or plastic container and refrigerate along with the bag of noodles for up to 3 days.

• • WHEN YOU'RE READY TO EAT:

Combine the pork mixture and soba noodles in a large skillet set over medium heat and simmer for 5 minutes to heat through. You can also reheat the noodles and pork mixture together in the microwave for 3 to 5 minutes on HIGH. Meanwhile, chop the cilantro. Remove from the heat, stir in the cilantro, and serve.

Prep day
PREP TIME: 10 MINUTES
ACTIVE COOKING TIME: 14 MINUTES

To finish the meal:
ACTIVE COOKING TIME: 5 MINUTES

8 ounces soba noodles or whole wheat spaghetti

4 teaspoons toasted sesame oil, divided

1 tablespoon minced pickled ginger

One 1¼-pound pork tenderloin, cut into 1-inch chunks

½ teaspoon salt

¼ teaspoon freshly ground black pepper

4 scallions (green and white parts), chopped

1 tablespoon sesame seeds

1 cup reduced-sodium chicken broth

¼ cup reduced-sodium soy sauce

½ cup sliced water chestnuts, drained

¼ cup chopped fresh cilantro

SHEPHERD'S PIE WITH CHEDDAR-SPIKED MASHED POTATOES

Prep day:
PREP TIME: 10 MINUTES
ACTIVE COOKING TIME: 10 MINUTES
WALK-AWAY TIME: 10 MINUTES

To finish the meal:
WALK-AWAY TIME: 20–25 MINUTES
RESTING TIME: 5 MINUTES

SERVES 4

My mom is the queen of meat stews. This shepherd's pie is no exception. The filling is a perfect blend of meat and vegetables, simmered together and then baked under a golden brown mashed potato topping—a true comfort meal. My whole family loves this dish. Let's face it, what toddler doesn't love mashed potatoes? If you don't eat red meat, substitute cubed chicken breast or thigh meat or turkey breast or tenderloin (the cooking time remains the same). Since this recipe has a longer walk-away time than most other recipes, take advantage of it and catch up with work or relaxation!

• •

Heat the oil in a large skillet over medium heat. Add the carrots, onions, and garlic and cook, stirring, until softened, about 3 minutes. Using a slotted spoon, remove the vegetables from the pan and set aside.

Add the beef to the hot skillet and brown on all sides, about 5 minutes. Add the flour, oregano, salt, and pepper and stir to coat the beef. Return the vegetables to the skillet and stir in the tomatoes. Bring to a simmer, reduce heat to medium-low, partially cover the pan, and simmer until the beef is cooked through, about 10 minutes.

Meanwhile, place the potatoes in a large saucepan and pour over enough water to cover. Set pan over high heat, bring to a boil, and boil until the potatoes are fork-tender, 8 to 10 minutes. Drain and return the potatoes to the pan. Add the cheese and sour cream and mash until smooth and well combined. Season to taste with

FILLING:

1 tablespoon olive oil

2 medium carrots, chopped

1 cup pearl onions (frozen or jarred, no need to thaw if frozen)

2 cloves garlic, minced

1¼ pounds lean beef round, cut into 1-inch cubes

1 tablespoon all-purpose flour

1 teaspoon dried oregano

½ teaspoon salt

½ teaspoon freshly ground black pepper

One 28-ounce can diced tomatoes

CHEDDAR-SPIKED MASHED POTATOES:

2 medium Idaho potatoes, peeled and cut into 1-inch chunks

½ cup shredded reduced-fat cheddar cheese

¼ cup low-fat sour cream

Salt and freshly ground black pepper

salt and pepper. At this point, the potatoes should be slightly thin and easy to spread over the beef mixture. If they're not, add more sour cream or low-fat milk.

Transfer the beef mixture to a deep dish pie plate or shallow casserole dish. Spoon the mashed potatoes over the top and, using the back of a spoon, make an even layer.

●●IF YOU'RE STOPPING HERE:

Let cool for 15 minutes, then cover the dish with plastic wrap and refrigerate up to 3 days or freeze up to 3 months. Thaw completely in the refrigerator or microwave before baking.

●●WHEN YOU'RE READY TO EAT:

Preheat the oven to 400°F. Place the casserole dish on a baking sheet and bake until top is golden brown and filling is bubbly, 20 to 25 minutes (the baking sheet prevents messy oven cleanups, in case the filling bubbles over). Let rest 5 minutes before serving.

TIME SAVER tip:

To split up the prep for this dish, make the filling on prep day and make the potato topping on the day you plan to eat, while the oven preheats.

GOOD HEALTH note:

The calories in the mashed potatoes are slashed by switching from regular cheddar cheese (1/2 cup: 228 calories and 19 grams of fat) to reduced-fat (140 calories and 9 grams of fat).

OLIVE-SPIKED
PORK TENDERLOIN

Prep day:
PREP TIME: 10 MINUTES

To finish the meal:
WALK-AWAY TIME: 30–35 MINUTES
RESTING TIME: 10 MINUTES

SERVES 4

One day I decided to jazz up plain pork tenderloin. I found some olives in the fridge and started poking holes all over the tenderloin so I could jam in the olives. Suffice to say, when the meal was served, the crowd roared! Seriously, now I can't make pork tenderloin without stuffing bits of sweet and savory ingredients inside it. I've used capers, sun-dried tomatoes, roasted red peppers, jalapeños, apricots, dried cranberries, and pepperoni! Not only does the "spiking" add incredible flavor, it keeps the flesh moist while the pork roasts. No doubt this dish will turn *you* into a "spiker," too.

For a complete meal, serve this with Garlic-Spiked Broccoli Rabe with Dried Mango (page 215) and Parmesan-Herb Dusted Polenta Rounds (page 233). Since you've got a fair amount of walkaway time, you can quickly whip up those side dishes and still have time to relax.

● ●

Season the pork all over with salt and pepper. Using a sharp knife, make several slits in it about ½ inch deep. Stuff the olives into the slits all over the pork (sometimes it's easiest to put the olives in as you make the slits, so you remember where they are!). Place the pork in a zip-top plastic bag.

In a small bowl, whisk together the vinegar, oil, brown sugar, mustard, and oregano until the sugar dissolves (if necessary, heat the mixture in the microwave for about 30 seconds to help melt it). Pour the mixture all over the pork and seal the bag.

One 1¼-pound pork tenderloin, trimmed of silverskin if necessary (see Prep Pointer on facing page)

Salt and freshly ground black pepper

½ cup stuffed green olives (stuffed with anything— pimiento, onion, garlic, jalapeño), cut in half crosswise

2 tablespoons balsamic vinegar

2 tablespoons olive oil

2 tablespoons light brown sugar

2 teaspoons Dijon mustard

1 teaspoon dried oregano

Cooking spray

• • IF YOU'RE STOPPING HERE:

Refrigerate the pork up to 3 days or freeze up to 3 months. Thaw completely in the refrigerator or microwave for about 5 minutes on LOW before baking.

• • WHEN YOU'RE READY TO EAT:

Preheat the oven to 400°F. Coat a roasting pan with cooking spray. Remove the tenderloin from the bag, place it in the pan, and pour the sauce over it. Bake until an instant-read thermometer inserted into the thickest part reads at least 160°F, 30 to 35 minutes. Let the pork stand 10 minutes before slicing crosswise into 1-inch-thick slices.

PREP POINTER:

Most pork tenderloin is very lean, meaning you won't find a layer of white fat like you would on a pork roast. If you do find fat, simply cut it away with a small, sharp knife. You will frequently find a thin, silvery membrane attached to the surface. This is called the silverskin and you should remove it because it shrinks during cooking and distorts the shape of the meat. To do so, run the tip of a sharp knife under the shiny membrane and peel it away.

BRAISED RED SNAPPER WITH TOMATOES, GREEK OLIVES, AND CAPERS

Prep day:
PREP TIME: 10 MINUTES
ACTIVE COOKING TIME: 7 MINUTES

To finish the meal:
ACTIVE COOKING TIME: 3–5 MINUTES

SERVES 4

This sauce is tomato-based and brimming with olives and capers. It's zesty, colorful, and downright wonderful! I like to serve this dish with rice or pasta on the side. Since the dish reheats in just a few minutes, choose quick-cooking rice or a small pasta shape (such as elbows or orzo) that cooks in 6 to 8 minutes.

• •

Heat the oil in a medium saucepan over medium heat. Add the garlic and cook, stirring, for 2 minutes. Add the oregano and red pepper and stir to coat. Stir in the tomatoes and wine and bring mixture to a simmer. Stir in the olives and capers and simmer for 5 minutes.

• • IF YOU'RE STOPPING HERE:

Let cool to room temperature, transfer mixture to a plastic container and refrigerate up to 3 days or freeze up to 3 months. Thaw completely in the refrigerator or microwave before cooking.

• • WHEN YOU'RE READY TO EAT:

Season the snapper all over with salt and black pepper to taste. Pour the sauce into a large skillet, set over medium-high heat, and bring to a simmer. Add the snapper fillets, cover, and cook until the fish is fork-tender, 3 to 5 minutes. Serve with the sauce spooned over the top of the snapper. Sprinkle with the basil.

2 teaspoons olive oil

4 cloves garlic, minced

1 teaspoon dried oregano

½ teaspoon crushed red pepper

One 28-ounce can diced tomatoes

½ cup red wine

½ cup pitted kalamata olives, drained and chopped

3 tablespoons drained capers

Four 6-ounce red snapper fillets

Salt and freshly ground black pepper

¼ cup chopped fresh basil

QUICK FIX IT YOUR WAY:

To reheat in the microwave, pour the sauce into a shallow microwave-safe dish, nestle the snapper in the sauce, and cover with plastic wrap. Microwave on HIGH for 3 to 5 minutes, until the fish is fork-tender.

CRUNCHY LEMON AND HERB-CRUSTED SCALLOPS

Prep day:
PREP TIME: 10 MINUTES

To finish the meal:
ACTIVE COOKING TIME: 6 MINUTES

SERVES 4

I love oyster crackers dunked in smokin' hot horseradish—they're fabulous with cocktails! Here I use crushed oyster crackers to create an herb-spiked, crunchy crust for moist scallops that are gorgeous enough for entertaining. I like to serve them with couscous that's been tossed with fresh lemon juice and green peas or Curried Couscous with Peas and Carrots (page 230) because both side dishes can be made in the time it takes for the scallops to cook.

● ●

Place the crackers in a large plastic bag and mash them into fine crumbs using a rolling pin, the flat side of a meat mallet, or the bottom of a heavy saucepan. Add the parsley, herb seasoning, salt, and cayenne and shake to combine.

In a separate plastic bag, combine the scallops and mustard. Seal the bag and squish around to coat the scallops with the mustard. Add the scallops to the cracker mixture, seal the bag, and shake to coat evenly.

● ● **IF YOU'RE STOPPING HERE:**

Refrigerate the scallops up to 2 days.

● ● **WHEN YOU'RE READY TO EAT:**

Heat the oil in a large skillet over medium heat. Remove the scallops from the bag, place in the skillet, and cook until golden brown on the outside and opaque on the inside, about 3 minutes per side.

4 cups oyster crackers (enough to yield 1 cup crushed)

2 tablespoons finely chopped fresh parsley

1½ teaspoons salt-free lemon and herb seasoning

½ teaspoon salt

¼ teaspoon cayenne pepper

1¼ pounds sea scallops (about 12 scallops), patted dry

2 tablespoons Dijon mustard

2 tablespoons olive oil

INGREDIENT note:

If you wonder what the difference between "wet" and "dry" scallops is, here's the deal. Wet scallops are stark white and unusually plump because they've been treated with a chemical phosphate to extend shelf life. If fresh dry scallops are available, opt for those (or buy frozen scallops and thaw them in the refrigerator). Wet scallops are acceptable for this dish, but they just might not brown as nicely.

CRAB-STUFFED ZUCCHINI BOATS

Prep day:
PREP TIME: 15 MINUTES

To finish the meal:
WALK-AWAY TIME: 5–15 MINUTES

SERVES 4

Fresh crabmeat rocks. Truth be told, I could eat two pounds of fresh crabmeat in one sitting. In this dish, I partner sweet, succulent crab with artichokes, Parmesan, Dijon mustard, and some seasonings to create a fantastic, refreshing salad. Nestled into a hollowed-out zucchini, it makes a stellar presentation, too!

• •

Using a spoon, scoop the seeds from the center of each zucchini half, making four long, canoe-like boats. Set aside.

In a medium bowl, combine the crabmeat, sour cream, artichoke hearts, ¼ cup of the Parmesan, the mustard, Creole seasoning, salt, and pepper. Mix gently to combine, being careful not to break up any crabmeat lumps. Spoon the mixture evenly into the zucchini boats. Transfer the zucchini to a shallow baking dish.

In a small bowl, combine the remaining 2 tablespoons Parmesan and the bread crumbs. Sprinkle over the crab mixture.

• • IF YOU'RE STOPPING HERE:

Cover the dish with plastic wrap and refrigerate up to 3 days.

• • WHEN YOU'RE READY TO EAT:

Preheat the oven to 400°F. Remove the plastic wrap from the baking dish and bake until the top is golden brown and the filling heated through, about 15 minutes.

DOLLAR SAVER tip:

Substitute thawed frozen small cooked shrimp or imitation crabmeat for the fresh crabmeat.

- 2 large zucchini, cut in half lengthwise
- 1 pound fresh lump crabmeat, picked over for shells and cartilage
- ⅓ cup low-fat sour cream
- ½ cup coarsely chopped artichoke hearts (oil or water-packed)
- ¼ cup plus 2 tablespoons grated Parmesan cheese, preferably freshly grated
- 1 teaspoon Dijon mustard
- 1 teaspoon Creole or Cajun seasoning
- ¼ teaspoon salt
- ¼ teaspoon freshly ground black pepper
- 2 tablespoons seasoned dry bread crumbs

QUICK FIX IT YOUR WAY:

If you don't want to take the time to preheat the oven, you can cook the stuffed zucchini in the micro-wave. Cover the baking dish with plastic wrap and cook on HIGH for 3 minutes, until hot. The tops won't be browned, but the filling will be hot and the zucchini boats tender.

PREP POINTER:

Turning a zucchini into a "boat" is simple: cut each zucchini in half lengthwise, then, using a small spoon, remove seeds and a little flesh, until there's a canoe shape and enough room for filling!

SAVORY TUNA BURGERS

Prep day:
PREP TIME: 10 MINUTES

To finish the meal:
ACTIVE COOKING TIME: 6–10 MINUTES

SERVES 4

Think beyond beef when you're making burgers. I make them with all kinds of things—wild mushrooms, tuna, salmon, turkey breast, chicken breast, crabmeat, you name it. Anything shaped into a patty and nestled on a bun is welcome in my home! For a complete meal, serve the burgers with Two-Cabbage Asian Slaw with Sesame Seeds (page 202). You can make the slaw up to 3 days ahead and refrigerate it until ready to serve.

• •

In a large bowl, combine the tuna, mayonnaise, bread crumbs, parsley, mustard, hot sauce, salt, and pepper. Mix well and shape the mixture into four equal patties, each about 1 inch thick.

• • IF YOU'RE STOPPING HERE:

Wrap the burgers tightly in plastic wrap and refrigerate up to 3 days or freeze up to 3 months. Thaw completely in the refrigerator or microwave for 3 to 4 minutes on LOW before cooking.

• • WHEN YOU'RE READY TO EAT:

Heat the oil in a large skillet over medium heat. Unwrap the burgers and cook until golden brown and heated through, 3 to 5 minutes per side. Serve the burgers on buns with sliced tomato and pickles.

"ANYTHING SHAPED INTO A PATTY AND NESTLED ON A BUN
is welcome in my home."

Three 6-ounce cans light tuna in water, drained

1/3 cup light mayonnaise

3 tablespoons seasoned dry bread crumbs

2 tablespoons chopped fresh parsley

1 teaspoon Dijon mustard

1 teaspoon hot sauce

1/4 teaspoon salt

1/4 teaspoon freshly ground black pepper

1 tablespoon olive oil

4 hamburger buns or kaiser rolls

1 beefsteak tomato, sliced

1/4 cup thinly sliced sweet pickles (such as gherkins)

CASHEW-LIME
CHICKEN WITH RICE

Prep day:
PREP TIME: 10 MINUTES
ACTIVE COOKING TIME: 14–16 MINUTES

To finish the meal:
ACTIVE COOKING TIME: 5 MINUTES

SERVES 4

My son Kyle calls cashews "moon nuts" because their little curve reminds him of a crescent moon. Shape aside, their salty, slightly sweet crunch is the perfect partner for otherwise bland chicken in this Asian-inspired winner. I like to serve this dish with a fresh salad of baby spinach leaves and mandarin oranges tossed with a light (store-bought!) vinaigrette—a salad that comes together while the dish reheats, now that's a Quick Fix!

• •

Cook the rice according to the package directions.

Meanwhile, heat the oil in a large skillet over medium heat. Add the ginger and garlic and cook, stirring, for 1 minute. Add the chicken and cook, stirring, until browned on all sides, about 5 minutes. Add the salt and pepper and stir to coat. Add the broth, hoisin, lime juice, and zest and bring to a simmer. Partially cover the pan and simmer until the chicken is cooked through and the sauce thickens, 8 to 10 minutes.

• • IF YOU'RE STOPPING HERE:

Let the rice and chicken mixture cool to room temperature, then transfer to separate plastic bags or plastic containers and refrigerate up to 3 days.

• • WHEN YOU'RE READY TO EAT:

Reheat the rice in the microwave. Reheat the chicken mixture in the microwave or a large saucepan over medium heat, simmering for 5 minutes to heat though. Meanwhile, chop the cashews. Serve the chicken mixture over the rice and top with the cashews.

1 cup basmati or jasmine rice

2 teaspoons peanut oil

1 tablespoon peeled and minced fresh ginger

3 cloves garlic, minced

1¼ pounds boneless, skinless chicken breasts, cut into 1-inch pieces

½ teaspoon salt

¼ teaspoon freshly ground black pepper

1½ cups reduced-sodium chicken broth

¼ cup hoisin sauce

1 tablespoon fresh lime juice

1 teaspoon finely grated lime zest

1 cup salted dry-roasted cashews

DOLLAR SAVER tip:

Buy cashew pieces instead of whole cashews and save money and precious time!

CHICKEN-CHEDDAR QUESADILLAS WITH WHITE BEAN-GREEN PEA GUACAMOLE

Prep day:
PREP TIME: 15 MINUTES
ACTIVE COOKING TIME: 6 MINUTES

To finish the meal:
WALK-AWAY TIME: 3–10 MINUTES

SERVES 4

I know, I know, you can order quesadillas at many restaurants. But why wait? Quesadillas are easy to make (it's basically an "assembly" meal) and *you* decide what goes inside! Vegan? No big deal. Substitute sliced portobello mushrooms for the chicken and use soy cheese instead of milk-based varieties. The guacamole on the side is a slam dunk, too. An interesting alternative to the usual avocado-based kind, it uses sweet peas mashed with white beans, garlic, and cilantro. Make a big batch; you'll want some for chip-dunking later in the week! The dip is so easy to make, you can wait until mealtime and prepare it while the quesadillas bake.

• •

Heat the oil in a large skillet over medium heat. Add the chicken and cook, stirring, until browned on all sides, about 5 minutes. Add the chiles and liquid smoke and cook 1 minute to heat through.

Arrange four tortillas on a flat surface. Top each one with an equal amount of the chicken mixture to within ¼ inch of the edges. Top the chicken with cheese (⅓ cup of cheese per tortilla). Top with a second tortilla and wrap each quesadilla in aluminum foil.

To make the guacamole, in a medium bowl or blender, combine the peas, beans, garlic, lime juice, and cumin. Mash with a fork or puree until larger lumps disappear (leave it as lumpy as you desire!). Fold in the cilantro and season to taste with salt and pepper.

CHICKEN-CHEDDAR QUESADILLAS:

2 teaspoons olive oil

1¼ pounds boneless, skinless chicken breasts, cut into 1-inch chunks

One 4-ounce can diced green chiles

1 teaspoon liquid smoke seasoning

Eight 8-inch flour tortillas

1⅓ cups shredded reduced-fat cheddar cheese

WHITE BEAN-GREEN PEA GUACAMOLE:

2 cups frozen peas, thawed

1 cup canned white beans, drained

2 cloves garlic, minced

2 teaspoons fresh lime juice

1 teaspoon ground cumin

¼ cup chopped fresh cilantro

Salt and freshly ground black pepper

TIME SAVER **tip:**

Buy rotisserie chicken and use that instead!

QUICK FIX IT YOUR WAY:

If you want, you can cook the quesadillas in the microwave instead of the oven. Remove the foil, wrap them in plastic wrap, and microwave on HIGH for 2 to 3 minutes, until the cheese melts.

● ● IF YOU'RE STOPPING HERE:

Refrigerate the quesadillas up to 3 days or freeze up to 3 months. Thaw completely in the refrigerator or microwave for 2 to 3 minutes on LOW before baking. Place the guacamole in a tightly covered container and refrigerate up to 3 days.

● ● WHEN YOU'RE READY TO EAT:

Preheat the oven to 400°F. Place the foil-wrapped quesadillas on a baking sheet and bake until the cheese melts, about 10 minutes. Slice each quesadilla into 4 wedges and serve with the guacamole on the side.

DOLLAR SAVER tip:

Buy chicken in bulk and individually wrap 1 or 2 breast halves in plastic wrap; store all the wrapped pieces in plastic bags in the freezer and thaw as needed.

GOOD HEALTH note:

White beans contain a large amount of fiber and folate, a B vitamin that protects against heart disease and birth defects.

APRICOT-JALAPEÑO CHICKEN WITH SESAME NOODLES

Prep day:
PREP TIME: 15 MINUTES

To finish the meal:
WALK-AWAY TIME: 25–30 MINUTES

SERVES 4

I've reinvented the globe and slammed continents together with this amazing meal. TexMex meets Tokyo and it's a match made in heaven. The bold flavors of jalapeños (sweetened with some apricot preserves) and cilantro pair beautifully with a noodle dish that boasts sesame, soy, and ginger. Joy to the world!

● ●

Cook the soba noodles according to the package directions, then drain.

Coat a shallow baking dish with cooking spray.

In a blender or food processor, combine the jalapeños, apricot preserves, cilantro, salt, and pepper and process until smooth.

Place the chicken in the prepared baking dish (or a zip-top plastic bag if you're planning on freezing it) and top with the jalapeño mixture.

● ● IF YOU'RE STOPPING HERE:

Let the noodles come to room temperature and transfer to a large zip-top plastic bag. Cover the baking dish with plastic wrap and refrigerate both up to 3 days or freeze up to 3 months. Thaw completely in the refrigerator or microwave for 3 to 4 minutes on LOW before baking.

12 ounces soba or somen noodles or whole wheat spaghetti

Cooking spray

½ cup sliced pickled jalapeños, drained

½ cup apricot preserves

¼ cup chopped fresh cilantro

½ teaspoon salt

½ teaspoon freshly ground black pepper

4 boneless, skinless chicken breast halves

3 tablespoons reduced-sodium soy sauce

2 teaspoons toasted sesame oil

¼ cup chopped scallions (green and white parts)

2 tablespoons minced pickled ginger

Preheat the oven to 400°F. Remove the plastic wrap from the chicken and bake until cooked through, 25 to 30 minutes.

Transfer the noodles to a microwave-safe bowl, cover with plastic wrap, and microwave on HIGH for 1 minute, until warm. Add the soy sauce, sesame oil, scallions, and pickled ginger and toss to combine. Season to taste with salt and pepper. Serve the chicken over the noodles.

GOOD HEALTH note:

Soba noodles are made with buckwheat flour (and, in some cases, wheat flour), so they boast more fiber than white-flour pasta.

PARMESAN-CRUSTED CHICKEN WITH SWEET-N-HOT MUSTARD DIP

Prep day:
PREP TIME: 10 MINUTES

To finish the meal:
WALK-AWAY TIME: 25–30 MINUTES

SERVES 4

There are few aromas better than Parmesan roasting in the oven—think baked lasagna! You'll get that same fantastic aroma from this dish. Chicken breasts are coated with a crunchy blend of oats, Parmesan cheese, herbs, and spices. The crust is golden and flavorful and the flesh is tender and juicy. Even better? A slightly hot, slightly sweet mustard dipping sauce on the side!

To make this a full meal, serve with Orzo Salad with Giardiniera and Sun-dried Tomato Vinaigrette (page 231), which you can make in the time it takes for the chicken to cook (the walk-away time) or precook and refrigerate it until you're ready to finish the salad right before dinner.

• •

In a shallow dish, combine the flour and ½ teaspoon each of the salt and pepper. Add the chicken to the mixture and turn to coat evenly and completely.

Whisk together the eggs and water in a separate shallow dish.

In a third shallow dish or plastic bag, combine the Parmesan, oats, garlic seasoning, and the remaining ¼ teaspoon each of salt and pepper.

Dip the flour-coated chicken into the eggs, then transfer to the Parmesan mixture. Turn until well coated.

PARMESAN-CRUSTED CHICKEN:

1 tablespoon all-purpose flour

¾ teaspoon salt, divided

¾ teaspoon freshly ground black pepper, divided

4 boneless, skinless chicken breast halves

2 large eggs, lightly beaten

1 tablespoon water

⅓ cup grated Parmesan cheese, preferably freshly grated

¼ cup quick-cooking oats

2 teaspoons salt-free garlic and herb seasoning

Cooking spray

SWEET-N-HOT MUSTARD DIP:

¼ cup Dijon mustard

2 tablespoons honey

1 tablespoon white wine vinegar

½ teaspoon hot mustard powder

¼ teaspoon garlic powder

••IF YOU'RE STOPPING HERE:

Wrap the chicken tightly in plastic wrap or transfer to plastic bags and refrigerate up to 3 days or freeze up to 3 months. Thaw completely in the refrigerator or microwave for about 4 minutes on LOW before baking.

••WHEN YOU'RE READY TO EAT:

Preheat the oven to 400°F. Coat a large baking sheet with cooking spray. Unwrap the chicken and place it on the prepared baking sheet. Spray the tops with cooking spray and bake until the crust is golden brown and chicken cooked through, 25 to 30 minutes. While the chicken cooks, whisk together the dip ingredients. Serve the chicken with the dip on the side.

> " THERE ARE FEW AROMAS BETTER THAN PARMESAN ROASTING IN THE OVEN—
> you'll get that fantastic aroma from this dish."

CHICKEN ENCHILADAS WITH REFRIED BEANS AND JACK CHEESE

SERVES 4

If it's gooey, count me in! And what's better than gooey cheese? My whole family adores these enchiladas—flour tortillas stuffed with chicken, refried beans, green chiles, salsa, and cilantro and baked under a thick layer of cheese. What's not to love? Plus, it gets your kids to eat heart-healthy beans!

• •

Heat the oil in a large skillet over medium heat. Add the onion and garlic and cook, stirring, until softened, about 2 minutes. Add the chicken and cook, stirring a few times, until golden brown on all sides, about 5 minutes. Stir in the refried beans, chiles, and salsa and simmer for 2 minutes to heat through. Remove from the heat and stir in the cilantro.

Arrange the tortillas on a flat surface. Top each with an equal amount of the chicken mixture. Roll up the tortillas and place side by side in a shallow baking dish. Top the tortillas with the shredded cheese.

• • IF YOU'RE STOPPING HERE:

Cover the dish with plastic wrap and refrigerate up to 3 days or freeze up to 3 months. Thaw completely in the refrigerator or microwave for about 4 minutes on LOW before baking.

• • WHEN YOU'RE READY TO EAT:

Preheat the oven to 400°F. Remove the plastic wrap from the baking dish and bake until the cheese is golden and gooey, 15 to 20 minutes.

2 teaspoons olive oil

½ cup chopped onion

2 cloves garlic, minced

1¼ pounds boneless, skinless chicken breasts, cut into ½-inch strips

One 15-ounce can refried beans

One 4-ounce can diced green chiles, drained if necessary

¼ cup prepared salsa, mild, medium, or hot

2 tablespoons chopped fresh cilantro

Four 8-inch flour tortillas

1½ cups shredded Mexican cheese blend (or any combination of Monterey Jack, cheddar, Colby, pepper Jack, and/or mozzarella)

QUICK FIX IT YOUR WAY:

To cook the dish in the microwave instead of the oven, leave the plastic wrap on the baking dish and microwave on HIGH for 3 to 5 minutes, until the dish is hot all the way through.

SESAME CHICKEN THIGHS
WITH GARLICKY BROCCOLI

Prep day:
PREP TIME: 5 MINUTES
ACTIVE COOKING TIME: 6–7 MINUTES
WALK-AWAY TIME: 5 MINUTES

To finish the meal:
ACTIVE COOKING TIME: 3–5 MINUTES

SERVES 4

Sounds like a take-out item from a Chinese restaurant, right? Perhaps, but my version doesn't require a cholesterol-lowering drug as a chaser. Don't worry, my lightened-up take on this classic still highlights the bold flavors of garlic and soy sauce (from bottled black bean sauce), and there's a nice crunch from sesame seeds toasted a golden brown. Serve this over somen or angel hair noodles for a complete meal. To prep the noodles, cook them according to the package instructions, then drain, let cool to room temperature, and zip up in a plastic bag until you're ready to reheat them with the chicken mixture.

● ●

Heat the sesame oil in a large skillet over medium heat. Add the chicken and cook, stirring, until golden brown on all sides, about 5 minutes. Add the sesame seeds and stir to coat the chicken with them. Cook 1 to 2 minutes, until the seeds turn golden. Add the broth, black bean sauce, and pepper and bring to a simmer. Cover the pan and cook until the chicken is cooked through, about 5 minutes.

● ● IF YOU'RE STOPPING HERE:

Let cool to room temperature, then transfer the chicken mixture to a large zip-top plastic bag or container and refrigerate up to 3 days.

● ● WHEN YOU'RE READY TO EAT:

Reheat the chicken mixture in a large skillet over medium heat. When the sauce is simmering, sprinkle the garlic powder all over the broccoli and arrange it over the simmering liquid. Cover and simmer until the broccoli is crisp-tender, 3 to 5 minutes, then serve.

1 tablespoon toasted sesame oil

1¼ pounds boneless, skinless chicken thighs, cut into 1-inch pieces

2 tablespoons sesame seeds

1 cup reduced-sodium chicken broth

½ cup Chinese black bean sauce

½ teaspoon freshly ground black pepper

1 to 2 teaspoons garlic powder, to your taste

4 cups broccoli florets

QUICK FIX IT YOUR WAY:

You can also reheat the dish in the microwave. Place the chicken mixture in a large, microwave-safe dish and cover with plastic wrap. Microwave on HIGH for 3 minutes, until hot. Place the broccoli on top of the chicken and sprinkle with the garlic powder. Cover and microwave again on HIGH for 2 minutes, until the broccoli is crisp-tender.

ORANGEY HERB AND OAT-CRUSTED CHICKEN TENDERS

Prep day:
PREP TIME: 10 MINUTES

To finish the meal:
WALK-AWAY TIME: 20 MINUTES

SERVES 4

My kids love these chicken "fingers" and I feel better serving them versus the frozen and fried varieties targeted to kids. Don't get me wrong, I have dinosaur-shaped nuggets sitting in my freezer right now, but when I have the time to prep ahead, I much prefer making these. It may seem weird to use marmalade to coat the chicken, but the sticky mixture keeps the crust stuck to the chicken while adding an incredible flavor of its own. You can use any fruit preserve, such as strawberry, raspberry, apricot, or blackberry—I just don't recommend grape jelly! Instead of chicken tenders, you can substitute boneless, skinless chicken breast halves cut into thin strips.

To make this a complete meal, serve it with Lettuce Wedges with Thousand Island Dressing (page 193) and Red Potatoes with Capers, Tomatoes, and Onion (page 219), or Mashed Acorn Squash with Sunflower Seeds (page 217). Any of these can be put together while the chicken cooks.

● ●

In a large zip-top plastic bag, combine the oats, flour, oregano, thyme, garlic powder, onion powder, salt, and black pepper. Seal the bag and shake to combine.

Using a brush or spoon, coat the chicken pieces all over with the marmalade. Add the chicken to the oat mixture, seal the bag, and shake to coat the pieces evenly.

½ cup quick-cooking oats

2 tablespoons all-purpose flour

1 teaspoon dried oregano

1 teaspoon dried thyme

1 teaspoon garlic powder

½ teaspoon onion powder

½ teaspoon salt

¼ teaspoon freshly ground black pepper

1¼ pounds chicken tenders (rib meat) or boneless, skinless chicken breasts cut into thin strips

⅓ cup orange marmalade

Cooking spray

• • IF YOU'RE STOPPING HERE:

Refrigerate the chicken up to 3 days or freeze up to 3 months. Thaw completely in the refrigerator or microwave for about 4 minutes on LOW before baking.

• • WHEN YOU'RE READY TO EAT:

Preheat the oven to 400°F. Coat a large baking sheet with cooking spray. Transfer the chicken pieces from the bag to the prepared baking sheet and spray the tops of them with cooking spray. Bake until golden brown and cooked through, about 20 minutes (no need to turn them). Serve hot.

GOOD HEALTH note:

To keep calories in check, the correct portion size for a serving of protein (such as chicken, turkey, beef, and pork) is approximately 3 to 4 ounces. When you start with 1 to 1¼ pounds of raw chicken for four people, it cooks down to about 3½ to 4 ounces per serving. The same is true of other meats.

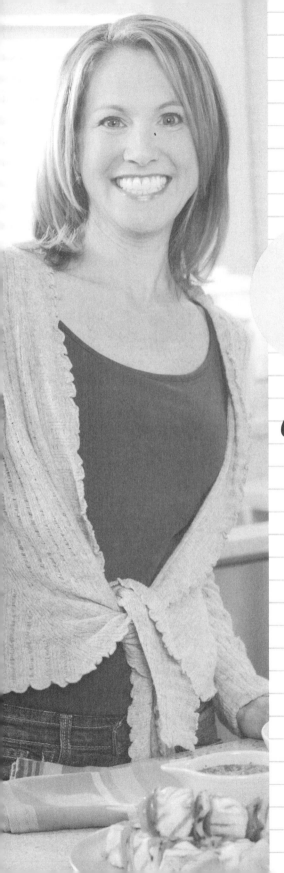

3

One recipe,

MORPH IT:

many meals

"MORPHING MEALS MAKES LIFE SO EASY, **YOU WILL BE TRANSFORMED** into a less stressful, more organized, HAPPY COOK!"

The word *morph* means "one of various distinct forms of an organism or species" and "to be transformed." Although the first definition doesn't sound all that appetizing, morphing is exactly what you'll do with the meals in this chapter. One dish amazingly and deliciously transforms into several different weeknight meals in minutes. Morphing meals makes life so easy, you will be transformed into a less stressful, more organized, happy cook! As I said in the beginning of the book, I'm not just going to give you recipes like roasting a big chicken and then using the extra meat for chicken salad sandwiches. I'm guessing you do that already and you don't need me to tell you how. What you *do* need is an inspirational, Quick Fix spin on reinventing dinner. My meals are unique, even when working with one main ingredient (like that perfect roasted chicken). My husband doesn't call me "MacGyver" for nothing. I can take yummy scraps from any meal and transform them into entirely new dishes. In fact, meals are so alive and refreshing, you could easily feel confident about serving them to guests! No one has to know you're working with leftovers!

●● THE NINE(TEEN) (HUNDRED) LIVES OF A PLASTIC BAG

Wondering what to do with all those plastic bags you're using? It seems a shame to toss them (especially if they've been holding things like chopped celery, carrots, or onions). Good news—you can use them again and again. Simply rinse out used plastic bags and turn them inside out to dry. Don't do this with bags that have held raw meat, fish, or poultry.

MAIN RECIPE

HERBED FISH CAKES

Total Time: 40 to 45 minutes
PREP TIME: 15 MINUTES
ACTIVE COOKING TIME: 4–5 MINUTES
WALK-AWAY TIME: 20 MINUTES

SERVES 4

My fish cakes are an excellent variation on the traditional crab cake. Not that I don't *adore* crab (I eat so much sometimes I walk sideways), but fish is a nice change. My fish cakes are a breeze to prepare and, if you make a huge batch, you can enjoy creamy Fish and Corn Chowder, Stuffed Red Bell Peppers, and Artichoke Salad with Capers and Red Lettuce later in the week. If you don't feel like eating all the fish in one week, simply freeze the leftovers and make those dishes another time. Or cut this recipe in half (cook just under 2 pounds of fish) and enjoy tonight's meal plus one additional meal (your choice from the morph recipes that follow).

The fish cakes, stuffed bell peppers, and salad also work well with tuna (not true of the chowder), so feel free to substitute fresh tuna steaks or an equal amount of canned light tuna for the halibut (reduce the quantity of tuna by about ¾ pound since you won't be making the chowder).

I serve these fish cakes with Brussels Sprouts with Bacon and Shallots (page 208) and warm dinner rolls.

● ●

Preheat the oven to 400°F.

Place the fish in a large stockpot and pour in enough water to cover. Set the pan over high heat and bring to a boil. Reduce the heat to low and simmer just until the fish is fork-tender, about 5 minutes. Drain.

You may also cook the fish in the microwave: Arrange the fillets in a single layer in a microwave-safe baking dish. Cover the dish with plastic wrap and microwave on HIGH for 4 minutes, until the fish is fork-tender. If the fish needs more cooking, cook in 1-minute intervals to prevent overcooking.

3½ pounds fresh or frozen halibut or cod fillets or steaks, thawed and skin removed if necessary

½ cup light mayonnaise

6 tablespoons seasoned dry bread crumbs

1 tablespoon Dijon mustard

1 tablespoon chopped fresh parsley

1 tablespoon chopped fresh basil

1½ teaspoons Old Bay® seasoning

1 teaspoon dried oregano

½ teaspoon freshly ground black pepper

2 tablespoons olive oil

STORAGE SAVVY:

To store the fish cakes in the freezer, place them on a baking sheet and set them in the freezer until frozen solid, then transfer to a freezer bag and label and date it. You'll then be able to open the bag and take out however many fish cakes you need. If you happen to really like this recipe, simply eat the fish cakes as is, instead of morphing them. Thaw in the microwave for a few minutes on LOW before reheating for a minute or so on HIGH.

Transfer the fish to a large bowl and fold in the mayonnaise, bread crumbs, mustard, parsley, basil, Old Bay, oregano, and pepper. Shape the mixture into 12 cakes, each about 1 inch thick. (At this point, you can cover the cakes with plastic wrap and freeze up to 3 months. Thaw completely in the refrigerator or microwave for 3 to 5 minutes on LOW before cooking.)

Heat the oil in a large, ovenproof skillet over medium-high heat. Add the fish cakes a few at a time and cook until golden brown, 2 to 3 minutes per side. Transfer the pan to the oven and bake 20 minutes.

Serve 4 cakes for this meal and refrigerate up to 3 days or freeze up to 3 months; thaw completely in the refrigerator or microwave for 3 to 5 minutes on LOW before using.

TIME SAVER tip:

Assemble the fish cakes and refrigerate up to 3 days before cooking.

MORPH RECIPE #1

ARTICHOKE SALAD WITH CAPERS AND RED LETTUCE

Total Time: 10 minutes
PREP TIME: 10 MINUTES

SERVES 4 TO 6

Fish and artichokes love each other. It must be all that time spent together in the Mediterranean region. Toss this concoction over colorful greens and you've got a hearty salad for any weeknight. For a beautiful "entertaining" salad, add ½ pound cooked small shrimp. I like to serve this with Quick Bruschetta with Tomatoes and Olives (page 192). If you don't want to fire up the oven for toasting the bruschetta, use melba toast squares or bagel chips as the base for the tomato-olive topping.

• •

In a large bowl, toss the fish cakes, artichoke hearts, capers, oregano, vinegar, and oil together until well combined. Season to taste with salt and pepper. Serve the fish mixture over the lettuce.

2 leftover Herbed Fish Cakes (facing page), crumbled

One 14-ounce can artichoke hearts, drained and chopped

2 tablespoons drained capers

2 tablespoons chopped fresh oregano or parsley

2 tablespoons cider vinegar

1 tablespoon olive oil

Salt and freshly ground black pepper

6 cups chopped red lettuce leaves

STUFFED RED BELL PEPPERS

Total Time: 20 to 22 minutes

PREP TIME: 10 MINUTES

WALK-AWAY TIME: 10–12 MINUTES

SERVES 4

This dish is so elegant looking, you could easily serve it to guests. Not that your family doesn't deserve elegance, I just mean it's gorgeous! Red bell peppers are sweet and wonderful and the perfect color contrast for the white-fleshed fish. You can stuff the peppers in advance (up to 3 days) and bake them just before serving. I like to serve these with Rice Pilaf with Tomatoes and Olives (page 209) because the pilaf comes together in the time it takes for the peppers to bake.

• •

Preheat the oven to 400°F. Coat a shallow roasting pan with cooking spray.

In a medium bowl, combine the fish cakes, sour cream, chiles, cilantro, and chili powder until well combined. Stuff the mixture into the pepper halves and arrange side by side in the prepared pan. Sprinkle the cheese over the filling. Bake until the filling is hot and the cheese golden and bubbly, 10 to 12 minutes, and serve.

Cooking spray

3 leftover Herbed Fish Cakes (page 64), crumbled

1/3 cup low-fat sour cream

One 4-ounce can diced green chiles, drained if necessary

2 tablespoons chopped fresh cilantro

1 teaspoon chili powder

4 red bell peppers, cut in half lengthwise and seeded

1 cup shredded Monterey Jack cheese

GOOD HEALTH note:

Bell peppers are incredibly rich in vitamin C. In fact, one bell pepper has more than twice the vitamin C of an orange (132 mg in the pepper versus 59 mg in the orange).

MORPH RECIPE #3 FISH AND CORN CHOWDER

Total Time: 17 minutes
PREP TIME: 10 MINUTES
ACTIVE COOKING TIME: 2 MINUTES
WALK-AWAY TIME: 5 MINUTES

SERVES 4

Simply toss together leftover fish cakes with a little corn, broth, and milk and you've got a creamy, thick chowder in minutes. There's no need for extra seasonings or lots of ingredients since all the flavor was baked into the cakes. Plus, since the cakes were made with bread crumbs, the starch from the bread helps thicken the broth without adding flour or butter. I like to serve this soup with a mixed green salad topped with cherry or grape tomatoes.

● ●

Heat the oil in a large saucepan over medium heat. Add the leeks and cook, stirring, until softened, about 3 minutes. Add the fish cakes, corn kernels, creamed corn, and bay leaves. Pour the broth over the fish mixture and bring to a simmer. Partially cover the pan and simmer for 5 minutes. Stir in the milk and simmer until hot, about 5 minutes. Remove the bay leaves, season to taste with salt and pepper, and serve.

2 teaspoons olive oil

2 leeks (white part only), rinsed well and chopped

3 leftover Herbed Fish Cakes (page 64), crumbled

2 cups frozen corn kernels

One 14-ounce can creamed corn

2 bay leaves

3 cups reduced-sodium chicken or vegetable broth

1½ cups low-fat milk

Salt and freshly ground black pepper

QUICK FIX IT YOUR WAY:

To make your own creamed corn, combine 1½ cups of canned or frozen corn and ½ cup low-fat milk in a blender and puree until almost smooth (leaving some smaller pieces of corn).

ROASTED SALMON WITH SWEET-N-HOT MUSTARD GLAZE

Total Time: 25 minutes
PREP TIME: 10 MINUTES
WALK-AWAY TIME: 15 MINUTES

SERVES 4

You can hold me to this: This salmon recipe is sure to win over even the non-fish eaters in the bunch. Sweet honey is blended with Dijon and hot mustard to create an unbelievable sauce for both fish and chicken. Fresh dill is added to extra sauce to use as a topping after cooking. As easy as it is elegant-looking, consider this for your next dinner party! Even better, the leftovers evolve into Asian Salmon Cakes with Sesame-Wasabi Cream, Mixed Seafood Paella with Sausage and Pink Beans, and Salmon Chowder with Yukon Gold Potatoes.

Serve this salmon with a fresh green salad and Parmesan-Crusted Cauliflower (page 209)—roast the cauliflower in the oven with the salmon and everything will be ready at the same time.

• •

Cooking spray

3½ pounds salmon fillets or steaks, skin on and pinbones removed (by your fish guy or you can do it using tweezers)

Salt and freshly ground black pepper

½ cup Dijon mustard

½ cup honey

2 tablespoons water

2 tablespoons fresh lemon juice

1 teaspoon hot mustard powder

1 teaspoon garlic powder

2 tablespoons chopped fresh dill

Preheat the oven to 400°F.

Coat a shallow baking dish with cooking spray. Season both sides of salmon with salt and pepper. Place salmon in prepared baking dish.

In a medium bowl, whisk together the mustard, honey, water, lemon juice, mustard powder, and garlic powder. Remove ½ cup of the mustard sauce and set aside. Pour the remaining sauce over the salmon fillets in the pan. Roast the salmon, uncovered, until fork-tender, about 15 minutes.

Stir the dill into the reserved mustard sauce. Serve one-third of the roasted salmon (four fillets, each about 4 ounces after cooking) with the dill-spiked mustard sauce spooned over the top. Refrigerate the remaining salmon up to 3 days or freeze up to 3 months; thaw it completely in the refrigerator or microwave for 3 to 5 minutes on LOW before using.

STORAGE SAVVY:

Prep the salmon for storage by peeling away the skin and breaking it into coarse pieces. Store the salmon in portions that make the most sense for you. You'll need 2 cups for the salmon cakes, 1 to 2 cups for the paella, and 1½ cups for the chowder. Label the plastic bag or container with the date and the name of the dish you intend to use it in.

ASIAN SALMON CAKES
WITH SESAME-WASABI CREAM

SERVES 4

Thanks to the mustard sauce on the roasted salmon, you just need a few ingredients to pull these sumptuous patties together. Look for tubes of wasabi paste in the Asian section of the super-market or, if your store sells sushi, alongside the sushi with the soy sauce. You can make these ahead and refrigerate up to 3 days before cooking. I like to serve the cakes on soft rolls, but they're also fine alone or on a bed of lightly dressed lettuce. I also serve them with a cucumber salad on the side (just sliced cuke, red onion, olive oil, and balsamic vinegar).

• •

In a medium bowl, gently combine the salmon, bread crumbs, egg, cilantro, cumin, and 2 tablespoons of the mayonnaise until combined. Shape mixture into four patties, each about 1 inch thick.

In a small bowl, add the sesame oil and wasabi paste to the remaining ¼ cup mayonnaise and mix well. Set aside.

Heat the olive oil in a large skillet over medium heat. Add the salmon cakes and cook until golden brown and cooked through, 3 to 5 minutes per side.

Serve the cakes with sesame-wasabi cream spooned over the top (1 tablespoon per salmon cake).

Total Time: 16 to 20 minutes
PREP TIME: 10 MINUTES
ACTIVE COOKING TIME: 6–10 MINUTES

2 cups leftover coarsely flaked salmon (facing page)

2 tablespoons seasoned dry bread crumbs

1 large egg, lightly beaten

1 tablespoon chopped fresh cilantro

1 teaspoon ground cumin

6 tablespoons light mayonnaise, divided

2 teaspoons toasted sesame oil

2 teaspoons wasabi paste

1 tablespoon olive oil

INGREDIENT note:

If you can't find wasabi paste (if you already have wasabi powder), make your own paste: combine equal parts wasabi powder and water and mix until you have a thick paste.

MORPH RECIPE #2 MIXED SEAFOOD PAELLA WITH SAUSAGE AND PINK BEANS

SERVES 4

This popular Spanish dish often boasts sausage, chicken, and shell-fish simmered in a tomato-based, saffron-infused sauce. Swap salmon for chicken and you can enjoy this traditional dish using leftovers (a true time saver)! You can certainly add cooked chicken breast to the dish if you want. If you're cutting calories and fat, substitute sweet or hot turkey or chicken sausage for the chorizo. This dish is so amazing you'll want to throw a party to celebrate it.

• •

Cook the rice according to the package directions.

Meanwhile, in a large saucepan, combine the salmon, shrimp, sausage, tomatoes, beans, bell pepper, oregano, and saffron, set over medium-high heat, and bring to a simmer. Let simmer until the shrimp are bright pink and cooked through, about 5 minutes. Stir in the cooked rice and cook for 2 minutes to heat through. Remove from the heat, stir in the parsley, season to taste with salt and pepper, and serve.

INGREDIENT note:

Saffron lends a pungent, bitter honey flavor to this dish. If you're wondering why it's a little pricey, it takes 75,000 blossoms or 225,000 hand-picked stigmas to make one single pound, making it the world's most expensive spice. Thankfully, a little goes a long way.

Total Time: 17 minutes
PREP TIME: 10 MINUTES
ACTIVE COOKING TIME: 7 MINUTES

1½ cups quick-cooking rice

1 to 2 cups leftover salmon (page 68), broken into pieces

1 pound medium shrimp, peeled and deveined

2 links chorizo or andouille sausage (or kielbasa), cut in half lengthwise, then cut crosswise into ¼-inch-thick slices

One 28-ounce can diced tomatoes

One 15-ounce can pink beans, drained

1 large green bell pepper, seeded and diced

1 teaspoon dried oregano

½ teaspoon saffron threads

¼ cup chopped fresh parsley

Salt and freshly ground black pepper

SALMON CHOWDER WITH YUKON GOLD POTATOES

SERVES 4

This recipe is so good it's worth making it from scratch with fresh or canned salmon if you don't have any leftover salmon, in the fridge or freezer. Rich, thick, and hearty, all you need to round out the meal is a light side salad (I also like to serve this soup in bread bowls—buy large bread rounds from the bakery section of your grocery store, hollow them out, and fill them with the soup for a fabulous presentation).

• •

Heat the oil in a large saucepan over medium heat. Add the leeks and garlic and cook, stirring, until softened, about 3 minutes. Add the tarragon and cook 1 minute, until fragrant. Add the potatoes and broth and bring to a simmer. Partially cover the pan and simmer until the potatoes are fork-tender, 8 to 10 minutes. Stir in the salmon and milk and simmer 2 minutes to heat through. Remove from the heat, season to taste with salt and pepper, and serve.

VARIATION:

No more salmon? Substitute 1½ cups of peeled and deveined small or medium cooked shrimp, fresh or frozen (no need to thaw first).

Total Time: 18 to 20 minutes
PREP TIME: 5 MINUTES
ACTIVE COOKING TIME: 5 MINUTES
WALK-AWAY TIME: 8–10 MINUTES

2 teaspoons olive oil

2 leeks (white part only), rinsed well and chopped

2 cloves garlic, minced

1 teaspoon dried tarragon

2 medium Yukon Gold potatoes, peeled and cut into 1-inch cubes

4 cups reduced-sodium chicken or vegetable broth

1½ cups leftover salmon (page 68), broken into pieces

One 12-ounce can evaporated fat-free milk or low-fat milk

Salt and freshly ground black pepper

TIME SAVER tip:

Use canned potatoes and simmer just 5 minutes (instead of 8 to 10 minutes).

BALSAMIC ROASTED PORK TENDERLOIN

SERVES 4

My husband loves pork tenderloin, as do my two little boys. After you roast the lean tenderloin in a sweet and tangy sauce of balsamic vinegar, honey, and mustard (livened up with fresh thyme), you not only enjoy an amazing dinner that night, you can use the tender leftover meat to make brothy Wonton Soup, colorful Pork Fried Rice, and super messy, super delicious Pork Sloppy Joes later in the week. Now that's a Quick Fix!

I like to serve the tenderloin with Soy-Sesame Green Beans with Ginger (page 211) and roasted new red or gold potatoes (pop halved small potatoes alongside the pork and they'll be ready when the pork is).

• •

Preheat the oven to 400°F.

Coat a shallow roasting pan with cooking spray. Place the pork in the prepared pan and season the top and sides with salt and pepper.

In a small bowl, whisk together the vinegar, honey, mustard, and thyme. Spoon the mixture all over the pork, then roast until an instant-read thermometer inserted into the thickest part reads at least 160°F (the pork may still be pink in the center and that's OK, so long as the temperature is right), about 45 minutes, basting every 15 minutes if possible.

Let the pork stand for 10 minutes before slicing one-third of it crosswise into 1-inch-thick slices. Serve the sliced pork for this meal and refrigerate the leftovers up to 3 days or freeze up to 3 months.

Cooking spray

Two 2-pound pork tenderloins, trimmed of silverskin if necessary (see Prep Pointer on page 45)

Salt and freshly ground black pepper

¼ cup balsamic vinegar

2 tablespoons honey

2 tablespoons Dijon mustard

2 teaspoons chopped fresh thyme

QUICK FIX IT YOUR WAY:

If you prefer, you can cut this recipe in half (cook just one pork tenderloin) and make tonight's recipe plus just one or two of the three morph recipes with the leftovers.

STORAGE SAVVY:

Prep the leftover pork for storage. For the fried rice, dice 1½ cups of the pork. For the wonton soup, shred 1 cup and, for the sandwiches, shred 3 cups. Place each recipe portion in its own zip-top plastic bag, date it, then label it with the name of the recipe it will be used in.

MORPH RECIPE #1 WONTON SOUP

Total Time: 20 minutes
PREP TIME: 5 MINUTES
ACTIVE COOKING TIME: 15 MINUTES

SERVES 4

If you think a soup like this is beyond your capability on a week-night, think again. First off, you can always stuff the wontons up to 3 days in advance and refrigerate them (a *must* if you want the soup ready in less than 15 minutes during the week). You can also stuff the wontons and freeze them up to 3 months (no need to thaw them before using). Second, you can certainly skip the "filling" of the wontons and just simmer everything together in the pot (this makes phenomenal soup—how can you lose with shredded veg-etables, pork, broth, pasta-like wontons, and a spike of scallions at the end?). But stuffing the wrappers and watching those adorable little dumplings tenderize in simmering broth is worth every min-ute. Trust me.

• •

Place the broth in a large saucepan, set over medium-high heat, and bring to a simmer.

Meanwhile, heat the oil in a large skillet over medium heat. Add the slaw mix and cook, stirring, for 1 minute. Add the pork and soy sauce and cook, stirring, until the cabbage wilts, about 2 minutes. Remove from the heat.

Arrange the wonton wrappers on a flat surface. Spoon 1 tea-spoon of the filling onto the center of each wrapper. Wet your fin-gers with water and run a wet finger along the outer edge of the wrapper. Pull up the edges of the wrapper and pinch together, mak-ing a beggar's purse–shaped wonton. When you run out of filling, place the stuffed wontons in the simmering broth and simmer until tender and translucent, about 5 minutes. Remove from the heat, stir in the scallions, and serve.

6 cups reduced-sodium chicken broth

1 tablespoon toasted sesame oil

1 cup shredded coleslaw mix

1 cup shredded leftover pork (facing page)

1 tablespoon reduced-sodium soy sauce

24 wonton wrappers (often sold in the refrigerated section of the produce aisle)

¼ cup chopped scallions (white and green parts)

DOLLAR SAVER tip:

Don't throw those leftover wonton wrappers out. If you tightly wrap them with plastic wrap, you can store them in the refrigerator for up to 1 month. Or, slip them into a freezer bag and freeze for up to 6 months (thaw them completely in the refrigerator or microwave for a few minutes on LOW before using). Use any leftover wrappers to make Wonton Chips. Spread them in a single layer on a baking sheet that's been coated with cooking spray, then give them a coating of spray and season evenly with salt, pepper, and garlic powder. Bake in a preheated 400°F oven until golden brown and crisp, 6 to 8 minutes. Serve with soft or melted cheeses and dips.

MORPH RECIPE #2 PORK FRIED RICE

SERVES 4

Just because the word "fried" is in a dish, it doesn't mean you actually have to fry anything. I don't like grease in my arteries *or* on my stove-top. In my lightened-up version of fried rice, I sauté vegetables in a little peanut oil and then add incredibly flavorful hoisin sauce, rice, and leftover pork. Since the rice is uncooked, it absorbs all the flavors of the veggies, sauce, and pork while it cooks to tender perfection. If you want to cut calories even further, instead of whole eggs use 4 egg whites or ½ cup fat-free liquid egg substitute.

• •

Heat 2 teaspoons of the oil in a large skillet over medium heat. Add the eggs and cook, stirring frequently, until cooked through and scrambled, 3 to 5 minutes. Remove the eggs to a plate and keep warm.

To the same skillet, still over medium heat, heat the remaining 2 teaspoons oil. Add the onion, carrots, and garlic and cook until softened, about 2 minutes. Add the rice and cook for 1 minute, stirring constantly to coat with the oil. Add the hoisin and stir to coat the rice. Add the broth, pork, and peas and bring to a boil. Remove from the heat, cover, and let stand until the liquid is absorbed and the rice tender, about 5 minutes. Fluff with a fork and season to taste with salt and pepper.

Transfer the fried rice to individual plates. Chop the cooked egg into small pieces and sprinkle over the rice just before serving.

4 teaspoons peanut oil, divided

2 large eggs, slightly beaten

½ cup chopped onion

½ cup shredded carrots

3 cloves garlic, minced

1 cup quick-cooking white rice

¼ cup hoisin sauce

2 cups reduced-sodium chicken broth

1½ cups diced leftover pork (page 72)

½ cup frozen green peas

Salt and freshly ground black pepper

GOOD HEALTH note:

To eliminate about 40 calories and 10 fat grams from the dish, substitute ½ cup fat-free liquid egg substitute for the 2 large eggs.

MORPH RECIPE #3 PORK SLOPPY JOES

SERVES 4

I must admit, I'm known for my Sloppy Joes. It's almost expected that I bring a batch to any gathering of friends (except maybe a beach party). I typically use ground turkey breast but I've been known to use leftover pork and other shredded meats to make Joes in minutes. If you're already out of pork for the week, simply brown a batch (about one pound) of ground turkey or chicken breast or lean ground beef. When you're ready to serve, break out the big rolls and even bigger napkins—this is one delightfully messy crowd pleaser.

● ●

In a large saucepan, combine the pork, tomatoes, ketchup, mustard, liquid smoke, basil, chili powder, cumin, salt, and pepper. Set the pan over medium heat, bring to a simmer, and simmer for 5 minutes. Add the corn and simmer 5 minutes to heat through.

Spoon the mixture onto rolls and serve hot.

"THIS IS ONE DELIGHTFULLY MESSY crowd pleaser."

3 cups shredded leftover pork (page 72; about 1 pound)

One 14-ounce can petite-cut diced tomatoes

½ cup ketchup

1 tablespoon Dijon mustard

1 teaspoon liquid smoke seasoning

1 teaspoon dried basil

1 teaspoon chili powder

1 teaspoon ground cumin

¼ teaspoon salt

¼ teaspoon freshly ground black pepper

1 cup frozen corn kernels

4 kaiser rolls

GOOD HEALTH note:

To add vitamin C (and some terrific green color), add one seeded and diced green bell pepper when you add the corn.

PORK TENDERLOIN WITH ANCHO-SPIKED MIXED BERRY SAUCE

Total Time: 45 to 50 minutes
PREP TIME: 5 MINUTES
ACTIVE COOKING TIME: 10 MINUTES
WALK-AWAY TIME: 20–25 MINUTES
RESTING TIME: 10 MINUTES

SERVES 4

Super-lean pork tenderloin couldn't be easier to prepare. A little salt and pepper, a quick roast in the oven, and you have a protein-packed meal in just about 30 minutes. Pork is also a wonderful "canvas" for adding all kinds of flavorful ingredients. I love pairing pork with fruits and this sauce is a unique combination of sweet berries and earthy cumin. I typically serve this dish with a steamed green vegetable (green beans, broccoli, or spinach) and rice or couscous. What do I do with the leftovers? Quick Cabbage Rolls with Pork and Hoisin Rice, Pan-Seared Pork with Pineapple-Kiwi Salsa, and Pork Tortilla Soup!

• •

Preheat the oven to 400°F. Coat a large roasting pan with cooking spray.

Season the pork all over with salt and pepper and place in the prepared pan. Roast until an instant-read thermometer inserted into the thickest part reads at least 160°F, 30 to 35 minutes. Let the pork stand 10 minutes before slicing crosswise into 1-inch-thick slices.

Meanwhile, in a medium saucepan, combine the berries, confectioners' sugar, vinegar, ancho chile, and cumin, set over medium heat, and bring to a simmer. Simmer until the sauce thickens and the berries break down, 10 minutes, stirring frequently. Remove from heat and discard the ancho chile.

Serve one-third of the pork with this meal, topped with the berry sauce, and refrigerate remaining pork up to 3 days or freeze up to 3 months; thaw in the refrigerator or microwave for 3 to 5 minutes on LOW before using.

Cooking spray

Three 1-pound pork tenderloins, trimmed of silverskin if necessary (see Prep Pointer on page 45)

Salt and freshly ground black pepper

One 10-ounce bag frozen raspberries (not in syrup)

One 10-ounce bag frozen blackberries (not in syrup)

2 tablespoons confectioners' sugar

2 tablespoons cider vinegar

1 whole ancho chile pepper

1 teaspoon ground cumin

STORAGE SAVVY:

For the seared pork dish, wrap one leftover pork tenderloin in plastic wrap and refrigerate or freeze (cover the plastic wrap with aluminum foil). Dice 4 cups of the remaining leftover pork and store 2 cups for the cabbage rolls and 2 cups for the soup. Date your containers and label with the name of the dish you plan to use it in.

MORPH RECIPE #1 QUICK CABBAGE ROLLS WITH PORK AND HOISIN RICE

SERVES 4

Cabbage rolls are incredibly easy to make and they're even more fun to eat! Who doesn't love to eat with their hands after a day of working with them? Feel free to add any vegetables you have handy to the rice mixture. This dish also works with leftover chicken and beef.

● ●

Cook the rice according to the package directions, adding the carrots, hoisin, and sesame oil to the boiling water when you add the rice.

When the rice is done, remove if from the heat and stir in the pork.

Bring 2 to 3 inches of water to a boil in a large stockpot.

Arrange the cabbage leaves on a flat surface. Top each leaf with an equal amount of the pork mixture. Fold over the sides of each leaf to partially cover the filling. Starting from the shorter end, roll up each leaf tightly. Place the rolls side by side in a colander or steamer basket and set over the simmering water. Cover and steam until the cabbage leaves are soft, about 5 minutes. Serve the rolls with the soy sauce on the side for dipping.

Total Time: 15 to 20 minutes
PREP TIME: 10–15 MINUTES
ACTIVE COOKING TIME: 5 MINUTES

1 cup quick-cooking white or brown rice

½ cup shredded carrots

1 tablespoon hoisin sauce

2 teaspoons toasted sesame oil

2 cups diced leftover roasted pork tenderloin (facing page)

8 leaves Napa cabbage

¼ cup reduced-sodium soy sauce

VARIATION:

Not a big cabbage fan? That's fine, you can still enjoy this dish—substitute 8 red lettuce leaves for the Napa cabbage and assemble as directed.

MORPH RECIPE #2

PAN-SEARED PORK WITH PINEAPPLE-KIWI SALSA

SERVES 4

Rejuvenate leftover pork slices by pan-searing them in olive oil (to create a golden brown crust) and then freshen everything up with a lively pineapple-kiwi salsa. If you want, you can also make this dish with boneless pork loin chops or lean sirloin steak (just cook the meat longer if you're starting from raw). I like to round out the dish with a store-bought mixed bean salad or combination of rice and black beans.

• •

In a medium bowl, combine the pineapple, kiwi, cilantro, jalapeño, and lime juice and toss to combine. Season to taste with salt and pepper and set aside.

Heat the oil in a large skillet over medium heat. Season both sides of the pork slices with salt and pepper. Rub the chili powder into both sides of the pork. Add the pork to the hot pan and sear 2 minutes per side, until golden brown. Serve the pork with the salsa spooned over the top.

Total Time: 14 to 19 minutes
PREP TIME: 10–15 MINUTES
ACTIVE COOKING TIME: 4 MINUTES

1 cup diced pineapple (fresh or canned in juice)

1 cup peeled and diced kiwi (2 or 3)

2 tablespoons chopped fresh cilantro

1 jalapeño, seeded and minced

1 tablespoon fresh lime juice

Salt and freshly ground black pepper

1 tablespoon olive oil

1 leftover roasted pork tenderloin (1 pound, page 76), sliced crosswise into 1-inch-thick slices

1 tablespoon chili powder

GOOD HEALTH note:

Kiwi is bursting with fiber and disease-fighting vitamin C—one kiwi boasts 120% of the RDA for vitamin C, a vitamin that not only boosts the immune system, but also protects your arteries from the damaging effects of free radicals.

MORPH RECIPE #3 PORK TORTILLA SOUP

Total Time: 15 minutes
PREP TIME: 5 MINUTES
ACTIVE COOKING TIME: 10 MINUTES

SERVES 4

This is a fantastic recipe for leftover anything. Use shredded or diced chicken, beef, even shrimp for a Quick Fix soup for any night of the week! You'll love the comforting, Tex-Mex–inspired broth that features *pico de gallo* (a rich combination of tomatoes, onion, and bell peppers) topped with crunchy corn chips. To complete the meal, serve a mixed green salad on the side.

● ●

Heat the oil in a large saucepan over medium heat. Add the garlic and cook, stirring, for 1 minute. Add the broth, *pico de gallo* sauce, pork, and corn and bring to a boil. Reduce the heat to medium-low, partially cover the pan, and simmer for 10 minutes.

Ladle the soup into bowls and sprinkle with the scallions and cilantro. Top with the tortilla strips just before serving.

"THIS IS A FANTASTIC RECIPE
for leftover anything."

- 2 teaspoons olive oil
- 2 cloves garlic, minced
- 7 cups reduced-sodium chicken broth
- 1 cup *pico de gallo* sauce (sold near the salsa in your supermarket)
- 2 cups diced leftover roasted pork tenderloin (page 76; about half of one tenderloin; ½ pound)
- 1 cup frozen corn
- ¼ cup chopped scallions (white and green parts)
- 2 tablespoons chopped fresh cilantro
- 2 cups tortilla strips or baked tortilla chips

QUICK FIX IT YOUR WAY:

To make your own baked corn chips, cut corn tortillas into wedges and place them on a baking sheet. Spray them with cooking spray, then season evenly with salt, pepper, and a little ground cumin. Bake in a preheated 400°F oven until golden brown and crisp, 6 to 8 minutes.

CITRUS-GLAZED HAM WITH ROASTED MANDARIN ORANGES

Total Time: 80 to 85 minutes
PREP TIME: 10–15 MINUTES
WALK-AWAY TIME: 1 HOUR
RESTING TIME: 10 MINUTES

SERVES 4

Ham is the quintessential "morphing" ingredient because it's typically sold in larger portions, it lasts for days, and it's simple to incorporate into other dishes. Ham also adds just enough salty-smokiness to a recipe while enabling you to make distinctly different meals from one baked ham, namely Penne with Ham, Green Peas, and Oregano; Honey Ham Wraps with Brie and Papaya; and Super-Cheesy Stove-Top Macaroni and Cheese with Ham.

I serve this ham with Green Beans with Pearl Onions and Parsley (page 212) and quinoa (both cook up in less than 15 minutes). So, let's ham it up!

• •

Preheat the oven to 325°F.

If the ham has skin, peel it away using a sharp knife, leaving a thin (⅛-inch) layer of fat on the surface. Score the fat (if there is any) with the knife by cutting diagonal lines (about ⅛ inch deep) from one side to the other, crisscrossing cuts to form diamond shapes on the surface. Transfer the ham to a large roasting pan.

In a small bowl, whisk together the marmalade, vinegar, and mustard. Brush the mixture all over the ham. Pour mandarin oranges and syrup from the can all over the ham, allowing the oranges to fall to the bottom of the pan. Bake for 1 hour (14 minutes per pound), basting every 15 minutes with the pan juices.

Remove the ham from the oven and let rest 10 minutes before cutting one-quarter of it crosswise into ¼-inch-thick slices. Serve the slices with this meal (topped with the roasted mandarin oranges) and refrigerate the remaining ham up to 3 days or freeze up to 3 months; thaw completely in the refrigerator or microwave for 3 to 5 minutes on LOW before serving.

One 4-pound fully cooked boneless ham

1 cup orange marmalade

2 tablespoons cider vinegar

½ teaspoon dry mustard

One 11-ounce can mandarin oranges in light syrup

STORAGE SAVVY:

If you plan on making the wraps, cut another 12 slices from the ham and place them in a large zip-top plastic bag. If you're going to be making the penne and/or macaroni, you need to cut the remaining ham into 1-inch cubes. You'll need 2 cups for the penne and 1 cup for the macaroni. Date your bags and label either as ham or with the name of the dish you plan to use it in.

PENNE WITH HAM, GREEN PEAS, AND OREGANO

Total Time: 16 to 21 minutes
PREP TIME: 10–15 MINUTES
ACTIVE COOKING TIME: 6 MINUTES

SERVES 4

This is an excellent brunch or take-along side dish for a party. Penne pasta cooks up fast and it's fantastic tossed with pan-seared, salty ham, sweet peas, and fresh oregano. The combination is light and phenomenal. If you can't find fresh oregano, substitute dried.

• •

Cook the pasta according to the package directions, adding the peas for the last 30 seconds of cooking. Drain and set aside.

Meanwhile, heat the oil in a large skillet over medium heat. Add the ham and cook, stirring, until golden brown, about 3 minutes. Add the garlic and cook, stirring, for 1 minute. Add the oregano and cook, stirring, for 1 minute, until fragrant. Add the broth, stir in the mustard, and bring to a simmer. Add the cooked pasta and simmer 1 minute to heat through.

Remove from the heat, season to taste with salt and pepper, and serve.

12 ounces penne pasta

1 cup frozen green peas

1 tablespoon olive oil

2 cups diced leftover ham (facing page)

2 cloves garlic, minced

2 tablespoons chopped fresh oregano or 1 teaspoon dried

1½ cups reduced-sodium chicken broth

1 tablespoon Dijon mustard

Salt and freshly ground black pepper

QUICK FIX IT YOUR WAY:

No leftover ham? Don't sweat it—swing by the market for deli ham or a ham steak and dice it at home. You may also substitute Canadian bacon or smoked turkey.

HONEY HAM WRAPS WITH BRIE AND PAPAYA

Total Time: 10 minutes
PREP TIME: 10 MINUTES

SERVES 4

My husband loves this simple sandwich because he loves to eat on the go and it doesn't drip! Not only a great lunchbox treat, this wrap goes well with a broth-based soup (minestrone comes to mind) for a complete dinner. Feel free to substitute any cheese for the Brie, such as vegetable cream cheese, spreadable cheddar, or slices of Monterey Jack, Gouda, or Swiss.

• •

Arrange the tortillas on a flat surface. Spread 1 tablespoon honey over each tortilla. Top the honey with one-quarter of the Brie (spread it with a knife). Top the Brie with one-quarter of the ham slices, papaya slices, and watercress leaves, making an even line down the center. Roll up and serve (or wrap in plastic and refrigerate for up to 2 days).

Four 8-inch flour tortillas

4 tablespoons honey

8 ounces Brie cheese

12 thin slices leftover ham (page 80)

1 cup peeled, seeded, and thinly sliced ripe papaya

1 cup watercress leaves

GOOD HEALTH note:

Papaya is an excellent source of vitamin C and beta-carotene, both potent antioxidants.

SUPER-CHEESY STOVE-TOP MACARONI AND CHEESE WITH HAM

SERVES 4

A family classic spruced up with baked ham. What's not to love? To make this in 15 minutes or less, cook the pasta ahead and refrigerate it until you're ready to assemble the meal. If you choose to do that, instead of adding the sour cream when the pasta is hot, add it when you add the other hot ingredients (the milk-and-cheese mixture) right before serving. You can also change the cheeses; if you want more cheddar, cut back on the Swiss and vice versa. If you want to add mozzarella or Gouda, please do! Just "say cheese" and you can't go wrong! Instead of baking the dish, I create a time-saving topping of bread crumbs and Parmesan that mimics the golden brown crust you get from baking (let's face it, that's the best part!).

• •

Cook the pasta according to the package directions. Drain and transfer to a large bowl. While the pasta is still hot, stir in the sour cream and set aside.

Scald the milk by heating in a small saucepan over medium heat until tiny bubbles just appear around the edges, about 3 minutes. Reduce the heat to low and add the cheddar and Swiss, mustard, pepper, salt, and nutmeg and simmer until the cheeses melt, stirring gently and constantly. Fold the cheese mixture into the pasta, along with the ham, and transfer the mixture to a serving dish.

Combine the bread crumbs and Parmesan in a dry skillet and set over medium heat. Cook 1 to 2 minutes, until both are golden brown. Sprinkle the mixture evenly over the macaroni and cheese and serve.

Total Time: 15 minutes
PREP TIME: 10 MINUTES
ACTIVE COOKING TIME: 5 MINUTES

1 pound elbow macaroni

½ cup low-fat sour cream

1½ cups low-fat milk

8 ounces reduced-fat cheddar cheese, shredded (2 cups)

4 ounces reduced-fat Swiss cheese, shredded (1 cup)

2 teaspoons Dijon mustard

½ teaspoon freshly ground black pepper

¼ teaspoon salt

⅛ teaspoon ground nutmeg

1 cup diced leftover ham (page 80)

2 tablespoons seasoned dry bread crumbs

2 tablespoons grated Parmesan cheese, preferably freshly grated

PREP POINTER:

Learn from my mistakes—make sure you combine the bread crumbs and Parmesan in the skillet at the same time. Otherwise, the cheese will melt and turn into one big clump, not the crumbly mixture you desire!

RED WINE AND BLACK PEPPER–GLAZED FILET MIGNON

SERVES 4

If this seems like a lot of steak, substitute chicken for half or all of the meat and use chicken in the morph recipes (Artichoke-Steak Melts with Smoked Provolone and Basil Mayo, Steak Soft Tacos with Asparagus-Spiked Guacamole, and Steak and Marinated Vegetable Salad over Acini di Pepe). I like to buy steak at the warehouse store so I can get good-quality meat in bulk. If you don't have that option, simply buy a box of frozen steaks from your favorite supermarket. I love to serve these steaks with baked potatoes and steamed broccoli that's been dusted with garlic powder. If you're not a wine enthusiast, substitute a nonalcoholic version or reduced-sodium beef broth.

• •

Coat a stove-top grill pan, griddle, or large skillet with cooking spray and set over medium-high heat.

Season the steaks all over with salt and cracked pepper. In a large shallow dish, whisk together the wine and honey. Add the steaks to the wine mixture and turn to coat. Cooking several at a time, place the steaks in the hot pan and cook 4 minutes per side for medium doneness. Serve 4 steaks for this meal and refrigerate the remaining steaks up to 3 days or freeze up to 3 months; thaw completely in the refrigerator or microwave for 3 to 5 minutes on LOW before using.

QUICK FIX IT YOUR WAY:

If desired, you can cut this recipe in half (cook 7 steaks or just under 2 pounds of chicken) and make tonight's recipe plus one of the morph recipes with the leftovers (you will have slightly less steak than called for but the recipe will be fine).

Total Time: 13 minutes
PREP TIME: 5 MINUTES
ACTIVE COOKING TIME: 8 MINUTES

Cooking spray

Fourteen 4- to 5-ounce filets mignons or lean steaks, trimmed of fat, or 3½ pounds boneless, skinless chicken breast halves

Salt and cracked black peppercorns

1 cup red wine

¼ cup honey

STORAGE SAVVY:

To store the leftover steaks, you can either set them on a baking sheet and place it in the freezer until they're frozen solid, then pop them all in one big bag and pull them out as you need them. Or you can divide them up according the morph recipes you plan to use them in: 4 steaks for the melts, 4 steaks for the tacos, and 2 steaks for the salad.

ARTICHOKE-STEAK MELTS WITH SMOKED PROVOLONE AND BASIL MAYO

SERVES 4

Rolls are piled high with tender steak, artichoke hearts, and smoked provolone cheese, then broiled until the cheese is gooey and golden. These sandwiches are so good you'll want to make the main recipe just to create them! If you don't have steak, try using leftover chicken instead. I like to serve these with coleslaw or pasta salad on the side.

● ●

Preheat the broiler.

Spread the mustard on bottom side of the rolls (2 teaspoons per roll). Top with equal amounts of the steak slices and artichoke hearts. Lay the cheese slices on top of the artichokes. Arrange sandwiches (open-faced) on a large baking sheet. Broil until the cheese is golden and bubbly (the open-faced, untopped side of the roll should be golden brown and toasted, too), about 3 minutes.

Meanwhile, combine the mayonnaise and basil in a blender or food processor and process until smooth (this will keep up to 3 days in the fridge; it's delicious spooned over grilled chicken or fish). Spread the mayo on the toasted side of the roll and serve.

Total Time: 8 to 13 minutes
PREP TIME: 5–10 MINUTES
ACTIVE COOKING TIME: 3 MINUTES

- 8 teaspoons coarse mustard
- 4 rolls (preferably submarine sandwich rolls)
- 4 leftover cooked filets mignons (facing page; or chicken breast halves), thinly sliced
- One 14-ounce can water-packed artichoke hearts, drained and chopped
- 8 ounces thinly sliced smoked or regular provolone cheese
- ½ cup light mayonnaise
- ¼ cup chopped fresh basil

GOOD HEALTH note:

There are 800 calories and 88 grams of fat in ½ cup of regular mayonnaise. There are 400 calories and 39 grams of fat in ½ cup of light mayonnaise— need I say more? In my opinion, the flavor is the same.

MORPH RECIPE #2

STEAK SOFT TACOS WITH ASPARAGUS-SPIKED GUACAMOLE

Total Time: 11 minutes
PREP TIME: 5 MINUTES
ACTIVE COOKING TIME: 6 MINUTES

SERVES 4

Soft tacos are a midweek cook's best friend! Why? Beyond the obvious (handheld food that eliminates the need to wash silverware), tacos are typically assembled by their owner. That means, once you provide the fillings and fixin's, your work is finished and the party begins! I've suggested my favorite additions to any kind of taco below, but feel free to add whatever you want (salsa, beans, green chiles, etc.). If you don't have a food processor to make the guacamole, simply mash all the ingredients together with a fork or potato masher.

• •

In a medium bowl, combine the asparagus, avocado, garlic, lemon juice, and cumin. Mash together with a fork until blended, leaving some small chunks. Stir in the tomato, cilantro, onion, and jalapeño and season to taste with salt and pepper. Set aside.

Heat the oil in a large skillet over medium heat. Add the chili powder and cook, stirring, for 1 minute, until fragrant. Add the steak and broth and cook until the beef is hot and liquid is absorbed, about 5 minutes. Spoon the beef mixture onto the tortillas and top with your favorite toppings and the guacamole.

1 cup canned or bottled asparagus spear pieces (1-inch pieces, drained)

2 ripe avocados, peeled and pitted

2 to 3 cloves garlic, to taste, minced

1 tablespoon fresh lemon juice

1 teaspoon ground cumin

1 small Roma or plum tomato, diced

2 tablespoons chopped fresh cilantro

2 tablespoons minced white onion

1 jalapeño, seeded and minced

Salt and freshly ground black pepper

1 tablespoon olive oil

1 tablespoon chili powder

4 leftover cooked filets mignons (page 84; or chicken breast halves), thinly sliced

½ cup reduced-sodium beef broth or water

Four 8-inch flour tortillas

ADDITIONS:

Shredded lettuce

Diced tomatoes

Shredded reduced-fat cheddar cheese

Chopped scallions

Sliced hot peppers

STEAK AND MARINATED VEGETABLE SALAD
OVER ACINI DI PEPE

SERVES 4

What a colorful salad over fun-shaped pasta! *Acini di pepe* is Italian for "peppercorns" and these little gems look like tiny beads. They're excellent for cold salads and soups. As for the vegetables, load up at the salad bar at lunch and you can enjoy an amazing dinner in just minutes! Steak is fantastic with this, but you can also use leftover chicken, turkey, ham, or shrimp.

● ●

Cook the pasta according to the package directions. Drain and set aside.

Meanwhile, fill a medium saucepan with water, add ¼ cup of the vinegar and the sugar and bring to a boil. Add the broccoli, cauliflower, and carrots and boil until just tender, about 1 minute. Drain and transfer to a large bowl.

Add the steak, roasted red peppers, basil, the remaining 2 tablespoons vinegar, and the olive oil and toss to combine. Season to taste with salt and pepper. Spoon the pasta onto a serving platter or individual plates and top with the steak mixture.

Total Time: 16 minutes
PREP TIME: 15 MINUTES
ACTIVE COOKING TIME: 1 MINUTE

1 pound acini di pepe or ditalini pasta or elbow macaroni

¼ cup plus 2 tablespoons red wine vinegar, divided

1 tablespoon sugar

2 cups broccoli florets

1 cup cauliflower florets

1 cup baby carrots

2 leftover cooked filets mignons (page 84; or chicken breast halves), cut into 1-inch chunks

1 cup chopped roasted red peppers (from water-packed jar)

¼ cup chopped fresh basil

1 tablespoon olive oil

Salt and freshly ground black pepper

MAIN RECIPE

BEEF AND NOODLES IN THAI PEANUT SAUCE

Total Time: 26 to 30 minutes
PREP TIME: 15 MINUTES
ACTIVE COOKING TIME: 11–15 MINUTES

SERVES 4

When my husband and I first started dating, we ate Thai food every Saturday night at the same restaurant, and I always ordered the crab salad and pad Thai. Both were incredible—so much so that I had withdrawal symptoms when we moved away! Here's my version of pad Thai, lightened up using broth instead of oil. The peanut sauce is so good this recipe makes a big batch and morphs into three completely different meals (Shrimp Satay, Chicken Salad with Peanut-Lime Vinaigrette, and Steamed Vegetable Spring Rolls).

● ●

Cook the noodles according to the package directions. Drain, transfer to a large bowl, and cover with aluminum foil or plastic wrap to keep warm.

Meanwhile, in a medium saucepan, whisk together the sauce ingredients until well blended and set the pan over medium heat. Bring to a simmer and let simmer for 10 minutes.

Heat the peanut oil in a large skillet over medium-high heat. Add the ginger and garlic and cook, stirring, for 2 minutes. Add the bell pepper and cook, stirring, for 2 minutes. Add the beef and cook, stirring, for 2 minutes. Add 1 cup of the peanut sauce and simmer until the beef is cooked through, about 5 minutes.

Transfer the beef mixture to the noodles and toss to combine, then serve on individual plates topped with the peanuts and scallions. The leftover peanut sauce will keep in the refrigerator up to 4 days or in the freezer up to 3 months; thaw completely in the refrigerator or microwave for about 3 minutes on LOW before using.

8 ounces somen or soba noodles or whole wheat spaghetti

THAI PEANUT SAUCE:

3 cups reduced-sodium beef broth

2 tablespoons reduced-sodium soy sauce

2 tablespoons creamy peanut butter

2 teaspoons toasted sesame oil

1 teaspoon hot sauce

PAD THAI:

1 tablespoon peanut oil

1 teaspoon peeled and minced fresh ginger

2 cloves garlic, minced

1 medium red bell pepper, seeded and diced

1¼ pounds lean beef steak (such as sirloin or flank), cut crosswise into ¼-inch-thick strips

¼ cup chopped dry-roasted peanuts

¼ cup chopped scallions (white and green parts)

STORAGE SAVVY:

Store the leftover peanut sauce in tightly covered plastic containers in the refrigerator or freezer in portion sizes that make sense to you, either 1-cup or all ½-cup measures, and date and label them.

MORPH RECIPE #1 SHRIMP SATAY

Total Time: 15 minutes
PREP TIME: 10 MINUTES
ACTIVE COOKING TIME: 5 MINUTES

SERVES 4

Not just for dinner, shrimp satay is fun finger food and a super addition to any party tray. You're going to use the leftover peanut sauce, thickened with black bean sauce and livened up with hot sauce, to make a great dip for your skewered shrimp. The sauce is also perfect with vegetables—simply place the sauce in a bowl and surround it with crudités (baby carrots, sliced cucumber, broccoli and cauliflower florets, cherry tomatoes, celery, zucchini, and/or yellow squash). I like to serve this with Asian noodles or rice and lightly sautéed sugar snap peas on the side.

• •

In a small saucepan, whisk together the peanut sauce, black bean sauce, and hot sauce. Set over medium-high heat, bring to a simmer, and simmer until reduced slightly, 5 to 7 minutes.

Meanwhile, coat a stove-top grill pan, griddle, or large skillet with cooking spray and set over medium-high heat. Skewer the shrimp, leaving a little space between each one to allow for even cooking. Place the skewers on the hot pan and cook until the shrimp are bright pink and cooked through, about 5 minutes, turning frequently.

Serve the shrimp with the warm peanut sauce on the side for dunking.

1 cup leftover Thai Peanut Sauce (facing page)

2 tablespoons Chinese black bean sauce

1 teaspoon hot sauce

Cooking spray

Wooden or metal skewers

1½ pounds large or jumbo shrimp, peeled and deveined

MORPH RECIPE #2

CHICKEN SALAD WITH PEANUT-LIME VINAIGRETTE

Total Time: 15 minutes
PREP TIME: 15 MINUTES

SERVES 4

Peanuts, chicken, and mayo? Sounds crazy but it works like magic. You'll love this Thai-inspired salad that partners fresh vegetables, chicken, and a lime-infused peanut dressing. It makes for a satisfying lunch or light dinner (light enough to save room for dessert!).

• •

In a large bowl, combine the chicken, tomatoes, celery, and onion. Add the peanut sauce, mayonnaise, and lime juice and toss to combine. Season to taste with salt and pepper. (At this point, you can refrigerate the salad for up to 3 days.)

Place the lettuce on four individual plates and top with the chicken mixture. Sprinkle the peanuts over the top just before serving.

1 pound cooked chicken (from rotisserie chicken, leftover roast chicken, or from the deli section of the supermarket), cubed

1 cup diced fresh tomatoes

½ cup diced celery

¼ cup diced red onion

½ cup leftover Thai Peanut Sauce (page 88)

¼ cup light mayonnaise

2 tablespoons fresh lime juice

Salt and freshly ground black pepper

6 cups shredded lettuce

¼ cup chopped dry-roasted peanuts

VARIATION:

For an added citrus flavor, add ¼ cup diced lemongrass. When using fresh lemongrass, peel away the tough outer skin and dice the portion close to the root end, where it's more tender. If you can't find fresh lemongrass, add 1 teaspoon finely grated lemon or lime zest.

MORPH RECIPE #3 STEAMED VEGETABLE SPRING ROLLS

Total Time: 18 minutes
PREP TIME: 10 MINUTES
ACTIVE COOKING TIME: 8 MINUTES

SERVES 4

Don't freak out when you see canned vegetables in this ingredient list. The fact is, canned vegetables and fruits are typically processed at their nutritional peak, so all the valuable nutrients are locked in. Quick Fix–wise, they're perfect for busy weeknights because you don't have to cook them first! Serve these with quick-cooking rice and Teriyaki Bok Choy with Cashews (page 214)—start both before you begin the spring rolls and everything will come together at the same time.

• •

Heat the oil in a large skillet over medium-high heat. Add the coleslaw mix and cook, stirring, until the cabbage wilts, about 3 minutes. Add the peanut sauce and mix well to combine. Remove from the heat.

Place 2 inches of water in the bottom of a steamer or large saucepan and set over medium-high heat.

Meanwhile, arrange the spring roll wrappers on a flat surface. Top each wrapper with an equal amount of the coleslaw mixture, water chestnuts, and asparagus, making an even layer down the center. Roll up the wrappers, tuck in the ends and place side by side in steamer basket or large colander. Set the steamer basket (or colander) over the now simmering water, cover, and steam until the wrappers are translucent, about 5 minutes.

Serve the spring rolls with soy sauce on the side for dipping.

- 2 teaspoons peanut or olive oil
- 2 cups shredded coleslaw mix
- ½ cup leftover Thai Peanut Sauce (page 88)
- 8 spring roll wrappers (sold in the refrigerated section of the produce aisle)
- One 6-ounce can sliced water chestnuts, drained and chopped
- One 11-ounce can asparagus, drained and cut into 1-inch pieces
- ¼ cup reduced-sodium soy sauce

INGREDIENT note:

You may find two types of spring roll wrappers at the market, those made from wheat flour and those made from rice (also called banh trang *or* banh da nem*). Both will work in this recipe, so the choice is yours. Leftover wrappers can be stored in plastic wrap in the refrigerator for up to 1 month or in a freezer bag in the freezer up to 6 months. Thaw completely in the refrigerator or microwave for a few minutes on LOW before using (avoid thawing and refreezing too many times or the wrappers will become hard). To keep wrappers pliable while working, cover them with a damp paper towel.*

SWEET AND TANGY BEEF ROAST WITH VEGETABLES

Total Time: 1¾ to 2¼ hours
PREP TIME: 15 MINUTES
WALK-AWAY TIME: 1¼–1¾ HOURS
RESTING TIME: 15 MINUTES

SERVES 4

This meal reminds me of my mom. She's the queen of hearty beef roasts with vegetables straight from her garden. When I make my own roasts, I try to think outside the traditional produce box when pairing the beef with vegetables. I can really use my imagination since I don't grow one single vegetable! Instead of regular onions, Idaho's, carrots, and celery, I use leeks, sweet potatoes, turnips, and celery root. The flavor completely changes and you'll love the variety! Even better, with the extra beef, you can enjoy French Dip Sandwiches, Asian Beef Salad with Cashews, and Beef Empanadas later in the week, month, or year!

● ●

Heat the oil in a large Dutch oven or stockpot over medium-high heat. Season the beef roast all over with salt and pepper. Add the roast to the pan and brown on all sides. Using tongs, remove it from the pan and set aside. To the same pan, add the leeks, sweet potatoes, turnip, and celery root and cook, stirring a few times, until the vegetables begin to brown, about 3 minutes. Return the beef to the pan.

Meanwhile, in a medium bowl, whisk together the remaining ingredients. Pour over the beef and vegetables and bring to a boil. Reduce the heat to low, cover, and simmer, turning the roast every 20 to 30 minutes, until the meat is tender, about 1¼ hours.

Let the beef roast rest for 15 minutes, then cut into ¼-inch-thick slices. Serve one-third of the beef with this meal (and all of the vegetables) and refrigerate the remaining beef up to 3 days or freeze up to 3 months; thaw completely in the refrigerator or microwave for 3 to 5 minutes on LOW before using.

1 tablespoon olive oil

One 5-pound boneless beef chuck or rump roast, trimmed of fat

Salt and freshly ground black pepper

2 leeks (white part only), rinsed well and chopped

2 large sweet potatoes, peeled and cut into 2-inch chunks

1 large turnip, peeled and chopped

1 celery root (celeriac), peeled and chopped

One 15-ounce can tomato sauce

⅓ cup firmly packed light or dark brown sugar

1 tablespoon cider vinegar

1 tablespoon chili powder

1 teaspoon ground cumin

1 teaspoon garlic powder

1 teaspoon onion powder

INGREDIENT note:

Celery root (not the real root of celery but a close cousin) is base-ball-sized, with brown, knotted skin. Sounds appetizing, huh? Thankfully, beneath the homely exterior lies a unique flavor combination of celery, lemon, and a little licorice.

MORPH RECIPE #1

FRENCH DIP SANDWICHES

Total Time: 10 minutes
PREP TIME: 5 MINUTES
ACTIVE COOKING TIME: 5 MINUTES

SERVES 4

On one of my first dates with my husband, we met friends at a bar in Philadelphia, a place known for their roast beef sandwiches. The place was delightfully grungy and the sandwiches were amazing. Roast beef was pulled with tongs from a vat of rich juice and placed on tender rolls. Extra "juice" was served on the side for dunking the sandwich. It wasn't pretty but it was memorable.

Although the sandwich isn't French, its inventor, Philippe Mathieu, was. According to legend, in 1918, Philippe (who owned a sandwich shop called "Philippe the Original" in Los Angeles) was making a sandwich for a policeman and accidentally dropped the sliced French roll into the roasting pan drippings. The policeman loved the sandwich so much he brought his friends back the next day and ordered the sandwich "dipped" in the meat pan. Thus, the French dip.

• •

In a medium saucepan, combine the broth, Worcestershire, garlic powder, and rosemary sprigs, set the pan over medium heat, and bring to a simmer. Add the beef and simmer 5 minutes to heat through.

Using a large fork or tongs, place the beef on the rolls. Serve the remaining broth mixture on the side in small individual bowls for dunking.

1 cup reduced-sodium beef broth

1 teaspoon Worcestershire sauce

½ teaspoon garlic powder

2 sprigs fresh rosemary

2 to 3 cups leftover sliced roast beef (facing page)

4 kaiser rolls

STORAGE SAVVY:

To store the leftover beef, divide the slices into three approximately equal portions and place in zip-top plastic bags or containers. Label with the date and "Sliced beef roast" or the name of the dish you intend to use it in.

MORPH RECIPE #2

ASIAN BEEF SALAD WITH CASHEWS

SERVES 4

If you don't have leftover beef, don't fret. This salad is terrific with deli-cut roast beef, roasted chicken and turkey, or cooked shrimp. Date night? Serve the salad with warm sake!

• •

Place the lettuce on a large serving platter or individual plates and top attractively with the beef, scallions, carrot, and cabbage.

In a small bowl, whisk together the broth, cilantro, vinegar, and sesame oil, then pour evenly over the salad. Top with the cashews and serve immediately.

- 6 cups chopped romaine lettuce
- 2 cups leftover sliced beef (page 92)
- 4 scallions (white and green parts), chopped
- ½ cup shredded carrot
- ½ cup shredded red cabbage
- ½ cup reduced-sodium chicken broth
- ¼ cup chopped fresh cilantro
- 1 tablespoon rice vinegar
- 1 tablespoon toasted sesame oil
- ½ cup cashew pieces

QUICK FIX IT YOUR WAY:

Make a double batch of the broth-based dressing and store leftovers for up to 4 days in the refrigerator. Save on cleanup and make the dressing in a jar with a lid—combine the ingredients, pop on the lid, then give the jar a shake. Store the leftovers right in the jar!

MORPH RECIPE #3 — BEEF EMPANADAS

Total Time: 18 to 20 minutes
PREP TIME: 10 MINUTES
WALK-AWAY TIME: 8–10 MINUTES

SERVES 4

There's no chance I'm making empanada dough on a busy week-night. In fact, there's little chance I'd take the time to do it on the weekend. But I can still enjoy these meat-filled patties by taking advantage of one of today's greatest convenience products—refrigerated pie crusts. Check out how few ingredients are necessary for a stellar feast! I like to serve these with a simple salad or slaw on the side.

● ●

Preheat the oven to 425°F. Coat a large baking sheet with cooking spray.

In a large bowl, combine the beef, cheese, chiles, and pimientos and mix well.

Unroll the pie crusts onto a flat surface. Top one of the crusts evenly with the beef mixture, spreading it out to within ½ inch of the edge. Top with the second pie crust. Using a pastry cutter or sharp knife, cut the circle into four equal wedges. Pinch around the edges of each wedge to seal (making four empanadas). (At this point, you can refrigerate the empanadas up to 3 days or freeze for up to 3 months before baking; there's no need to thaw the empanadas before baking.)

Transfer the empanadas to the prepared baking sheet and make small slits in the top of each one to allow steam to escape during cooking. Bake until the crust is golden brown, 8 to 10 minutes (if the empanadas are frozen, this may take another 5 minutes). (At this point, you can let the cooked empanadas come to room temperature and freeze up to 3 months. Reheat thawed cooked empanadas in the microwave or a preheated 350°F oven for 15 minutes.)

Cooking spray

2 cups leftover sliced beef (page 92), finely chopped

1 cup shredded reduced-fat Monterey Jack cheese

One 4-ounce can diced green chiles

One 4-ounce jar diced pimientos, drained

Two 9-inch refrigerated pie crusts

SMOKED CHEDDAR-STUFFED BURGERS

SERVES 4

I typically buy ground beef at a warehouse store, so I come home with tons of it. I like to season a big batch of the meat and shape it into burgers or meatballs. I often stuff a bunch of them with cheese, olives, roasted red peppers, pepperoni (whatever I have on hand). After shaping, I cook the whole batch, so I can create great meals from them during the week in just minutes: Greek Pita Pockets with Yogurt-Cucumber Sauce, Vegetable-Beef Stew with Yukon Gold Potatoes, and Spaghetti and "Meatballs." If I'm "beefed out" by midweek, I freeze both the uncooked and cooked burgers and meatballs; they freeze well for up to 3 months.

I serve these burgers with elbow macaroni that's been tossed with light Italian dressing and jazzed up with cut-up vegetables from the salad bar.

• •

In a large bowl, combine the beef and herb seasoning until well mixed. Shape the mixture into 12 patties, each about 1 inch thick. Press a chunk of cheese into the center of four patties, covering it well with the meat. (At this point, you can refrigerate the uncooked burgers up to 3 days or freeze up to 3 months; thaw completely in the refrigerator or microwave for 3 to 5 minutes on LOW before using.)

Heat the oil in a large skillet over medium-high heat. Add the burgers several at a time and cook 4 to 6 minutes per side for medium to medium-well done.

Serve the four cheese-stuffed burgers with this meal (on buns) and refrigerate the remaining burgers for up to 3 days or freeze up to 3 months; thaw completely in the refrigerator or the microwave for 3 to 5 minutes on LOW before using.

- 3½ pounds lean ground beef
- 2 teaspoons garlic-and-herb seasoning
- Four 1-inch chunks smoked cheddar cheese
- 1 tablespoon olive oil
- 4 hamburger buns

QUICK FIX IT YOUR WAY:

If you prefer, you can cut this recipe in half (cook just under 2 pounds of beef) and make tonight's recipe plus the pita pockets or tonight's recipe and both the stew and the spaghetti and "meatballs."

STORAGE SAVVY:

To store the leftover burgers, you can set them on a baking sheet and place it in the freezer until they're frozen solid, then pop them all in one big bag and pull them out as you need them. Or place two burgers each in smaller zip-top plastic bags so you can just grab a bag (or two) and go. You'll need 4 burgers for the pita pockets, 2 for the stew, and 2 for the "meatballs."

MORPH RECIPE #1

GREEK PITA POCKETS WITH YOGURT-CUCUMBER SAUCE

SERVES 4

Want to enjoy carnival street food in your own home in just minutes? A few simple ingredients can turn regular burgers into a traditional Greek sandwich that boasts allspice, cumin, and yogurt. To make the pita pockets soft, I warm them in a 200°F oven while preparing the filling.

• •

Heat the oil in a large skillet over medium heat. Break the burgers up into small pieces and add them to the skillet. Add the water, allspice, cumin, and oregano and mix well. Cook until the liquid is absorbed and the meat is hot, about 5 minutes, stirring a few times.

Meanwhile, in a small bowl, combine the yogurt, cucumber, dill, and garlic powder.

Spoon the beef mixture into the pita pockets, top with the yogurt sauce, and serve.

TIME SAVER tip:

If you use an English cucumber (the ones that are usually sold wrapped in plastic), you don't need to peel it or seed it.

Total Time: 15 minutes
PREP TIME: 10 MINUTES
ACTIVE COOKING TIME: 5 MINUTES

1 tablespoon olive oil

4 leftover cooked burgers (facing page)

¼ cup water

1 teaspoon ground allspice

1 teaspoon ground cumin

1 teaspoon dried oregano

½ cup low-fat plain yogurt

¼ cup peeled, seeded, and shredded cucumber

2 teaspoons chopped fresh dill

1 teaspoon garlic powder

4 pita pockets (preferably the "pillowy" pockets that are slightly thicker than traditional pita pockets)

MORPH RECIPE #2

VEGETABLE-BEEF STEW WITH YUKON GOLD POTATOES

SERVES 4

Since you've already precooked a bunch of burgers, you can create a comforting, hearty soup (one usually reserved for weekends) on any busy weeknight. The only ingredient that needs cooking is the potatoes and by the time you change out of your work clothes, they'll be tender and perfect! I like to serve this with an arugula salad topped with a light vinaigrette.

● ●

In a large stockpot or saucepan, combine the broth, burger pieces, potatoes, onion, celery, carrots, and bay leaves, set over high heat, and bring to a boil. Reduce the heat to medium, partially cover the pan, and simmer until the potatoes are fork-tender, 8 to 10 minutes.

Remove from the heat, remove the bay leaves, and stir in the parsley. Season to taste with salt and pepper and serve. At this point, you can refrigerate up to 3 days or freeze up to 3 months; there's no need to thaw before reheating in a large saucepan or microwave. To thaw in the microwave, cook for 3 to 5 minutes on LOW before reheating for 3 to 4 minutes on HIGH.

6 cups reduced-sodium beef broth

2 leftover cooked burgers (page 96), cut into bite-size pieces

2 cups peeled and diced Yukon Gold or Idaho potatoes

1 cup chopped onion

1 cup chopped celery

1 cup chopped carrots

2 bay leaves

2 tablespoons chopped fresh parsley

Salt and freshly ground black pepper

MORPH RECIPE #3

SPAGHETTI AND "MEATBALLS"

Total Time: 15 minutes
PREP TIME: 10 MINUTES
ACTIVE COOKING TIME: 5 MINUTES

SERVES 4

There's no question that the spaghetti-and-meatball meal is a family favorite. But let's face it, who has the time (or energy) to make meatballs during the week? Those frozen meatballs, albeit convenient, just aren't the same. Thankfully, you've got leftover burgers that can evolve into meatballs and save the day. Save even more time and cook the spaghetti when you make the hamburgers on the weekend. Refrigerate the cooked pasta in a plastic bag or a plastic container until you're ready to reheat it in the microwave. Sometimes I don't even reheat the spaghetti; I just smother it with the hot sauce, studded with these amazing "meatballs"!

● ●

Cook the spaghetti according to the package directions. Drain and set aside.

Meanwhile, in a large saucepan, combine the tomato sauce, tomato paste, and Italian seasoning, set over medium-high heat, and bring to a simmer. Stir in the burger pieces and simmer 5 minutes to heat through. Remove from the heat and stir in the basil. Spoon the sauce and meat over the spaghetti. Sprinkle with the Parmesan just before serving.

12 ounces spaghetti

One 28-ounce can tomato sauce

One 6-ounce can tomato paste

1 teaspoon Italian seasoning

2 leftover cooked burgers (page 96), cut into 2-inch pieces

¼ cup chopped fresh basil

¼ cup grated Parmesan cheese, preferably freshly grated

TIME SAVER tip:

Use store-bought sauce instead of making it.

TIME SAVER tip:

Italian seasoning is a blend of dried herbs and spices including basil, oregano, rosemary, savory, sage, marjoram, and thyme. It's a one-stop-shop for this recipe and many others.

PERFECT ROASTED CHICKEN WITH FRESH HERBS

Total Time: 2³/₄ to 3¹/₄ hours
PREP TIME: 10 MINUTES
WALK-AWAY TIME: 2¹/₂–2³/₄ HOURS
RESTING TIME: 10 MINUTES

SERVES 4

Ready for the most deliciously simple roasted chicken you've ever made? Yes, the ingredient list is small, and that's one reason the chicken is so divine. The fact is, it's not the quantity of ingredients, it's the quality. Fresh herbs and onion season the chicken just enough to lend incredible flavor, not incredible legwork. If you want to switch herbs (fresh oregano instead of rosemary, fresh sage instead of thyme), please do! I serve this chicken with Quick Fix Mashed Potatoes (page 218) or roasted potatoes (roast the potatoes with the chicken) and frozen peas and carrots. With the leftovers, I enjoy Teriyaki Chicken with Soba Noodles, Chicken Reubens with Swiss and Kraut, and Mustard-Glazed Chicken over Couscous.

● ●

One 7- to 8-pound roaster, giblets removed and discarded

2 tablespoons chopped fresh rosemary, or 1 teaspoon dried

2 tablespoons chopped fresh thyme, or 1 teaspoon dried

½ teaspoon salt

½ teaspoon freshly ground black pepper

2 cups sliced onion

½ cup reduced-sodium chicken broth

Preheat the oven to 450°F.

Coat the chicken all over with the rosemary, thyme, salt, and pepper. Transfer to a shallow roasting pan and arrange the onion all around the chicken, covering the bottom of the pan. Pour the broth into the pan, covering the onion slices. Insert an oven-safe meat thermometer deep into the thickest part of the thigh next to the body, not touching the bone. Place the chicken in the oven and immediately reduce the oven temperature to 325°F. Roast 20 minutes per pound, or until the thermometer reads 180 to 185°F, basting every 30 minutes after the first 30 minutes of cooking.

Let the chicken stand 10 minutes before carving. Serve one-quarter of the chicken with this meal and refrigerate the remaining carved chicken up to 3 days or freeze up to 3 months; thaw completely in the refrigerator or microwave for 3 to 5 minutes on LOW before using.

STORAGE SAVVY:

Prep your chicken before storing it. For the teriyaki chicken and mustard-glazed chicken, you'll need to dice it (2 cups and 4 cups respectively). For the reubens, you'll need to shred 2 cups of chicken. Date your zip-top bags and label them with the name of the dish you intend to use it for.

MORPH RECIPE #1

TERIYAKI CHICKEN WITH SOBA NOODLES

Total Time: 18 minutes
PREP TIME: 10 MINUTES
ACTIVE COOKING TIME: 8 MINUTES

SERVES 4

Every day I thank the manufacturers of convenience products. Asian bottled sauces like soy, teriyaki, hoisin, duck, and sweet-and-sour sauce make our lives much easier come mealtime. The sauces are fabulous on their own, but I like to jazz things up with fresh ingredients such as garlic, ginger, and cilantro. Here's a perfect example—this dish is outstanding!

• •

Cook the soba noodles according to the package directions. Drain and transfer to a serving platter or individual plates (cover with aluminum foil to keep warm, if necessary).

Meanwhile, heat the oil in a large skillet over medium heat. Add the garlic and ginger and cook, stirring, for 1 minute. Add the bell pepper and cook, stirring, for 2 minutes. Add the teriyaki sauce and chicken, bring to a simmer, and simmer until heated through, about 5 minutes. Remove from the heat and stir in the cilantro. Pour the chicken mixture over the noodles and serve.

12 ounces soba noodles

2 teaspoons peanut oil

3 cloves garlic, minced

1 tablespoon peeled and finely grated fresh ginger

1 medium red bell pepper, seeded and chopped

1 cup reduced-sodium teriyaki sauce

2 cups diced leftover roast chicken (facing page)

2 tablespoons chopped fresh cilantro

MORPH RECIPE #2 CHICKEN REUBENS WITH SWISS AND KRAUT

Total Time: 13 minutes
PREP TIME: 10 MINUTES
ACTIVE COOKING TIME: 3 MINUTES

SERVES 4

It's hard to believe that a sandwich with so much flavor contains so few ingredients. This reminds me of the sandwiches I used to enjoy when I lived near one of the hottest delis in New York. Throw a bunch of celebrity pictures on your walls, sit down to this meal, and you can enjoy the same experience! I like to serve the sandwiches with macaroni salad or potato salad and a mixed green salad with a thick dressing (like blue cheese).

• •

Preheat the broiler.

Top the bottom half of the rolls with the dressing (2 teaspoons per roll). Place an equal amount of sauerkraut on top of each roll and then top with the chicken and a slice of cheese. Place the sandwiches on a baking sheet (open-faced so the tops get toasted, too) and broil until the cheese melts, about 3 minutes. Serve hot.

4 kaiser rolls

8 teaspoons low-fat Thousand Island dressing

1 cup sauerkraut, drained and rinsed if desired

2 cups shredded leftover roast chicken (page 100)

4 thick slices Swiss cheese

MUSTARD-GLAZED CHICKEN OVER COUSCOUS

SERVES 4

Adding just a little pungent cumin to couscous really creates tremendous flavor. Add a savory sweet-and-sour sauce of Dijon mustard and honey to your perfectly roasted chicken and send the whole meal soaring! I like to serve this winner with wilted greens (bok choy, kale, chard) and steamed carrots.

● ●

Cook the couscous according to the package directions, adding the cumin and a pinch of salt and pepper to the simmering water when you add the couscous.

Meanwhile, in a medium saucepan, combine the chicken, broth, mustard, honey, and thyme and set over medium heat. Bring to a simmer. Partially cover and simmer for 5 minutes to heat through.

Fluff the couscous with a fork and transfer to a serving platter or individual plates. Serve the chicken mixture over the couscous.

1 cup couscous

1 teaspoon ground cumin

Salt and freshly ground black pepper

4 cups diced leftover roast chicken (page 100)

1 cup reduced-sodium chicken broth

¼ cup Dijon mustard

2 tablespoons honey

1 teaspoon dried thyme

ROASTED CHICKEN WITH SMOKEY APRICOT SAUCE

Total Time: 45 minutes
PREP TIME: 10 MINUTES
WALK-AWAY TIME: 35 MINUTES

SERVES 4

The simple sauce for this chicken has such an incredible aroma and flavor, it's hard to believe it's made with three simple ingredients that you may already have in your fridge. If you have orange marmalade instead of apricot preserves, that works, too. In fact, any fruit preserve will work. Liquid smoke seasoning is sold near the Worcestershire sauce at the grocery store. Enjoy this meal tonight and later in the week (or month!) by making Chicken and Mushroom Quesadillas, Thai Chicken Salad with Peanuts and Lime, and Chicken Curry with Chickpeas and Tomatoes. Serve this dish with Red Potatoes with Capers, Tomatoes, and Onion (page 219)—make the side dish while the chicken cooks.

• •

Preheat the oven to 400°F.

Coat a large roasting pan with cooking spray. Season the chicken all over with salt and pepper and arrange in the prepared pan.

In a small bowl, combine the preserves, soy sauce, and liquid smoke until well blended, then pour over the chicken. Roast until the breasts are cooked through, about 35 minutes.

Serve four chicken breast halves with this meal and refrigerate the remainder up to 3 days or freeze up to 3 months.

INGREDIENT note:

Bone-in chicken is often less expensive than boneless chicken. Thing is, the money saved at the market could be time lost in the kitchen when it comes to prepping. I like to save the bone-in chicken pieces for recipes like this—those that cook the chicken with the bone. It's much easier to pull meat from a cooked chicken breast than a raw one!

Cooking spray

10 skinless bone-in chicken breast halves

Salt and freshly ground black pepper

1½ cups apricot preserves

2 tablespoons reduced-sodium soy sauce

1 teaspoon liquid smoke seasoning

QUICK FIX IT YOUR WAY:

If you prefer, you can cut this recipe in half (cook 5 chicken breast halves instead of 10) and make tonight's recipe plus 2 of the 3 morph recipes with the leftovers.

STORAGE SAVVY:

To store the leftover chicken, you can set the breasts on a baking sheet and place it in the freezer until they're frozen solid, then pop them all in one big bag and pull them out as you need them. Or place two breast halves each in smaller zip-top plastic bags so you can just grab a bag and go. Remember to date and label your bags.

MORPH RECIPE #1

CHICKEN AND MUSHROOM QUESADILLAS

Total Time: 16 minutes
PREP TIME: 10 MINUTES
ACTIVE COOKING TIME: 6 MINUTES

SERVES 4

Turn this assembly-style meal into a family event by letting each person choose what they want inside their own quesadilla. When kids get involved, they're more likely to try new flavors and eat their creations. Just make sure the cheese is melted and gooey and you'll get kids to eat practically any vegetable that's stuffed inside! Serve these with a mixed green salad sprinkled with fruit, nuts, and cheese for a complete meal.

• •

Coat a large griddle or skillet with cooking spray and set over medium heat to preheat (a griddle will take slightly longer to pre-heat, so if you plan to use a large skillet instead of a griddle, wait until your quesadillas are assembled before preheating the pan).

Using a fork, pull the chicken meat from the bone in shreds. Arrange the tortillas on a flat surface. Top one tortilla with an equal amount of chicken, mushrooms, and tomatoes, and sprinkle with shredded cheese (⅓ cup per tortilla). Top with a second tortilla. Place the quesadillas in (or on) the prepared pan—however many will fit—and cook until the tortillas are golden brown and the cheese melts, about 3 minutes per side.

Cut each tortilla into four wedges and serve.

Cooking spray

2 leftover roasted chicken breast halves (facing page)

Eight 8-inch flour tortillas

2 cups sliced mushrooms (any combination of shiitake, cremini, oyster, porcini, portobello, etc.)

1 cup thinly sliced oil-packed sun-dried tomatoes

1⅓ cups shredded reduced-fat Monterey Jack cheese

QUICK FIX IT YOUR WAY:

You can assemble the quesa-dillas in advance, wrap them in plastic, and refrigerate for up to 3 days or freeze for up to 3 months; thaw in the refrigerator or microwave for a few minutes on LOW before cooking.

THAI CHICKEN SALAD WITH PEANUTS AND LIME

SERVES 4

I love this combination: sweet and salty peanuts, tart fresh lime juice, and colorful vegetables. The chicken adds a dash of protein to round out the meal. It's light and refreshing and works with beef, pork, and shrimp, too. I like to serve crunchy sesame breadsticks on the side.

• •

Pull the chicken meat from the bone and cut into ½-inch cubes. Set aside.

In a medium bowl, whisk together the mayonnaise, peanut butter, soy sauce, lime juice, and sesame oil. Add the chicken and toss to coat. Fold in the celery, red pepper, and scallions until well combined. Season to taste with salt and black pepper. (At this point, you can refrigerate the chicken mixture for up to 3 days.)

Place the lettuce on a serving platter or individual plates and top with the chicken mixture. Sprinkle with the peanuts just before serving.

2 leftover roasted chicken breast halves (page 104)

⅓ cup light mayonnaise

2 tablespoons smooth peanut butter

1 tablespoon reduced-sodium soy sauce

1 tablespoon fresh lime juice

2 teaspoons toasted sesame oil

1 cup diced celery

1 medium red bell pepper, seeded and chopped

¼ cup chopped scallions (white and green parts)

Salt and freshly ground black pepper

4 cups chopped lettuce (such as romaine, Bibb, red leaf, Boston)

¼ cup chopped dry-roasted peanuts

GOOD HEALTH note:

To cut out about 6 grams of fat per serving, substitute reduced-fat peanut butter for regular.

MORPH RECIPE #3

CHICKEN CURRY WITH CHICKPEAS AND TOMATOES

Total Time: 15 minutes
PREP TIME: 10 MINUTES
ACTIVE COOKING TIME: 5 MINUTES

SERVES 4

A real curry dish would ideally cook all day long. Since I rarely (if ever) have that luxury, I found a Quick Fix solution that delivers the same flavors. The leftover chicken is jazzed up with chickpeas and a creamy curry-cilantro sauce. I like to serve this over rice or couscous with steamed asparagus or zucchini on the side. Curry in a hurry, now that's a weekday solution!

• •

Cook the rice according to the package directions.

Meanwhile, using a fork, pull the chicken meat from the bone into shreds and place in a medium saucepan. Add the chickpeas, tomatoes, curry powder, and cumin and mix well. Set over medium heat, bring to a simmer, and simmer until heated through, 3 to 5 minutes. Stir in the sour cream and simmer 1 minute to heat through.

Remove from the heat and stir in the cilantro. Season to taste with salt and pepper and serve over the rice.

"CURRY IN A HURRY, NOW THAT'S A
weekday solution!"

2 cups quick-cooking white or brown rice

2 leftover roasted chicken breast halves (page 104)

One 15-ounce can chickpeas, drained and rinsed

One 15-ounce can diced tomatoes, drained

1½ teaspoons curry powder

1 teaspoon ground cumin

½ cup low-fat sour cream

¼ cup chopped fresh cilantro

Salt and freshly ground black pepper

GOOD HEALTH note:

Also known as garbanzo beans, chickpeas are a rich source of heart-protective folate, iron, and vitamin B-6.

OVEN-FRIED CHICKEN

Total Time: 40 to 45 minutes
PREP TIME: 10–15 MINUTES
WALK-AWAY TIME: 30 MINUTES

SERVES 4

Nothing beats the crunch of fried food—except maybe the nutrient stats for baked chicken. I found a way to enjoy both: an herb-infused, crispy crust for moist chicken that boasts respectable nutrition numbers and so much flavor it rivals the Colonel's on his best day. When I make a big batch like this, I can enjoy Chicken Taco Salad with Cilantro-Ranch Dressing, Strawberry-Chicken Salad with Mixed Greens and Walnuts, and White "Antipasto" Pizza with Chicken whenever I want. Serve this chicken with Swiss Chard with Garlic and Pine Nuts (page 213) and baked Idaho or sweet potatoes—bake cut-up potatoes in the oven with the chicken and they'll be ready at the same time.

●●

Preheat the oven to 400°F. Coat a large baking sheet with cooking spray.

In a large shallow dish, combine the flour, cornmeal, garlic powder, onion powder, oregano, basil, salt, and pepper, mixing it together with a fork. Add the chicken to the mixture and turn to coat evenly, tapping off any excess. Transfer the chicken breasts to the prepared baking sheet and spray their tops with cooking spray. Bake until the chicken is golden brown and cooked through, about 30 minutes.

Serve four chicken breast halves for this meal and refrigerate the remainder up to 3 days or freeze up to 3 months; thaw completely in the refrigerator or microwave for 3 to 5 minutes on LOW before using.

Cooking spray

1 cup all-purpose flour

½ cup yellow cornmeal

2 teaspoons garlic powder

2 teaspoons onion powder

2 teaspoons dried oregano

2 teaspoons dried basil

1 teaspoon salt

½ teaspoon freshly ground black pepper

12 boneless chicken breast halves

QUICK FIX IT YOUR WAY:

If desired, you can cut this recipe in half (cook 6 chicken breast halves instead of 12) and make tonight's recipe plus one morph recipe (either the taco salad or pizza) with the leftovers.

STORAGE SAVVY:

To store the leftover chicken, you can set the breasts on a baking sheet and freeze until they're frozen solid, then pop them in one big bag and pull them out as you need them. Or place two breast halves each in smaller zip-top plastic bags so you can just grab a bag (or two) and go. You'll need 2 breast halves for the taco salad, 4 for the chicken salad, and 2 for the pizza. Remember to date and label your bags.

CHICKEN TACO SALAD WITH CILANTRO-RANCH DRESSING

SERVES 4

My son Kyle adores taco salad and I love the fact that he's eating shredded chicken, cheese, beans, and vegetables. One caveat: I make sure he finishes the chicken before devouring the taco shell "bowl"! And I make sure Luke doesn't steal all his olives! When I make taco salad at home, I turn the corn tortillas into "plates" rather than bowls because it's faster and easier. I also spruce up bottled dressing with the distinct flavor of fresh cilantro.

● ●

Preheat the oven to 400°F. Coat a large baking sheet with cooking spray.

Arrange the tortillas on the prepared baking sheet and spray them with cooking spray. Bake until golden brown and crisp, about 6 minutes.

Transfer the tortillas to individual plates and top with equal amounts of the lettuce, chicken, tomatoes, green pepper, beans, olives, and jalapeños. Sprinkle the cheese over the top.

In a small bowl, whisk together the ranch dressing and cilantro and drizzle over the salad just before serving.

Total Time: 16 minutes
PREP TIME: 10 MINUTES
WALK-AWAY TIME: 6 MINUTES

Cooking spray

Four 6-inch corn tortillas

4 cups shredded lettuce

2 leftover Oven-Fried Chicken breast halves (facing page), shredded with 2 forks

2 cups diced fresh tomatoes

1 medium green bell pepper, seeded and diced

1 cup canned black beans, rinsed and drained

½ cup sliced black olives, drained

¼ cup sliced pickled jalapeños, drained

½ cup shredded reduced-fat cheddar cheese

1 cup reduced-fat ranch dressing

2 tablespoons chopped fresh cilantro

QUICK FIX IT YOUR WAY:

No time to preheat the oven? Make the tortillas up to 3 days in advance and store in an airtight container. Or, substitute baked corn chips or regular tortilla chips for the tortillas.

TIME SAVER tip:

If you don't want to take the time to preheat your oven, use baked corn tortilla chips instead of toasting the corn tortillas. Use about 1 to 2 cups of chips per serving as a base for the salad.

STRAWBERRY-CHICKEN SALAD WITH MIXED GREENS AND WALNUTS

SERVES 4

My husband loves strawberries so much, he'd eat an entire crate if someone didn't stop him. He's also crazy about chicken, so I created this dish with him in mind. Sweet strawberries are partnered with vinegar and Dijon mustard to create a sensational dressing for chicken. If you don't have strawberry preserves, fresh raspberries and raspberry preserves work, too. You can also use leftover turkey instead of chicken.

● ●

In a large bowl, gently toss together the chicken, strawberries, celery, and chives to combine.

In a small bowl, whisk together the preserves, oil, vinegar, and mustard. Add to the chicken mixture and toss to combine. Season to taste with salt and pepper.

Arrange the lettuce on individual plates. Spoon the chicken salad over the lettuce and sprinkle the walnuts over the top just before serving.

Total Time: 10 to 15 minutes
PREP TIME: 10–15 MINUTES

4 leftover Oven-Fried Chicken breast halves (page 108), cut into 1-inch chunks

1 cup hulled and sliced fresh strawberries

1 cup chopped celery

¼ cup chopped fresh chives

½ cup strawberry preserves

2 tablespoons olive oil

2 tablespoons cider vinegar

1 teaspoon Dijon mustard

Salt and freshly ground black pepper

6 cups mixed lettuce greens (any combination of romaine, Bibb, red leaf, Boston, etc.)

¼ cup chopped walnuts

GOOD HEALTH note:

Strawberries aren't just a rich source of vitamin C; thanks to the little seeds, they're also loaded with fiber.

MORPH RECIPE #3

WHITE "ANTIPASTO" PIZZA WITH CHICKEN

SERVES 4

Think of this as antipasto on a pizza crust. Use whatever you have in your fridge to create a unique pizza any night of the week. This recipe calls for a prepared pizza crust, but you can substitute thawed frozen pizza or bread dough or you can swing by your favorite pizza shop and buy uncooked dough from them.

• •

Preheat the oven to 450°F.

Place the pizza crust on a large baking sheet and top with the chicken, salami, red peppers, and olives. Sprinkle the mozzarella and Parmesan evenly over the top. Sprinkle on the oregano. Bake until the cheese melts, 8 to 10 minutes.

Total Time: 18 to 20 minutes
PREP TIME: 10 MINUTES
WALK-AWAY TIME: 8–10 MINUTES

1 prepared pizza crust (such as Boboli®; about 15 inches in diameter)

2 leftover oven-fried chicken breast halves (page 108), cut into 1-inch chunks

1 cup diced salami

1 cup sliced roasted red peppers (from water-packed jar)

½ cup pitted and sliced green olives, drained

1 cup shredded part-skim mozzarella cheese

¼ cup grated Parmesan cheese, preferably freshly grated

1 teaspoon dried oregano

STORAGE SAVVY:

You can assemble the pizza up to 2 days in advance, cover with plastic wrap, and refrigerate until ready to bake.

MORPH IT **111**

CHICKEN CACCIATORE WITH WILD MUSHROOMS

Total Time: 36 to 38 minutes
PREP TIME: 15 MINUTES
ACTIVE COOKING TIME: 11–13 MINUTES
WALK-AWAY TIME: 10 MINUTES

SERVES 4

Chicken cacciatore is a Miller family staple. I have created lots of different variations, but I love the combination of bell peppers, mushrooms, garlic, and chicken simmered in a mildly spicy, curried tomato sauce. I use wild mushrooms for their earthy flavor. The meal is hearty, rich, and lasts for days in the fridge (if you can keep it around that long!). I also love the sauce because it lends its deep, wonderful flavor to Quick Fix recipes later in the week (Seared Tilapia with Tomato-Cream Sauce, Pasta e Fagioli, and Tuna Salad in Cucumber Canoes).

• •

Heat 1 tablespoon of the oil in a large saucepan over medium heat. Add the onion, bell peppers, mushrooms, and garlic and cook, stirring, until softened, about 5 minutes. Add the basil, curry powder, bay leaves, salt, and red pepper and cook 1 minute, until the curry is fragrant. Add the tomatoes and broth and bring to a boil. Reduce the heat to low, partially cover the pan, and simmer for 20 minutes.

Meanwhile, cook the rice according to the package directions.

Heat the remaining 1 tablespoon oil in a large skillet over medium-high heat. Add the chicken and cook, stirring, until golden brown on all sides, 5 to 7 minutes. Add 2 cups of the cacciatore sauce and simmer until the chicken is cooked through, about 10 minutes.

Divide the rice among four individual shallow bowls and spoon the chicken mixture over the top. Refrigerate the remaining cacciatore sauce up to 4 days or freeze up to 3 months; thaw in the refrigerator or a microwave for 3 to 5 minutes on LOW before using.

2 tablespoons olive or vegetable oil, divided

1 cup chopped onion

1 medium green bell pepper, seeded and diced

1 medium red bell pepper, seeded and diced

2 cups sliced wild mushrooms, such as shiitake, oyster, chanterelle, or porcini

3 cloves garlic, minced

2 teaspoons dried basil

2 teaspoons curry powder

2 bay leaves

½ teaspoon salt

¼ teaspoon crushed red pepper

Two 28-ounce cans diced tomatoes

2 cups reduced-sodium chicken broth

2 cups quick-cooking white rice

1¼ pounds boneless, skinless chicken breasts, cut into 2-inch pieces

STORAGE SAVVY:

Store the sauce in the portions you'll need: 1 cup for the tilapia, 2 cups for the pasta, and ½ cup for the tuna salad. Date the container and label it as Cacciatore Sauce or with the name of the recipe you plan on using it for.

MORPH RECIPE #1

SEARED TILAPIA WITH TOMATO-CREAM SAUCE

Total Time: 10 minutes
PREP TIME: 5 MINUTES
ACTIVE COOKING TIME: 5 MINUTES

SERVES 4

No need to wait for a rich cream sauce to come together—you did the work already, now reap the rewards! You can use any type of fish or shellfish for this dish. The sauce is also excellent over pasta. Serve the tilapia with quick-cooking rice or Lemon-Curry Rice with Golden Raisins (page 228)—start the rice before starting the fish so everything is ready at the same time.

• •

Heat the oil in a large skillet over medium-high heat. Season the tilapia fillets all over with salt and pepper, place in the hot pan, and sear 1 minute on each side, until golden brown. Add the cacciatore sauce, heavy cream, and lemon zest and simmer until the fish is fork-tender, about 3 minutes.

Remove from the heat, transfer the fish and sauce to individual plates, sprinkle with the parsley, and serve.

1 tablespoon olive oil

Four 6-ounce tilapia fillets

Salt and freshly ground black pepper

1 cup leftover Cacciatore Sauce (facing page)

¼ cup heavy cream

1 teaspoon finely grated lemon zest

¼ cup chopped fresh parsley

GOOD HEALTH note:

To cut out 170 calories and 22 grams of fat, substitute ¼ cup fat-free half-and-half for the heavy cream. But be careful; since there's little or no fat, fat-free milks and "creams" have a serious "curdle factor," so keep an eye on the sauce and stir frequently.

MORPH RECIPE #2   PASTA E FAGIOLI

Total Time: 11 to 13 minutes
PREP TIME: 5 MINUTES
ACTIVE COOKING TIME: 6–8 MINUTES

SERVES 4

This is Quick Fix comfort for any crazy weeknight. My version of this Italian winner boasts beans and tender pasta simmered in my well-seasoned cacciatore sauce. Serve the soup at the end of a long day and watch your stress melt away. The addition of ripe tomatoes adds a distinctly fresh taste, even when you use a "well-aged" container of cacciatore sauce out of the freezer! I like to serve this with a Caesar salad on the side (buy a Caesar salad kit from the produce aisle to save time).

● ●

In a large saucepan, combine the cacciatore sauce, broth, and tomato puree. Set over high heat and bring to a boil. Add the beans and pasta, partially cover, and cook until the pasta is al dente, 6 to 8 minutes, stirring frequently.

Remove from the heat and stir in the tomatoes and basil. At this point, you can let cool to room temperature and refrigerate up to 3 days or freeze up to 3 months—there's no need to thaw before reheating it in a large saucepan over medium heat or in the microwave for 4 to 5 minutes on HIGH.

Ladle the soup into bowls and top with the Parmesan just before serving.

2 cups leftover Cacciatore Sauce (page 112)

3 cups reduced-sodium vegetable or chicken broth

One 15-ounce can tomato puree

One 15-ounce can white beans, drained

1 cup ditalini pasta or elbow macaroni

1 cup diced fresh tomatoes

¼ cup chopped fresh basil

¼ cup grated Parmesan cheese, preferably freshly grated

MORPH RECIPE #3 TUNA SALAD IN CUCUMBER CANOES

Total Time: 10 to 15 minutes
PREP TIME: 10–15 MINUTES

SERVES 4

Just a bit of leftover cacciatore sauce lends loads of flavor to this simple salad. This salad is fancy enough for guests and it works with shrimp, lobster, and lump crabmeat, too.

● ●

In a medium bowl, combine the tuna, celery, cacciatore sauce, mayonnaise, relish, and mustard and mix well. Season to taste with salt and pepper. (At this point, you can cover and store in the refrigerator up to 2 days in advance.)

Using a small spoon, remove the seeds from the center of the cucumber halves, making hollowed-out "canoes." Spoon the tuna mixture into the cucumbers just before serving.

Four 6-ounce cans chunk white tuna in water, drained

½ cup diced celery

½ cup leftover Cacciatore Sauce (page 112)

2 tablespoons light mayonnaise

2 teaspoons hamburger relish

1 teaspoon Dijon mustard

Salt and freshly ground black pepper

2 large cucumbers, cut in half lengthwise

MAIN RECIPE

CHICKEN PARMESAN

Total Time: 45 to 50 minutes
PREP TIME: 10 MINUTES
ACTIVE COOKING TIME: 10 MINUTES
WALK-AWAY TIME: 25–30 MINUTES

SERVES 4

Let's face it, making chicken Parmesan from scratch can be time-consuming. First you make a sauce. Then you dip the chicken in the flour, eggs, and bread crumbs. Then you sear the chicken in hot oil before topping it with sauce and cheese. Next comes the baking. I'm exhausted just writing about it. But, since you're going to all that effort, wouldn't it make sense to make a big batch of extra chicken for meals later in the week (or month)? In this recipe, just four of the chicken pieces get topped with sauce and cheese (for tonight's meal) and the rest are cooked alongside (in the bread crumb coating) so it's ready to go when you are! A little extra prep and you can quickly enjoy Stuffed Butternut Squash with Chicken, Rice, and Fresh Herbs; Tequila Chicken Kebabs with Jalapeño-Lime-Cilantro Vinaigrette; and Greek Chicken Salad with Feta and Oregano.

I serve this chicken with angel hair pasta that's been tossed with basil-flavored olive oil.

● ●

Preheat the oven to 400°F. Coat a large roasting pan with cooking spray.

In a medium saucepan, combine the tomatoes, tomato paste, basil, oregano, and garlic powder, set over medium heat, bring to a simmer, and let simmer until ready to use (about 10 minutes).

Meanwhile, in a shallow dish, combine the flour, salt, and pepper. Place the eggs in a separate shallow dish and the bread crumbs in a third shallow dish. Dredge the chicken in the flour, evenly coating both sides and tapping off any excess. Dip both sides of the flour-coated chicken in the eggs and then in the bread crumbs.

Heat 1 tablespoon of the oil in a large skillet over medium-high heat. Working in batches, add the chicken to the hot pan and cook

Cooking spray

One 14-ounce can crushed tomatoes

One 6-ounce can tomato paste

2 teaspoons dried basil

2 teaspoons dried oregano

1 teaspoon garlic powder

1 cup all-purpose flour

1 teaspoon salt

½ teaspoon freshly ground black pepper

2 large eggs, lightly beaten

1 cup seasoned dry bread crumbs

12 boneless skinless chicken breast halves

1 to 2 tablespoons olive oil

1 cup shredded part-skim mozzarella cheese

4 teaspoons grated Parmesan cheese, preferably freshly grated

QUICK FIX IT YOUR WAY:

If desired, you can cut this recipe in half (cook 6 chicken breast halves instead of 12) and make tonight's recipe plus one of the morph recipes with the leftovers.

until golden brown, 2 to 3 minutes per side. Transfer the chicken to the prepared roasting pan. Top four chicken pieces equally with the tomato sauce, mozzarella, and Parmesan (leave the remaining chicken untopped).

Cover the pan with aluminum foil and bake for 20 minutes. Uncover and bake 5 to 10 more minutes, until the chicken is cooked through and the cheese is golden and bubbly. Serve the Parmesan chicken for this meal and refrigerate the remaining chicken up to 3 days or freeze up to 3 months.

STORAGE SAVVY:

To store the leftover chicken, you can set the breasts on a baking sheet and place it in the freezer until they're frozen solid, then pop them all in one big bag and pull them out as you need them. Or place two breast halves each in smaller zip-top plastic bags so you can just grab a bag and go. Remember to date and label your bags.

MORPH RECIPE #1

GREEK CHICKEN SALAD WITH FETA AND OREGANO

Total Time: 15 minutes
PREP TIME: 15 MINUTES

SERVES 4

This is a refreshing, color-blasted salad that boasts the fresh flavors of cucumber, tomato, scallions, and salty feta cheese. Notice that I recommend adding the feta last—if you add it to hot pasta, it will quickly melt, leaving you without the unique little lumps of feta we all know and love.

• •

Cook the orzo according to the package directions. Drain and transfer to a large bowl. Add the chicken, cucumber, tomato, and scallions and toss to combine.

In a small bowl, whisk together the oil, vinegar, mustard, and oregano. Add to the pasta mixture and toss to combine. Season to taste with salt and pepper. Fold in the feta just before serving.

1 pound orzo pasta

2 leftover cooked chicken breast halves (facing page), cut into 1-inch chunks

1 cup peeled, seeded, and diced cucumber

1 cup diced fresh tomato

½ cup chopped scallions (white and green parts)

3 tablespoons olive oil

1 tablespoon red wine vinegar

1 teaspoon Dijon mustard

1 tablespoon chopped fresh oregano or 1 teaspoon dried

Salt and freshly ground black pepper

½ cup crumbled feta cheese

TEQUILA CHICKEN KEBABS WITH JALAPEÑO-LIME VINAIGRETTE

SERVES 4

This dish is sure to shake your maracas! If your palate has been dozing, wake it up with this powerful combination of flavors. As a plus, the meal is *fast*. The chicken is already cooked, so you just need to heat the skewers long enough to soften the vegetables. Because the vinaigrette is so incredibly tasty, you can skip the tequila glaze if you don't indulge. I serve the skewers with rice or couscous or even inside pita pockets—I like to have something to soak up the delicious vinaigrette so not a drop is left behind!

● ●

Coat a stove-top grill pan, griddle, or large skillet with cooking spray and set over medium-high heat.

Alternate pieces of chicken, colors of bell pepper, and the onion on metal or wooden skewers. Brush the tequila all over the chicken and vegetables and place the skewers on the hot pan. Cook until the vegetables are crisp-tender, about 5 minutes, turning frequently.

Meanwhile, in a blender or food processor, combine the broth, jalapeños, cilantro, honey mustard, and lime juice and process until smooth. Season to taste with salt and pepper. Serve the skewers with the vinaigrette drizzled over the top (or alongside for dunking!).

STORAGE SAVVY:

Make a double batch of the broth-based vinaigrette and store in the refrigerator for up to 1 week. Use over salads or as a marinade for chicken, fish, shellfish, and/or pork tenderloin. You can also freeze leftover vinaigrette in a plastic container for up to 3 months. Thaw in the microwave for a few minutes on LOW before using.

Total Time: 15 to 20 minutes
PREP TIME: 10–15 MINUTES
ACTIVE COOKING TIME: 5 MINUTES

Cooking spray

2 leftover cooked chicken breast halves (page 116), cut into 2-inch chunks

1 medium red bell pepper, seeded and cut into 2-inch pieces

1 medium green bell pepper, seeded and cut into 2-inch pieces

1 medium yellow or orange bell pepper, seeded and cut into 2-inch pieces

1 medium red onion, cut into 2-inch chunks

¼ cup tequila

½ cup reduced-sodium chicken broth

One 4-ounce can sliced jalapeños, drained

3 tablespoons chopped fresh cilantro leaves

2 tablespoons honey mustard

1 tablespoon fresh lime juice

Salt and freshly ground black pepper

MORPH RECIPE #3

STUFFED BUTTERNUT SQUASH WITH CHICKEN, RICE, AND FRESH HERBS

SERVES 4

This is not only beautiful to look at, you'll adore the combination of flavors: sweet butternut squash, aromatic cumin, fresh parsley, chives, and salty goat cheese, all mixed with a perfectly roasted chicken. It's as colorful as it is savory (and easy!). Feel free to use any fresh herbs you have. You can also substitute acorn squash for the butternut if desired. This is certainly a complete meal, but sometimes I serve fresh or steamed spinach on the side for something green.

• •

Preheat the oven to 400°F. Coat a shallow roasting pan with cooking spray.

Cook the rice according to the package directions, adding the cumin when you add the rice to the boiling water.

Meanwhile, using a spoon, remove the seeds from the center of the squash halves. Place the squash, flesh side down, in a microwave-safe baking dish and cover the dish with plastic wrap. Microwave on HIGH for 5 minutes, until the squash is tender.

Once the rice is cooked, stir in the diced chicken, sour cream, parsley, and chives until well combined. Season to taste with salt and pepper. Spoon the mixture into the squash halves (mound up the filling) and transfer the stuffed squash to the prepared roasting pan. Top each squash half with 2 tablespoons of the goat cheese. Bake until the cheese is golden and filling hot, 10 to 12 minutes.

Total Time: 25 to 32 minutes
PREP TIME: 10–15 MINUTES
WALK-AWAY TIME: 15–17 MINUTES

Cooking spray

2 cups quick-cooking brown rice

1 teaspoon ground cumin

2 large butternut squash, cut in half lengthwise

2 leftover cooked chicken breast halves (page 116), diced

½ cup low-fat sour cream

2 tablespoons chopped fresh parsley

2 tablespoons chopped fresh chives

Salt and freshly ground black pepper

½ cup crumbled goat cheese

GRILLED CHICKEN WITH TANGY TOMATO RAGOUT AND MELTED SWISS

SERVES 4

The actual definition of ragout is "a well-seasoned meat or fish stew, usually with vegetables." Mine is certainly well seasoned, and it definitely has vegetables. My twist is, I keep the meat out so I can use the incredible sauce in countless meals during the week. In this dish, I cook lean chicken breasts on a stove-top grill pan, but feel free to use your outdoor grill or broiler if you want! Had too much chicken already this week? Substitute a white-fleshed fish, such as flounder, halibut, or tilapia; simply pan-sear the fish until fork-tender and top with the ragout and cheese. Serve with a spinach salad on the side.

• •

Heat the oil in a large saucepan over medium heat. Add the onion, bell pepper, and garlic and cook, stirring, until softened, about 5 minutes. Stir in the diced tomatoes, tomato paste, vinegar, and oregano and bring to a simmer. Reduce the heat to low, partially cover the pan, and simmer for 10 minutes (and up to 1 hour).

Meanwhile, coat a stove-top grill pan or skillet with cooking spray and set it over medium-high heat. Season both sides of the chicken with salt and pepper. Place the chicken on the hot grill pan and grill until cooked through, 3 to 5 minutes per side.

Preheat the broiler.

Transfer the chicken to a shallow baking dish. Top each chicken breast half with ½ cup of the ragout and an equal amount of the shredded Swiss. Broil until the cheese is golden and bubbly, about 3 minutes.

Refrigerate the leftover ragout up to 4 days or freeze for up to 3 months.

Total Time: 20 minutes
PREP TIME: 10 MINUTES
ACTIVE COOKING TIME: 10 MINUTES

1 tablespoon olive oil

1 cup diced onion

1 large red or yellow bell pepper, seeded and chopped

3 cloves garlic, minced

Three 28-ounce cans diced tomatoes

One 6-ounce can tomato paste

1 tablespoon balsamic vinegar

1 teaspoon dried oregano

Cooking spray

4 boneless, skinless chicken breast halves

Salt and freshly ground black pepper

1 cup reduced-fat Swiss cheese

STORAGE SAVVY:

Store the sauce in portions that make sense to you. You'll need 3 cups for the Turkey Bolognese, 1 cup for the Shrimp Fra Diavolo, and 1 cup for the chutney, so store it in 1-cup portions or one 3-cup portion and the rest in 1-cup portions. Label them with the date and either Tangy Tomato Ragout or the name of the dish you plan to use it in.

MORPH RECIPE #1

TURKEY BOLOGNESE OVER RIGATONI

Total Time: 20 to 27 minutes
PREP TIME: 10 MINUTES
ACTIVE COOKING TIME: 5–7 MINUTES
WALK-AWAY TIME: 5 MINUTES

SERVES 4

Rigatoni is my dad's favorite pasta shape and every rigatoni meal I see reminds me of him! You can substitute any pasta shape for this dish, as long as it's hearty enough to stand up to a thick, rich sauce. Speaking of the sauce, I may lighten up my Bolognese by using ground turkey breast, but I blast flavor into the sauce with pancetta (Italian salt-cured bacon). Feel free to use ground beef if that's what you have. To save time, cook the pasta ahead and refrigerate it in a plastic bag or a plastic container. Just reheat the pasta in the microwave and spoon the wonderful sauce over it!

● ●

12 ounces rigatoni pasta, or any tube-shaped pasta

2 teaspoons olive oil

¼ cup diced pancetta or turkey bacon

1¼ pounds ground turkey breast

3 cups leftover Tangy Tomato Ragout (facing page)

¼ cup chopped fresh basil

¼ cup grated Parmesan cheese, preferably freshly grated

Cook the pasta according to the package directions. Drain and set aside.

Meanwhile, heat the oil in large saucepan over medium heat. Add the pancetta and cook for 3 minutes, stirring a few times. Add the ground turkey and cook 5 to 7 minutes, until cooked through, breaking up the meat as it cooks. Add the ragout, bring to a simmer, and simmer for 5 minutes to heat through. Remove from the heat and stir in the basil.

Divide the pasta between four individual shallow bowls. Spoon the sauce over the pasta, top with the Parmesan, and serve.

SHRIMP FRA DIAVOLO OVER LINGUINE

Total Time: 18 minutes
PREP TIME: 10 MINUTES
ACTIVE COOKING TIME: 8 MINUTES

SERVES 4

Traditional shrimp Fra Diavolo is often greased up with olive oil. I prefer to give those lip-smacking crustaceans a break by creating a lightened-up sauce, swapping broth for oil. After that, I boost flavor with the leftover ragout (you can certainly enjoy the dish without the ragout added, too). Bottom line? You'll enjoy the same, decadent-tasting shrimp dish without the devastating effects of saturated fat and calories!

• •

Cook the linguine according to the package directions. Drain and set aside.

Meanwhile, heat the oil in a large skillet over medium heat. Add the shallots and garlic and cook, stirring, until softened, about 2 minutes. Add the shrimp and red pepper and cook for 1 minute. Add the ragout, broth, and vermouth and bring to a simmer. Partially cover the pan and continue to simmer until the shrimp are bright pink and cooked through, about 5 minutes. Remove from the heat and stir in the basil. Season to taste with salt and pepper. Spoon over the pasta and serve.

- 12 ounces linguine
- 1 tablespoon olive oil
- 2 medium shallots, minced
- 2 to 4 cloves garlic, to taste, minced
- 1½ pounds large or jumbo shrimp, peeled and deveined
- 1 teaspoon crushed red pepper
- 1 cup leftover Tangy Tomato Ragout (page 120)
- ½ cup reduced-sodium chicken broth
- ¼ cup dry vermouth or dry white wine
- ¼ cup chopped fresh basil
- Salt and freshly ground black pepper

TIME SAVER tip:

I like to use large or jumbo shrimp (21 to 40 shrimp per pound) in recipes where shrimp is the main ingredient. Smaller shrimp (61 to 80 shrimp per pound) are better in casseroles and salads. Larger shrimp, though more expensive, cut back on prep time (there are fewer to clean). I also save money by purchasing peeled and deveined frozen shrimp. You can also prepare this dish with already cooked shrimp—although it doesn't save much cooking time, it eliminates prep work. Reduce the simmering time by 3 minutes when starting with cooked shrimp.

MORPH RECIPE #3
PAN-SEARED PORK CHOPS WITH TOMATO CHUTNEY

SERVES 4

Brown sugar and sweet raisins are balanced with tangy vinegar and smoky cumin to take the tomato ragout over the top. The whole concoction is simmered and reduced to a thick paste, making it the ideal topping for chicken, fish, beef, and pork. It's even excellent with cheese and crackers! If you want to make this and don't have any leftover ragout in the fridge or freezer, simply swap one cup of diced tomatoes (fresh or canned) for the ragout. You can make this chutney with practically any dried fruit you have on hand; instead of raisins, try currants, golden raisins, chopped dates, and/or dried cherries.

Serve these chops with Broccoli Puree with Parmesan (page 210)—start the side dish before making the chutney and everything will be ready at the same time.

• •

1 cup leftover Tangy Tomato Ragout (page 120)

⅓ cup raisins

2 tablespoons balsamic vinegar

2 tablespoons brown sugar

1 teaspoon ground cumin

1 tablespoon olive oil

Four 4-ounce boneless pork loin chops

Salt and freshly ground black pepper

Place the ragout in a small saucepan and stir in the raisins, vinegar, brown sugar, and cumin. Set the pan over medium heat, bring to a simmer, and simmer until the mixture thickens and reduces to about 1 cup, 8 to 10 minutes.

Meanwhile, heat the oil in a large skillet over medium-high heat. Season both sides of the pork with salt and pepper. Add the pork to the skillet and pan-sear until cooked through, 3 to 4 minutes per side.

Serve the pork with the chutney spooned over the top.

HERB-CRUSTED TURKEY TENDERLOIN

Total Time: 55 to 60 minutes
PREP TIME: 10 MINUTES
WALK-AWAY TIME: 35–40 MINUTES
RESTING TIME: 10 MINUTES

SERVES 4

Turkey tenderloin is a protein-packed, excellent way to get a healthy meal on the table fast. There's no fat to trim off, no bones to remove, no major prep work at all. Just add a few pantry staples and you can take this lean winner over the top. If you don't have fresh herbs handy, use dried (1 teaspoon instead of 1 tablespoon). I love turkey for this dish, but pork tenderloin works, too. I like to serve this with Israeli (pearl) couscous and steamed green beans or Balsamic Roasted Asparagus (page 207)—roast the asparagus in the oven with the turkey.

As for leftovers, turkey takes on a whole new life with Turkey Quesadillas with Cranberry Sauce and Swiss; Mesquite-Rubbed Turkey Medallions; and Pan-Seared Turkey with Apples, Melted Blue Cheese, and Pecans.

• •

Preheat the oven to 400°F. Coat a shallow roasting pan with cooking spray.

Season the turkey tenderloins all over with salt and pepper. Brush the mustard all over both tenderloins, then coat them with the lemon zest, rosemary, thyme, and oregano. Transfer the turkey to the prepared pan and roast until an instant-read thermometer inserted into the thickest part reads at least 160°F, 35 to 40 minutes.

Let rest for 10 minutes before slicing half of one of the tenderloins crosswise into thin slices. Serve the slices for this meal and refrigerate the remainder up to 3 days or freeze up to 3 months; thaw completely in the refrigerator or microwave for 3 to 5 minutes on LOW before using.

Cooking spray

Two 2-pound boneless skinless turkey tenderloins

Salt and freshly ground black pepper

2 tablespoons honey mustard

2 tablespoons finely grated lemon zest

2 tablespoons chopped fresh rosemary

2 tablespoons chopped fresh thyme

4 teaspoons dried oregano

QUICK FIX IT YOUR WAY:

If desired, you can cut this recipe in half (cook one turkey tenderloin) and make tonight's recipe plus one of the morph recipes with the leftovers.

STORAGE SAVVY:

Dice the half tenderloin for the quesadillas. Cut the remaining tenderloin into 1/2-inch-thick slices and divide it evenly between two small zip-top plastic bags for use in the medallions and the pan-seared turkey recipes. Date each one and label it with the name of the dish you plan on using it for.

MORPH RECIPE #1

TURKEY QUESADILLAS WITH CRANBERRY SAUCE AND SWISS

SERVES 4

This is such a deliciously untraditional way to use leftover turkey! Think of this as a Mexican staple with an American twist—turkey, cranberries, and cheese with green chiles and cilantro! Incredible.

● ●

Coat a large griddle or skillet with cooking spray and set over medium-high heat (a griddle will take slightly longer to preheat, so if you plan to use a large skillet instead of a griddle, wait until your quesadillas are assembled before preheating the pan).

Arrange four of the tortillas on a flat surface. Top each with an equal amount of turkey and spread it out to within ½ inch of the edge.

In a small bowl, combine the cranberry sauce, chiles, and cumin until well blended, then spoon the mixture over the turkey. Top with equal amounts of the Swiss. Place a second tortilla over the top of each and place the quesadillas—however many will fit—on the hot griddle. Cook until golden brown and the cheese melts (make sure the cheese is starting to melt before flipping or the filling may fall out!), 3 to 5 minutes per side.

Cut each tortilla into four wedges and sprinkle with the cilantro just before serving.

Total Time: 16 to 20 minutes
PREP TIME: 10 MINUTES
ACTIVE COOKING TIME: 6–10 MINUTES

Cooking spray

Eight 8-inch flour tortillas

Half of 1 roasted turkey tenderloin (facing page), diced

1 cup prepared cranberry sauce

One 4-ounce can diced green chiles

1 teaspoon ground cumin

1 cup shredded reduced-fat Swiss cheese

¼ cup chopped fresh cilantro

STORAGE SAVVY:

You can assemble the quesa-dillas in advance, wrap in plastic, and refrigerate up to 3 days or freeze up to 3 months. Thaw in the refrigerator or microwave for 2 to 3 minutes on LOW before cooking.

MORPH RECIPE #2 — MESQUITE-RUBBED TURKEY MEDALLIONS

Total Time: 12 to 14 minutes
PREP TIME: 5 MINUTES
ACTIVE COOKING TIME: 7–9 MINUTES

SERVES 4

This is a zesty meal that will make it to the table in just minutes. The turkey slices are dusted with mesquite seasoning (sold in the spice section in the supermarket), seared in olive oil, and then braised in a fabulous tomato sauce. I love to serve this with rice or pasta and a fresh green salad.

• •

Heat the oil in a large skillet over medium heat. Season both sides of the turkey slices with salt and pepper. Rub the mesquite seasoning into both sides of the slices. Place in the hot pan and cook 1 to 2 minutes per side, until golden brown. Add the tomatoes, bring to a simmer, and simmer 5 minutes to heat through. Remove from the heat, stir in the scallions, and serve.

2 teaspoons olive oil

Half of 1 roasted turkey tenderloin (page 124), cut crosswise into ½-inch-thick slices

Salt and freshly ground black pepper

1 tablespoon mesquite seasoning

One 14-ounce can diced tomatoes with onion and green pepper

2 tablespoons chopped scallions (white and green parts)

INGREDIENT note:

Mesquite seasoning is a tasty blend of salt, garlic, onion, red bell peppers, sugar, paprika, grill flavor, and spices. It's a one-stop-shop for intense flavor.

PAN-SEARED TURKEY WITH APPLES, MELTED BLUE CHEESE, AND PECANS

SERVES 4

This may seem like an unusual combination, but each ingredient has a natural affinity (call it a love affair) with the others—mild turkey, apples and applesauce, bold blue cheese, and fresh thyme. What could be better? How about adding a nice crunch from pecans? I like to serve this comforting meal with mashed potatoes and green or snap peas (yes, frozen peas are fine).

● ●

Heat the oil in a large skillet over medium heat. Season both sides of the turkey slices with salt and pepper. Rub the thyme into both sides of the slices. Place the turkey in the hot pan and cook 1 to 2 minutes per side, until golden brown. Add the applesauce, apples, and onion, bring to a simmer, and simmer for 5 minutes, until the onion and apples are tender. Stir in the blue cheese and cook for 1 minute, until the cheese melts.

Transfer the turkey and sauce to individual plates (or a serving platter) and top with the pecans just before serving.

Total Time: 17 to 18 minutes
PREP TIME: 10 MINUTES
ACTIVE COOKING TIME: 7–8 MINUTES

2 teaspoons olive oil

Half of one roasted turkey tenderloin (page 124), cut crosswise into ½-inch-thick slices

Salt and freshly ground black pepper

1 tablespoon chopped fresh thyme or 1 teaspoon dried

1 cup applesauce

2 apples (McIntosh or Granny Smith), cored, peeled, and diced

¼ cup chopped onion

½ cup crumbled blue cheese

¼ cup chopped pecans

GOOD HEALTH note:

Turkey is an excellent source of low-fat protein (there's a whopping 30 grams in just 3½ ounces of turkey breast). It's also a good source of iron, zinc, phosphorus, potassium, and B vitamins.

SAVORY TURKEY AND TWO-BEAN CHILI

Total Time: 57 minutes
PREP TIME: 15 MINUTES
ACTIVE COOKING TIME: 12 MINUTES
WALK-AWAY TIME: 30 MINUTES

SERVES 4

Everyone loves chili. It's warm, comforting and spicy. I always cook up a huge batch when I know friends are coming over. But be sure to make enough for leftovers that will morph into Turkey and Cheese Burritos with Red Sour Cream, Spinach and Cheese Lasagna, and Mexican Flautas with Green Chili Salsa. This recipe uses turkey but feel free to use lean ground beef instead.

• •

Heat 2 teaspoons of the oil in a large stockpot over medium-high heat. Add the ground turkey and cook until browned and cooked through, 5 to 7 minutes, breaking up any clumps. Transfer to a bowl and set aside.

Heat the remaining 2 teaspoons oil in the same pot over medium heat. Add the onion, garlic, and jalapeño and cook, stirring, until tender and golden, about 4 minutes. Return the turkey to the pot and add the chili powder, cumin, oregano, bay leaves, salt, and red pepper and stir to coat the vegetables and turkey with the seasoning. Add the tomatoes, broth, tomato sauce, and both beans and bring to a boil. Reduce the heat to low, partially cover the pot, and simmer for at least 30 minutes and up to 2 hours.

Discard the bay leaves, ladle the chili into bowls, and top with the shredded cheddar, sour cream, and scallions. Serve 4 to 6 cups of chili for this meal and refrigerate the leftovers up to 3 days or freeze up to 3 months; thaw completely in the refrigerator or microwave for 3 to 5 minutes on LOW before using.

STORAGE SAVVY:

Store the leftover chili in the portion sizes you'll need. You'll need 4 cups for the lasagna, 2 for the burritos, and 1 for the flautas. Date the containers and label Turkey Chili or with the name of the recipe you plan to use it for.

4 teaspoons olive oil, divided

2 pounds ground turkey breast

1 cup chopped onion

4 cloves garlic, minced

1 jalapeño, seeded and minced

¼ cup chili powder

2 tablespoons ground cumin

2 teaspoons dried oregano

2 bay leaves

½ teaspoon salt

½ teaspoon crushed red pepper, or more to taste

Two 28-ounce cans diced tomatoes

3 cups reduced-sodium chicken broth

Two 8-ounce cans tomato sauce

Two 15-ounce cans red kidney beans, rinsed and drained

Two 15-ounce cans black beans, rinsed and drained

GARNISHES:

Shredded cheddar cheese (regular or reduced-fat)

Sour cream (regular or low-fat)

Chopped scallions (white and green parts)

MORPH RECIPE #1

TURKEY AND CHEESE BURRITOS WITH RED SOUR CREAM

SERVES 4

Just a few additions turn leftover chili into a mouthwatering Mexican staple. Making the chili ahead means all the work's been done and this is a simple "assembly" meal. For the finicky eaters in your clan, it's also a nice way to sneak in vegetables (though I wouldn't try Brussels sprouts here!).

● ●

Preheat the oven to 400°F. Coat a shallow baking dish with cooking spray.

In a large bowl, combine the leftover chili, 1 cup of the cheese, the succotash, and chiles. Arrange the tortillas on a flat surface. Top each one with an equal amount of the chili mixture, making an even layer down the center. Roll up the tortillas and place side by side in the prepared pan. Top the tortillas with the remaining 1 cup cheese. Bake until the cheese is golden and bubbly, 10 to 12 minutes.

Meanwhile, in a small bowl, combine the sour cream and chili sauce. Serve the burritos with sour cream sauce spooned over the top.

Total Time: 20 to 22 minutes
PREP TIME: 10 MINUTES
WALK-AWAY TIME: 10–12 MINUTES

Cooking spray

2 cups leftover Turkey Chili (facing page)

2 cups shredded reduced-fat Monterey Jack cheese, divided

1 cup frozen succotash (corn and lima beans), thawed

One 4-ounce can diced green chiles

Four 8-inch flour or whole wheat tortillas

1 cup low-fat sour cream

2 tablespoons prepared chili sauce

INGREDIENT note:

Chili sauce is a blend of tomatoes, chiles, herbs, and spices and it's often sold near the ketchup or ethnic ingredients at the grocery store.

MORPH RECIPE #2

SPINACH AND CHEESE LASAGNA

Total Time: 55 minutes
PREP TIME: 15 MINUTES
WALK-AWAY TIME: 35 MINUTES
RESTING TIME: 5 MINUTES

SERVES 6

Surprise! There's no need to precook noodles before making lasagna! What a pain that can be. The fact is, when you use uncooked noodles, they soak up the sauce, not water, making them *much* more flavorful. My mom doesn't precook any of her noodles anymore— all her pasta is cooked directly in the sauce!

• •

Preheat the oven to 350°F.

In a medium bowl, combine the leftover chili and tomato sauce. In another bowl, combine the ricotta, spinach, 1 cup of the mozzarella, and the garlic powder.

Pour 1 cup of the chili mixture into a 13x9-inch lasagna pan, evenly coating the bottom. Arrange 4 lasagna noodles on top of the chili, overlapping them slightly to cover the bottom. Spoon half of the cheese mixture over the noodles, spreading it evenly. Top with 1 cup of the chili and 4 more noodles. Top the second layer of noodles with the remaining cheese mixture, 1 cup of the chili and 4 more noodles. Top the noodles with the remaining 1 cup chili and the remaining 1 cup mozzarella. Sprinkle evenly with the Parmesan. (At this point, you can tightly wrap the lasagna in plastic wrap and refrigerate up to 2 days before baking or freeze up to 3 months; thaw completely in the refrigerator before baking.)

Bake until the top is golden and bubbly, about 35 minutes. Let stand for 5 minutes before slicing.

4 cups leftover Turkey Chili (page 128)

One 8-ounce can tomato sauce

One 15-ounce container part-skim ricotta cheese

One 10-ounce box frozen chopped spinach, thawed and well drained (squeeze spinach to remove excess water)

8 ounces (2 cups) shredded part-skim mozzarella cheese, divided

1 teaspoon garlic powder

12 uncooked lasagna noodles

¼ cup grated Parmesan cheese, preferably freshly grated

GOOD HEALTH note:

By using part-skim ricotta cheese rather than the whole milk variety, you'll dodge 21 grams of fat (15 ounces of whole milk ricotta has 55 grams of fat while the same amount of part-skim ricotta has just 34 grams).

MORPH RECIPE #3

MEXICAN FLAUTAS WITH GREEN CHILE SALSA

Total Time: 25 minutes
PREP TIME: **15 MINUTES**
WALK-AWAY TIME: **10 MINUTES**

SERVES 4

Flautas are flute-shaped stuffed tortillas. To make the "flutes," corn tortillas are deep-fried and then held in place with toothpicks. Since I wanted flautas without fat (or the work and mess of deep-frying), I created a baked version using flour tortillas that's simply divine!

• •

Preheat the oven to 400°F. Coat a shallow baking pan with cooking spray.

In a small bowl, combine the chili and cheddar and mix well.

Arrange the tortillas on a flat surface. Top each one with an equal amount of the chili mixture, making an even line down the center. Roll up the tortillas and secure with toothpicks. Place the flautas side by side in the prepared pan. (At this point, you can cover the pan tightly with plastic wrap and refrigerate up to 3 days.)

Spray the top of the tortillas with cooking spray, then bake until they are golden brown, about 10 minutes.

Meanwhile, in a medium bowl, combine the salsa ingredients and mix well to combine.

Serve the flautas with the green chile salsa on the side.

Cooking spray

1 cup leftover Turkey Chili (page 128)

½ cup shredded reduced-fat cheddar cheese

Eight 8-inch flour tortillas

Toothpicks

GREEN CHILE SALSA:

Two 4-ounce cans diced green chiles (drained for a less watery salsa)

1 Roma tomato, diced

¼ cup chopped fresh cilantro

1 tablespoon fresh lime juice

1 teaspoon ground cumin

TIME SAVER tip:

You can assemble the flautas in advance and refrigerate them (in the baking pan) up to 3 days before baking.

4

From pantry to table

DINNER
EXPRESS:

in 30 minutes or less

**"LET'S FACE IT, WHEN TIME'S
AT A MINIMUM,** you NEED
a chapter like this."

If your sanity truly depends on getting a healthful, delicious dinner to the table in about 20 minutes, this chapter is for you. Let's face it, when time's at a minimum (as are your fridge's contents), you need a chapter like this. Depending on how well-stocked your pantry is, you can enjoy these meals *any* night of the week. They're fast, delicious, and versatile enough so that if you're missing an ingredient or two you won't miss out on dinner. Feel free to leave ingredients out or substitute what you have to make your life easier. Don't have pork for the pork chops? No big deal, use chicken. No beans for the soup? Oh well, leave 'em out. Don't want to fuss with spaghetti squash? Fine, stuff the savory chicken mixture into acorn squash or simply throw it over pasta or rice. There are no hard and fast rules in a Quick Fix kitchen. Don't stress out, you *can* enjoy an amazing dinner while having some fun!

CHEDDAR-POTATO SOUP

Total Time: 22 to 24 minutes
PREP TIME: 10 MINUTES
ACTIVE COOKING TIME: 4 MINUTES
WALK-AWAY TIME: 8–10 MINUTES

SERVES 4

Cheesy, creamy, and rich potato soup is the perfect midweek stress-reliever. Using a broth that's been infused with the intense flavor of roasted garlic really sends the flavors soaring without sending you to the garlic press or roasting pan. I typically serve this with a fresh spinach salad topped with diced fruit and berries and a nice sourdough baguette.

• •

Heat the oil in a large saucepan over medium heat. Add the leeks and cook, stirring, until softened, about 4 minutes. Add the potatoes, broth, and bay leaves and bring to a boil. Partially cover the pan and boil until the potatoes are fork-tender, 8 to 10 minutes.

Remove the bay leaves. Working carefully so as not to burn yourself and in batches, puree the soup in a blender or food processor or use a handheld blender and do it right in the pot. Return the puree to the pan over medium heat. Add the cheese and stir until it melts. Season to taste with salt and pepper. Ladle the soup into bowls and top with the chives.

2 teaspoons olive oil

2 leeks (white part only), rinsed well (see Prep Pointer on page 222) and chopped

2 large Idaho potatoes, peeled and diced

6 cups reduced-sodium roasted garlic–flavored chicken broth or regular chicken broth

2 bay leaves

1 cup shredded reduced-fat cheddar cheese

Salt and freshly ground black pepper

2 tablespoons chopped fresh chives

STORAGE SAVVY:

If you have leftovers, let the soup cool to room temperature, then store it in plastic containers in the refrigerator for up to 3 days. Potatoes don't freeze particularly well so I don't recommended freezing this soup. Reheat leftovers in the microwave for about 3 minutes on HIGH or in a saucepan over medium heat.

MINESTRONE SOUP
WITH PASTA, BEANS, AND VEGETABLES

Total Time: 11 to 13 minutes
PREP TIME: 5 MINUTES
ACTIVE COOKING TIME: 6–8 MINUTES

SERVES 4

My dad's mom (I called her "Nanny") was an amazing cook. She was "old school"—never sat, only served. The women ate in the kitchen after their husbands were taken care of. I'm sure she would have spent all day Sunday making a soup like this. Thankfully, you can enjoy the same flavors in a fraction of the time!

● ●

In a large stockpot, combine the broth and tomatoes, set over high heat, and bring to a boil. Add the macaroni, beans, vegetables, oregano, thyme, and bay leaves and cook until the macaroni is tender, stirring frequently, 6 to 8 minutes.

Remove the bay leaves and season to taste with salt and pepper. Ladle the soup into bowls, sprinkle the Parmesan over the top, and serve.

6 cups reduced-sodium vegetable or chicken broth

One 28-ounce can diced tomatoes

2 cups elbow macaroni

One 15-ounce can white (cannellini or navy) beans

4 cups chopped vegetables (any combination of onions, carrots, bell peppers, broccoli, etc., either from your Quick Fix freezer or the bagged varieties from the market)

1 teaspoon dried oregano

1 teaspoon dried thyme

2 bay leaves

Salt and freshly ground black pepper

¼ cup grated Parmesan or Romano cheese

STORAGE SAVVY:

If you have leftovers, let the soup cool to room temperature, then store it in plastic containers in the refrigerator for up to 3 days or freeze up to 3 months; thaw in the microwave for 3 to 4 minutes on LOW, then reheat for 3 to 4 minutes on HIGH or in a saucepan over medium heat.

CREAMY ROASTED RED PEPPER SOUP WITH CRUMBLED FETA

SERVES 4

Roasted red peppers from a jar absolutely belong in a Quick Fix cook's pantry. I use them in everything, from roasted chicken, fish, and pork dishes to dressings, dips, and salsas. In this recipe, they're pureed, then simmered with onion, garlic, mushrooms, and herbs for a super creamy soup that's crammed with flavor. For a complete meal, serve with grilled ham and cheese sandwiches and a fresh green salad. This soup is excellent served warm or chilled.

● ●

Place the red peppers in a blender or food processor and process until smooth. Set aside.

Heat the oil in a large saucepan over medium-high heat. Add the onion and garlic and cook, stirring, for 1 minute. Add the mushrooms and cook until softened and their liquid is released, about 3 minutes. Stir in the thyme, oregano, and bay leaves. Add the red pepper puree and broth and bring to a boil. Reduce the heat to medium, partially cover the pan, and simmer for 5 minutes. Add the milk and simmer for 1 minute to heat through. Remove from the heat, remove the bay leaves, and stir in the basil. Season to taste with salt and cayenne. Ladle the soup into bowls and top with the feta.

STORAGE SAVVY:

You can make the soup up to 3 days in advance and refrigerate until ready to serve. It also freezes well—let the soup cool to room temperature, transfer to plastic containers, and freeze up to 3 months; reheat in a saucepan or thaw in the microwave for 3 to 4 minutes on LOW, then reheat for 3 minutes on HIGH.

Two 16-ounce jars roasted red peppers, drained

1 tablespoon olive oil

½ cup chopped onion

3 cloves garlic, minced

1 cup sliced mushrooms

1 teaspoon dried thyme

1 teaspoon dried oregano

2 bay leaves

6 cups reduced-sodium vegetable broth

½ cup low-fat milk

¼ cup chopped fresh basil

Salt and cayenne pepper

¼ cup crumbled feta cheese

TIME SAVER tip:

Add chicken, vegetable, and beef bouillon cubes to soups, stews, chilis, and sauces for chicken, turkey, pork, and beef to create a concentrated, rich flavor (like you get from long simmering) without actually cooking for long periods of time. MSG-free and reduced-sodium varieties are widely available.

ASIAN CHICKEN SOUP WITH WATERCRESS

Total Time: 11 to 18 minutes
PREP TIME: 5–10 MINUTES
ACTIVE COOKING TIME: 6–8 MINUTES

SERVES 4

This is a blast for your palate, from one continent to the other. The best thing is, all the ingredients are readily available at your local market (or already sitting in your pantry). The distinct taste of toasted sesame oil kicks things off and then the soup is infused with the classic flavors of garlic and ginger. Serve with a side of steamed rice or sesame bread sticks to round out the meal.

● ●

Heat the oil in a large saucepan over medium-high heat. Add the garlic and ginger and cook, stirring, for 1 minute. Add the chicken and cook until golden brown on all sides, 3 to 5 minutes, stirring frequently. Add the broth and soy sauce and bring to a boil. Add the udon noodles and carrots, partially cover the pan, and cook until the noodles are just tender, about 2 minutes. Remove from the heat and stir in the watercress and lime juice. Season to taste with salt and pepper and serve.

2 teaspoons toasted sesame oil

2 cloves garlic, minced

1 tablespoon peeled and minced fresh ginger

1¼ pounds boneless, skinless chicken breasts, cut into 1-inch chunks

6 cups reduced-sodium chicken broth

3 tablespoons reduced-sodium soy sauce

6 ounces udon noodles

1 cup shredded carrots

2 cups packed watercress leaves

1 tablespoon fresh lime juice

Salt and freshly ground black pepper

GOOD HEALTH note:

Watercress is a great source of the antioxidant vitamin A and potassium.

TIME SAVER tip:

Use store-bought cooked chicken or leftover chicken instead of starting with raw.

MANHATTAN CLAM CHOWDER

Total Time: 26 minutes
PREP TIME: 10 MINUTES
ACTIVE COOKING TIME: 16 MINUTES

SERVES 4

I love clam chowder but I prefer the tomato-based version, not the cream-laden one. This one is hearty enough to be a complete meal, but I like to serve it with a fresh baguette or garlic bread.

• •

Heat the oil in a stockpot over medium heat. Add the shallots and garlic and cook, stirring, for 1 minute. Add the bell pepper and cook, stirring, until softened, about 2 minutes. Stir in the thyme and bay leaves. Add the clams to the pot (with the liquid from the cans) along with the broth, tomatoes, potato, and wine. Bring to a boil, partially cover the pot, and boil until the potato is fork-tender, about 8 minutes. Remove from the heat, remove the bay leaves, and stir in the parsley. Season to taste with salt and pepper. Ladle the soup into bowls and top with the crackers.

VARIATION:

You can certainly make this soup with fresh clams—either on a weeknight or weekend when you have more time. Substitute 3 dozen littleneck clams for the canned. Select clams with shells that are tightly closed and scrub them to remove debris (soak them in cold water if necessary to remove excess grit). Place the clams in a large pot of boiling water, cover, and steam until the shells open, about 5 minutes. Drain and discard any shells that have not opened. When cool enough to handle, pull the clams from the shells and chop into ¼-inch pieces (discard the shells). Use as directed in the recipe, adding more broth if necessary (since you won't have the liquid from the canned clams).

2 teaspoons olive oil

2 medium shallots, chopped

2 cloves garlic, minced

1 medium green bell pepper, seeded and chopped

2 teaspoons dried thyme

2 bay leaves

Four 6-ounce cans baby clams

4 cups reduced-sodium chicken or vegetable broth

One 28-ounce can crushed tomatoes

1 large Idaho potato, peeled and cut into 1-inch cubes

¼ cup dry white wine or vermouth

2 tablespoons chopped fresh parsley

Salt and freshly ground black pepper

1 cup oyster crackers

QUICK POBLANO-CORN CHOWDER WITH TORTILLA STRIPS

Total Time: 20 minutes
PREP TIME: 10 MINUTES
ACTIVE COOKING TIME: 10 MINUTES

SERVES 4

This is a quick corn chowder that boasts the intense flavors of spicy poblano and smoky chipotle chiles—it's a palate-stoker if ever there was one. The addition of cheese creates a thick, rich soup in just minutes. I love to serve this with a fresh green salad that's been topped with ripe avocado slices and a squirt of fresh lime juice.

● ●

Heat the oil in a large saucepan over medium heat. Add the onion and garlic and cook for 1 minute. Stir in the poblano, chipotle, and oregano. Add the broth, corn, potato, bay leaves, and salt, bring to a boil, and boil until the potato is fork-tender, about 8 minutes. Stir in the milk and cheese and simmer until the cheese melts.

Remove the bay leaves and puree about 1 cup of the chowder in a blender or food processor until smooth. Return the puree to the pot and mix well. Remove from the heat and stir in the cilantro. Ladle the soup into bowls, top with the tortilla strips, and serve.

2 teaspoons olive oil

½ cup diced yellow onion

3 cloves garlic, minced

1 poblano chile, seeded and chopped

1 teaspoon minced canned chipotle chile in adobo sauce

1 teaspoon dried oregano

6 cups reduced-sodium chicken or vegetable broth

3 cups fresh or frozen corn

1 large Idaho potato, peeled and diced

2 bay leaves

½ teaspoon salt

½ cup low-fat milk

½ cup shredded Monterey Jack cheese (regular or reduced-fat)

¼ cup chopped fresh cilantro

1 cup tortilla strips or tortilla chips

GOOD HEALTH note:

Corn is one of the best dietary sources of two antioxidants, lutein and zeaxanthin. Like their carotenoid cousins (such as vitamin A), both play a role in preventing heart disease and cancer and reducing the risk of macular degeneration.

INGREDIENT note:

Poblanos are dark (sometimes almost black) chile peppers that range in size (2 to 3 inches wide and 4 to 5 inches long) and flavor (from mildly sweet to downright hot). The darker the poblano, the richer the flavor. As is the case with all peppers, they're a great source of vitamin C.

GREEK PASTA SALAD
WITH FETA AND SHRIMP

Total Time: 14 minutes
PREP TIME: 10 MINUTES
ACTIVE COOKING TIME: 4 MINUTES

SERVES 4

The best Greek salad I ever tasted was in a little restaurant in Queens, New York. The place was a tiny gem and people would wait outside for hours just to get a table. The secret to the salad was simple: Use fresh, colorful ingredients. Here's my take on it.

● ●

Cook the pasta according to the package directions. Drain and transfer to a large bowl.

Meanwhile, heat the oil in a large skillet over medium heat. Add the bell pepper and garlic and cook, stirring, for 1 minute. Add the shrimp and oregano and cook until the shrimp are bright pink and cooked through, about 3 minutes. Transfer to the bowl with the pasta.

In a small bowl, whisk together the broth, mint, vinegar, mustard, thyme, salt, and pepper. Pour over the pasta and shrimp and toss to combine and coat everything with the dressing. Top with the feta just before serving.

12 ounces ditalini or penne pasta

1 tablespoon olive oil

1 medium green bell pepper, seeded and chopped

2 cloves garlic, minced

1¼ pounds medium shrimp, peeled and deveined

1 teaspoon dried oregano

½ cup reduced-sodium chicken broth

¼ cup chopped fresh mint

1 tablespoon red wine vinegar

1 teaspoon Dijon mustard

½ teaspoon dried thyme

½ teaspoon salt

¼ teaspoon freshly ground black pepper

½ cup crumbled feta cheese

QUICK FIX IT YOUR WAY:

You can turn this into a Meal Kit. Make the pasta up to 3 days in advance and store it in a plastic bag in the refrigerator. Prepare the bell pepper–shrimp mixture up to 2 days in advance and refrigerate it in a separate plastic bag. Come meal time, make the broth-based dressing and mix everything together.

CHICKEN TOSTADAS

Total Time: 18 minutes
PREP TIME: 10 MINUTES
ACTIVE COOKING TIME: 8 MINUTES

SERVES 4

In my Quick Fix kitchen, a tostada is the best taco salad you could ever imagine. Cumin-dusted corn tortillas are baked until crisp, then topped with salsa-infused chicken, lettuce, tomatoes, cheese, olives, and jalapeños. If you feel something's missing, toss it on top! I give you some ideas (sour cream, guacamole, and ranch dressing), but feel free to empty your cabinets on this winner!

• •

Preheat the oven to 400°F. Coat a large baking sheet with cooking spray.

Place the chicken in a large saucepan and add enough water to cover. Set the pan over high heat, bring to a boil, reduce the heat to medium, and let simmer until the chicken is just cooked through, about 8 minutes. Drain and, using two forks, pull the chicken meat apart into shreds. Transfer it to a bowl, add the salsa, and stir to combine.

Meanwhile, arrange the tortillas on the prepared baking sheet, spray them with cooking spray, sprinkle with the cumin, and salt and pepper to taste. Bake until golden brown, 6 to 8 minutes.

Transfer the tortillas to individual plates (2 per plate) and top with the chicken mixture, shredded lettuce, tomato, cheddar cheese, olives, jalapeños, and whatever else you want.

Cooking spray

1¼ pounds boneless, skinless chicken breasts

1 cup prepared salsa of your choice

Eight 6-inch corn tortillas

1 teaspoon ground cumin

Salt and freshly ground black pepper

2 cups shredded romaine lettuce

1 cup diced fresh tomato

1 cup shredded reduced-fat cheddar cheese

½ cup sliced pitted black olives

¼ cup sliced pickled jalapeños

ADDITIONS TO THE TOSTADAS, IF DESIRED:

Low-fat sour cream

Prepared guacamole

Low-fat ranch dressing

TIME SAVER tip:

Use a rotisserie chicken from the market to slash cooking time. Alternatively, purchase any fully cooked chicken breast and shred it as instructed. You can also cook the chicken up to 3 days in advance, combine it with the salsa as instructed, and refrigerate until ready to assemble the tostada.

QUICK FIX IT YOUR WAY:

Cook two extra chicken breast halves and use them to make the White "Antipasto" Pizza with Chicken (page 111) later in the week.

SHRIMP SALAD WITH HEARTS OF PALM AND PAPAYA

Total Time: 10 to 15 minutes

PREP TIME: 10–15 MINUTES

SERVES 4

In this dish, tender, succulent shrimp enjoy the company of papaya and tangy hearts of palm, tossed in a slightly sweet cider vinegar dressing with fresh chives. To make this a more substantial meal, I often serve it with a wedge of sourdough or pumpernickel bread smeared with an herb-spiked butter.

• •

Place 2 to 3 inches of water in a large stockpot, set the pan over high heat, and bring to a boil. Place the shrimp in a colander and place it in the pot over the boiling water. Cover and steam until the shrimp are bright pink and cooked through, about 5 minutes. Transfer the shrimp to a large bowl. Add the hearts of palm, papaya, chives, oil, and vinegar and toss to combine. Season to taste with salt and pepper and serve.

TIME SAVER tip:

Buy shrimp already cooked and skip the steaming step.

- 1¼ pounds medium shrimp, peeled and deveined
- 1 cup sliced canned hearts of palm (cut crosswise into ¼-inch-thick slices)
- 1 cup peeled, seeded, and diced papaya
- 2 tablespoons chopped fresh chives
- 1 tablespoon olive oil
- 1 tablespoon cider vinegar
- Salt and freshly ground black pepper

INGREDIENT note:

To pick a ripe papaya, select one that is mostly yellow with a bit of green. When fully ripe, the skin is bright yellow and the flesh is firm but will yield to gentle pressure from your fingers (you can ripen a papaya at home by placing it in a paper bag—it should soften in one or two days). When in doubt, use your nose; a ripe papaya will have a sweet aroma.

WHITE PIZZA WITH BASIL PESTO AND PINE NUTS

Total Time: 25 minutes
PREP TIME: 10 MINUTES
WALK-AWAY TIME: 10 MINUTES
RESTING TIME: 5 MINUTES

SERVES 4

Not that I don't love tomato sauce on pizza, but sometimes a "white" pizza is just what the doctor ordered! If you think working with bread or pizza dough is too hard or time consuming, think again. I like to work with raw dough instead of an already baked crust because I often "spike" it with things like Parmesan cheese, garlic, sun-dried tomatoes, and fresh herbs.

Serve the pizza with Baby Spinach, Fennel, and Grapefruit Salad with Shallot Vinaigrette (page 197)—make the salad while the pizza bakes and everything will be ready at the same time.

• •

Preheat the oven to 450°F.

Punch the dough down with your fist and transfer to a lightly floured work surface (you can also cover your work surface with parchment or waxed paper to prevent the dough from sticking). Using a rolling pin, roll it out into an 18-inch circle. Transfer the dough to a large baking sheet and spread the pesto evenly over the top, to within ½ inch of the edge. Sprinkle the mozzarella, Parmesan, and pine nuts evenly over the top. Bake until the cheese melts and the crust is golden brown, about 10 minutes. Let stand for 5 minutes before cutting into slices.

QUICK FIX IT YOUR WAY:

Since this pizza is a snap to prepare, I suggest making two at a time—you can eat leftover slices cold or reheat the slices in the microwave. Wrap the slices in plastic wrap and refrigerate up to 4 days or freeze up to 3 months. There's no need to thaw before reheating in the microwave for 1 to 2 minutes on HIGH.

1 pound fresh or frozen pizza dough, thawed according to package directions

¾ cup prepared basil pesto

1½ cups shredded part-skim mozzarella cheese

¼ cup grated Parmesan cheese, preferably freshly grated

⅓ cup pine nuts

INGREDIENT note:

You can use fresh or frozen pizza dough for this recipe, or you can swing by your favorite pizza shop and give them dough for their dough!

GOOD HEALTH note:

Basil is low in calories (5 leaves have just 1 calorie!), has almost no fat, and is a good source of vitamins A and C, both powerful antioxidants.

DEEP DISH PIZZAS
WITH MIXED TOPPINGS

Total Time: 22 to 25 minutes
PREP TIME: 10 MINUTES
WALK-AWAY TIME: 12–15 MINUTES

SERVES 4 TO 6

This is true comfort food in the comfort of your own home. Sure, you could have pizza delivered, but I'm positive that after you try my version, you'll be using that speed dial to the pizza joint less often (if ever). Not only do you control the ingredients, you'll have the pizza to the table in less than 25 minutes! I give you a few ideas for great toppings, but the choice is yours. In no time, you can have a custom-made, sensational pizza!

• •

Preheat the oven to 450°F. Coat two 9-inch round cake pans with cooking spray.

Divide the dough in half and press each half into the bottom of a prepared pan.

In a small bowl, combine the diced tomatoes, tomato paste, and oregano, then spoon evenly over each crust. Sprinkle the pizzas equally with the mozzarella and then the Parmesan. Top with desired toppings. Bake until the crusts are golden brown and the cheese is bubbly, 12 to 15 minutes. Let rest a few minutes for the cheese to settle.

Cooking spray

1 pound bread or pizza dough, thawed if necessary

One 15-ounce can diced tomatoes

2 tablespoons tomato paste

1 teaspoon dried oregano

1 cup shredded part-skim mozzarella cheese

2 tablespoons grated Parmesan cheese

OPTIONAL TOPPINGS:

Sliced mushrooms

Sliced bell peppers

Broccoli florets

Sliced black olives

Turkey pepperoni slices

Thinly sliced onion

Frozen chopped spinach, thawed and well drained (squeeze to remove excess water)

Diced fresh tomatoes

TIME SAVER tip:

For a variety of toppings, grab a bunch of extras at the salad bar at lunch. All the prep work of cutting, dicing, slicing, and rinsing has been done, and the only thing left to do is the fun of assembling your masterpiece!

SICILIAN FOCACCIA WITH CAPICOLA, MORTADELLA, SALAMI, PROVOLONE, AND PEPERONCINI

SERVES 4 TO 6

Think of this as an Italian-inspired party on a prepared pizza crust. Feel free to add any fillings you want. This is also great party food cut into bite-size pieces when you want to impress your friends and family!

● ●

Preheat the oven to 450°F.

Place one half of the pizza crust on a large baking sheet. Top with half of the provolone and then all of the capicola, mortadella, salami, and peppers. Top with remaining provolone and the second half of the pizza crust. Bake until the cheese melts, about 8 to 10 minutes. Slice crosswise into thick slices and serve.

"THINK OF THIS AS AN ITALIAN-INSPIRED PARTY
on a prepared pizza crust."

Total Time: 18 to 20 minutes
PREP TIME: 10 MINUTES
WALK-AWAY TIME: 10 MINUTES

One 12-inch prepared thin pizza crust (such as Boboli), cut in half crosswise

12 ounces thinly sliced provolone cheese

4 ounces thinly sliced capicola ham

4 ounces thinly sliced mortadella ham

4 ounces thinly sliced salami

½ cup thinly sliced peperoncini peppers (from jar)

VARIATION: MAKE IT A PANINI

If desired, you can weigh down the stuffed pizza crust, making a panini-type sandwich. Before baking, place a baking sheet on top of the stuffed pizza crust and place a heavy, ovenproof pan (a skillet or saucepan) on the baking sheet. Bake as directed.

ROTELLE WITH BROILED FETA, SNOW PEAS, AND YELLOW BELL PEPPER

SERVES 4

Take a simple ingredient, like feta cheese, and pop it under the broiler to create a completely new experience! You can do this with almost any cheese to create a golden brown, caramelized crust with a moist, creamy interior. I've had fantastic results with goat cheese, blue cheese, and hunks of smoked cheddar. This salad is a complete meal, but feel free to toss in cooked shrimp or chicken for added protein.

● ●

Cook the pasta according to the package directions. Drain and transfer to a large bowl.

Meanwhile, preheat the broiler. Arrange the feta slices on an aluminum foil–lined baking sheet and place under the broiler. Broil until the cheese is golden brown on top, about 2 minutes. Set aside.

Heat 1 tablespoon of the oil in a large skillet over medium heat. Add the onion and garlic and cook, stirring, for 1 minute. Add the snow peas and bell pepper and cook, stirring, until crisp-tender, about 5 minutes. Add the tomatoes and cook until just softened, about 1 minute. Transfer the vegetables to the pasta, add the remaining 1 tablespoon oil and the vinegar, and toss to combine. Fold in the basil. Season to taste with salt and pepper. Transfer the pasta to a serving platter or individual plates, top with the broiled feta slices, and serve.

12 ounces rotelle or any spiral-shaped pasta

8 ounces feta cheese, cut crosswise into 1/2-inch-thick slices

2 tablespoons olive oil, divided

1/2 red onion, sliced into half-moons

2 cloves garlic, minced

1 1/2 cups snow peas (fresh or frozen)

1 medium yellow bell pepper, seeded and cut into thin strips

1 1/2 cups cherry or grape tomatoes, cut in half

2 tablespoons balsamic vinegar

1/4 cup chopped fresh basil

Salt and freshly ground black pepper

TIME SAVER tip:

Pasta water often takes forever to boil: cook pasta (and rice) on the weekends and refrigerate for later in the week.

GOOD HEALTH note:

Snow peas have the lowest carbs of all peas (1/2 cup has just 35 calories and 6 grams of carbs) and they're a good source of fiber (2 grams in 1/2 cup).

QUICK FIX IT YOUR WAY:

You can turn this into a Meal Kit. Cook the pasta and snow pea mixture up to 3 days in advance. Store them in separate plastic bags in the refrigerator. Reheat them together in the microwave for 3 to 4 minutes on HIGH (or skip reheating and serve the salad chilled or room temperature). Broil the feta just before serving.

PLUM-GLAZED
PORK MEDALLIONS

Total Time: 14 minutes
PREP TIME: 5 MINUTES
ACTIVE COOKING TIME: 9 MINUTES

SERVES 4

Pork loves fruit as much as the next guy, and plum preserves are a wonderful way to enjoy that fruit whether they're in season or not! This creative combination melds them with Dijon mustard and onion flakes. Chicken broth helps thin the sauce slightly, giving the pork a chance to braise in the sauce as it tenderizes.

I like to serve this with Broccoli Puree with Parmesan (page 210) —start boiling the potato first and the side dish will be ready when the pork is finished cooking.

• •

In a small bowl, combine the plum preserves, broth, mustard, and onion. Set aside.

Heat the oil in a large skillet over medium-high heat for 2 to 3 minutes. Season the pork all over with salt and pepper. Add the pork to the hot pan and cook until golden brown, about 2 minutes per side.

Add the preserves mixture to the skillet and bring to a simmer. Partially cover the pan and simmer until the pork is just cooked through, about 5 minutes.

½ cup plum preserves

½ cup reduced-sodium chicken broth

2 teaspoons Dijon mustard

2 teaspoons onion flakes

2 teaspoons olive oil

One 1¼-pound pork tenderloin, silverskin removed if necessary (see Prep Pointer on page 45) and cut crosswise into 1-inch-thick medallions

Salt and freshly ground black pepper

PORK CHOPS WITH APPLES AND ROSEMARY

Total Time: 14 minutes
PREP TIME: 5 MINUTES
ACTIVE COOKING TIME: 9 MINUTES

SERVES 4

Pork enjoys basking in both sweet and savory ingredients. Here, I've partnered lean chops with apples and raisins, smoky cumin, and pine-like rosemary. Partner this with mashed red potatoes and Balsamic Roasted Asparagus (page 207). Start boiling the potatoes before starting the pork (as you would if making my Quick Fix Mashed Potatoes (page 218) and everything will be ready at the same time.

● ●

Heat the oil in a large skillet over medium-high heat. Season the pork chops on both sides with salt and pepper, then place them in the hot pan and sear until golden brown, about 2 minutes per side. Add the applesauce, broth, raisins, rosemary, and cumin, bring to a simmer, and simmer until the pork is just cooked through, about 5 minutes. Serve the chops with extra sauce spooned over the top.

2 teaspoons olive oil

4 boneless pork loin chops, trimmed of fat

Salt and freshly ground black pepper

1 cup chunky applesauce

½ cup reduced-sodium chicken broth

¼ cup dark raisins

1 tablespoon chopped fresh rosemary

1 teaspoon ground cumin

GOOD HEALTH note:

Pork is an excellent source of thiamin, niacin, riboflavin, vitamin B-6, phosphorus, and protein, as well as zinc and potassium.

SWEET-N-SOUR PORK CHOPS

Total Time: 14 minutes
PREP TIME: 5 MINUTES
ACTIVE COOKING TIME: 4 MINUTES
WALK-AWAY TIME: 5 MINUTES

SERVES 4

In my house, we have pork at least once a week. Since super-lean cuts of pork loin are widely available these days, I've put it back on our regular menu. I have no doubt you're going love this dish as much as my family does. Sometime I double this recipe so I have leftover pork to shred and turn into pulled pork sandwiches. I serve this with Shredded Carrots and Currants with Rosemary Dressing (page 205) and Quick Fix Mashed Potatoes (page 218) because I can pull both side dishes together in the time it takes for the pork to cook (assuming I prepped the potatoes in advance!).

● ●

Heat the oil in a large skillet over medium-high heat. Season the pork chops on both sides with salt and pepper to taste, add to the hot pan, and cook until golden brown, about 2 minutes per side. Stir in the apricot preserves, soy sauce, and ginger and bring to a simmer. Reduce the heat to low, partially cover the pan and simmer until the pork is just cooked through, about 5 minutes. Remove from the heat, stir in the scallions, and serve.

1 tablespoon toasted sesame oil

4 boneless pork loin chops

Salt and freshly ground black pepper

1 cup apricot preserves

2 tablespoons reduced-sodium soy sauce

1 teaspoon peeled and minced fresh ginger

¼ cup chopped scallions (white and green parts)

INGREDIENT note:

When shopping for pork, read labels (or ask your butcher) and opt for pork that hasn't been injected with water or solutions that enhance color and give the illusion of freshness. If the pork has been treated, there will be ingredients on the label beyond just pork.

TROPICAL FRUIT–GLAZED HAM WITH SWEET ONIONS AND YUKON GOLD POTATOES

Total Time: 20 minutes
PREP TIME: 10 MINUTES
ACTIVE COOKING TIME: 10 MINUTES

SERVES 4

Fully baked hams are wonderful—half of the work has been done for you. All that's left is to season the salty meat with your favorite flavors. Ham has a natural affinity for sweet ingredients, so here it's paired with sweet Vidalia onions, mixed tropical fruit (chunks of pineapple, guava, and papaya in passion fruit nectar), and brown sugar. Serve this with steamed green beans on the side.

● ●

Place the potatoes in a large saucepan and add enough water to cover. Set over high heat, bring to a boil, and boil until the potatoes are fork-tender, about 8 minutes. Drain and set aside.

Meanwhile, heat the oil in a large skillet over medium heat. Add the onion and cook, stirring, until softened, about 3 minutes. Add the fruit along with the juice from the can, the brown sugar, soy sauce, and pepper, bring to a simmer, and simmer until the liquid thickens and reduces slightly, about 5 minutes. Add the ham slices and potatoes, simmer for 2 minutes to heat through, and serve.

4 medium Yukon Gold potatoes, unpeeled and cut into 2-inch pieces

2 teaspoons peanut oil

½ Vidalia or red onion, cut in half and thinly sliced into half-moons

One 8-ounce can tropical fruit salad in passion fruit nectar

1 tablespoon brown sugar

1 tablespoon reduced-sodium soy sauce

½ teaspoon freshly ground black pepper

1 pound thick-cut deli ham

QUICK FIX IT YOUR WAY:

You can turn this into a Meal Kit. Cook the potatoes and fruit sauce up to 3 days in advance and refrigerate in separate plastic bags or containers, until ready to reheat. Reheat everything together (including the ham slices) in a large skillet or in the micro-wave for 3 to 4 minutes on HIGH.

GRILLED STEAKS, WITH PEPPERCORN MÉLANGE AND SWEET ONION MARMALADE

Total Time: 14 to 16 minutes
PREP TIME: 5 MINUTES
ACTIVE COOKING TIME: 9–11 MINUTES

SERVES 4

Peppercorn mélange is a combination of four different peppercorns: black, green, white, and pink. The black lends a signature "black pepper" flavor; the green boasts a mild, fresh taste; the white is hot and gingery; and the pink is slightly sweet. You could buy all four varieties separately, but why bother? Peppercorn mélange is convenient and it's sold in the spice aisle with other peppercorns. The onion marmalade is the perfect partner for the robust, peppery, and mildly salty steak.

Serve this up with Teriyaki Bok Choy with Cashews (page 214) and/or Sautéed Wild Mushrooms (page 223) and steamed acorn squash (steam one quartered and seeded acorn squash in the microwave for 5 minutes, until tender, then season with salt and black pepper—the squash will cook in the time it takes for the steak to cook).

• •

Place the peppercorns in a large plastic bag and mash them with the flat side of a meat mallet or rolling pin until finely crushed. Season both sides of the steaks with salt to taste and add to the bag with the crushed peppercorns. Press the peppercorns into the meat until both sides are coated.

Heat the oil in a large skillet over medium-high heat for 1 minute, until hot. Add the steaks and cook until nicely seared, about 2 minutes per side. Remove from the pan and set aside.

In a small bowl, combine the marmalade, onion, and soy sauce. Add the mixture to the same pan used for the steak and set over medium heat. Bring to a simmer and cook until the onion softens, about 3 minutes. Return the steaks to the pan and simmer 2 minutes for medium-rare to 5 minutes for well done. Serve the steaks with the onion marmalade spooned over the top of each.

2 tablespoons peppercorn mélange

4 boneless sirloin steaks (about 1¼ pounds total)

Salt

1 tablespoon olive oil

1 cup orange marmalade

½ red onion, sliced into half-moons

1 tablespoon reduced-sodium soy sauce

PREP POINTER:

Use the flat side of a meat mallet or rolling pin to smash the peppercorns or you'll pop holes in your plastic bag. Trust me, it can make quite a mess!

Stove-Top Jambalaya with Andouille Sausage, Chicken, and Shrimp (IN THE BAG, page 36)

Wild Mushroom Tart with Broccoli Rabe and Goat Cheese (IN THE BAG, page 38)

Sesame-Ginger Pork with Soba Noodles (IN THE BAG, page 41)

Shepherd's Pie with Cheddar-Spiked Mashed Potatoes
(IN THE BAG, page 42)

Braised Red Snapper with Tomatoes, Greek Olives, and Capers
(IN THE BAG, page 46)

Crunchy Lemon and Herb–Crusted Scallops (IN THE BAG, page 47)
and Garlic-Spiked Broccoli Rabe with Dried Mango (SIMPLE SIDES, page 215)

Crab-Stuffed Zucchini Boats
(IN THE BAG, page 48)

Cashew-Lime Chicken with Rice (IN THE BAG, page 51)

Chicken-Cheddar Quesadillas with White Bean–Green Pea Guacamole (IN THE BAG, page 52)

● ● **Parmesan-Crusted Chicken with Sweet-n-Hot Mustard Dip**
(IN THE BAG, page 56)

Roasted Salmon with Sweet-n-Hot Mustard Glaze (MORPH IT, page 68) and Parmesan-Crusted Cauliflower (SIMPLE SIDES, page 209)

"YOU'RE GOING TO LOVE THIS ROASTED SALMON. AND YOU WON'T BELIEVE HOW EASY IT IS TO MORPH IT into one of these other delicious dishes."

Balsamic Roasted Pork Tenderloin (MORPH IT, page 72)
and Warm Spinach Salad with Pancetta and Gorgonzola (SIMPLE SIDES, page 196)

"MY FAMILY LOVES THIS PORK TENDERLOIN AND CAN'T WAIT UNTIL I MORPH IT INTO PORK SLOPPY JOES for a quick Friday night meal."

● ● **Citrus-Glazed Ham with Roasted Mandarin Oranges** (MORPH IT, page 80) and **Soy-Sesame Green Beans with Ginger** (SIMPLE SIDES, page 211)

- ● ● Penne with Ham, Green Peas, and Oregano (MORPH IT, page 81)

- ● ● Honey Ham Wraps with Brie and Papaya (MORPH IT, page 82)

- ● ● Super-Cheesy Stove-Top Macaroni and Cheese with Ham (MORPH IT, page 83)

"WHO DOESN'T LOVE A BIG GLAZED HAM? HERE ARE THREE EASY COMFORT FOOD MORPHS to stretch that Sunday ham a little longer."

Sweet and Tangy Beef Roast with Vegetables (MORPH IT, page 92)

"MY HOMEY ROAST BEEF DINNER CAN MORPH INTO ANY OR ALL OF THESE SIMPLY DELICIOUS MEALS with just a little planning."

- ● ● Asian Beef Salad with Cashews (MORPH IT, page 94)

- ● ● Beef Empanadas (MORPH IT, page 95)

- ● ● French Dip Sandwiches (MORPH IT, page 93) with Shredded Carrots and Currants with Rosemary Dressing (SIMPLE SIDES, page 205)

Creamy Roasted Red Pepper
Soup with Crumbled Feta (DINNER
EXPRESS, page 136)

Quick Poblano-Corn Chowder
with Tortilla Strips (DINNER
EXPRESS, page 139)

White Pizza with Basil Pesto and
Pine Nuts (DINNER EXPRESS, page 143)

● ● **Rotelle with Broiled Feta, Snow Peas, and Yellow Bell Pepper** (DINNER EXPRESS, page 147)

Curried Lamb Chops with Cucumber Relish (DINNER EXPRESS, page 160)
and Mashed Acorn Squash with Sunflower Seeds (SIMPLE SIDES, page 217)

Grilled Steaks with Peppercorn Mélange
and Sweet Onion Marmalade
(DINNER EXPRESS, page 152)

Chicken Piccata with Olives
(DINNER EXPRESS, page 163)
**and Red Potatoes with Capers,
Tomatoes, and Onion**
(SIMPLE SIDES, page 219)

**Bacon-Wrapped Turkey Burgers
with Blue Cheese Sauce**
(DINNER EXPRESS, page 171)

Cornmeal-Crusted Flounder with Spicy Pink Beans (DINNER EXPRESS, page 176)

Grilled Tuna Steaks with Tangerine-Roasted
Red Pepper Salsa (DINNER EXPRESS, page 180)
and Balsamic Roasted Asparagus
(SIMPLE SIDES, page 207)

Pineapple-Shrimp Skewers with Rum Sauce (DINNER EXPRESS, page 187)
and Coconut Rice (SIMPLE SIDES, page 227)

Chocolate-Dunked Bananas with Peanuts (THERE'S ALWAYS TIME FOR DESSERT, page 237)

Apricot Puff-Pastry Twists (THERE'S ALWAYS TIME FOR DESSERT, page 241)

Brown Sugar–Glazed Pineapple with Toasted Coconut (THERE'S ALWAYS TIME FOR DESSERT, page 238)

● ● Peach-Cherry Galette (THERE'S ALWAYS
TIME FOR DESSERT, page 242)

Frozen Lime Pie (THERE'S ALWAYS TIME FOR DESSERT, page 246)

PAN-SEARED STEAKS WITH GARLIC-ROSEMARY GLAZE

Total Time: 15 to 16 minutes
PREP TIME: 5 MINUTES
ACTIVE COOKING TIME: 10–11 MINUTES

SERVES 4

What's a glaze? In this recipe, it's an easy-to-make, thick sauce that clings to every fiber of the steak's being. That's great news because the sauce is brimming with the wonderful flavors of garlic, shallots, rosemary, and vermouth. This dish also works with boneless chicken breasts and pork loin chops. I often serve this with Sautéed Cabbage with Apples and Cinnamon (page 204) or Creamed Spinach My Way (page 216) and a nice sourdough baguette. Start the side dishes before the steak so everything makes it to the table at the same time (the side dishes can be made up to 3 days in advance, stored in the refrigerator, and reheated in the microwave).

● ●

Season both sides of the steaks with salt and pepper. Melt the butter in a large skillet over medium-high heat. Add the steaks and cook until well seared, about 2 minutes per side. Remove the steaks from the pan and set aside.

To the same pan, add the shallots and garlic and cook, stirring, for 2 minutes. Add the rosemary and cook until fragrant, about 1 minute. Add the vermouth and cook 1 minute. Dissolve the cornstarch in the broth, add to the pan, and bring to a simmer. Return the steaks to the pan and cook until medium, 2 to 3 minutes (or longer for more well-done meat). Serve the steaks with the glaze drizzled over the top.

4 ribeye steaks, each about 1 inch thick (about 1¼ pounds total)

Salt and coarsely ground black pepper

1 tablespoon butter

¼ cup finely chopped shallots

3 cloves garlic, minced

1 tablespoon chopped fresh rosemary

½ cup dry vermouth or white wine

1 teaspoon cornstarch

½ cup reduced-sodium beef broth or water

QUICK FIX IT YOUR WAY:

Cook a double batch of steaks and use the leftovers in Artichoke-Steak Melts with Smoked Provolone and Basil Mayo (page 85) or Steak Soft Tacos with Asparagus-Spiked Guacamole (page 86).

HOISIN BEEF WITH VEGETABLES

Total Time: 24 minutes
PREP TIME: 10 MINUTES
ACTIVE COOKING TIME: 9 MINUTES
WALK-AWAY TIME: 5 MINUTES

SERVES 4

This meal belongs on a Quick Fix cook's list of the top 10 recipes for crazy weeknights. Why? It's got incredible flavor, color, and nutrients and you can swap ingredients to fit what you have in your fridge. Ginger and garlic lay the groundwork, then beef is sautéed with fresh bell pepper, crunchy water chestnuts, and fresh asparagus. Don't have those things? No big deal. Use hot peppers, canned baby corn, broccoli, and cauliflower. Use chicken or shrimp instead of beef. Use this recipe as an outline and make your own version any night of the week. I like to serve all variations over white or brown rice (quick-cooking, of course!).

● ●

In a small bowl, whisk together the broth, hoisin, and cornstarch. Set aside.

Heat the oil in a large skillet or wok over medium-high heat. Add the garlic and ginger and stir-fry for 1 minute. Add the steak and stir-fry until browned on all sides, about 5 minutes. Add the bell pepper, carrots, water chestnuts, and asparagus and stir-fry for 3 minutes.

Add the broth mixture to the skillet, bring to a simmer, and simmer until the sauce thickens and the vegetables are crisp-tender, about 5 minutes.

¾ cup reduced-sodium beef broth

2 tablespoons hoisin sauce

2 teaspoons cornstarch

1 tablespoon peanut oil

3 to 4 cloves garlic, to taste, minced

1 tablespoon peeled and minced fresh ginger

1¼ pounds boneless lean sirloin steak, cut into 1-inch cubes

1 medium red bell pepper, seeded and chopped

1 cup shredded carrots

One 8-ounce can sliced water chestnuts, drained

12 asparagus spears, woody bottoms snapped off and spears cut into 2-inch lengths

QUICK FIX IT YOUR WAY:

Cook an extra ¾ pound of beef and use the leftovers in the Asian Beef Salad with Cashews (page 94).

STIR-FRIED STEAK WITH ARTICHOKE HEARTS, CAPERS, AND OLIVES

Total Time: 21 minutes
PREP TIME: 10 MINUTES
ACTIVE COOKING TIME: 11 MINUTES

SERVES 4

If you're tired of the same old Asian-inspired stir-fry, I've got the perfect antidote: one with the flavors of the Mediterranean, boasting garlic, oregano, bell peppers, artichokes, olives, and capers. Serve over rice or couscous so you don't miss a drop of the sauce.

● ●

Heat the oil in a large skillet or wok over medium-high heat. Add the scallions and garlic and stir-fry for 1 minute. Add the steak and stir-fry until browned on all sides, about 3 minutes. Add the oregano and stir to coat. Add the bell pepper, artichokes, olives, and capers and stir-fry for 2 minutes. Add the marsala and simmer for 2 minutes.

While that's simmering, dissolve the cornstarch in the broth and add to the pan. Continue to simmer until the sauce thickens and the beef is cooked through, about another 3 minutes.

QUICK FIX IT YOUR WAY:

To turn this into a Meal Kit, prepare the beef mixture and store it in a plastic container or bag in the refrigerator for up to 3 days. Store the cooked rice, noodles, or couscous in a separate container. Reheat both separately in the microwave (3 minutes on HIGH) and serve the beef mixture over the "starch." You can also prep all the ingredients up to 3 days in advance (before cooking), store everything in plastic bags or containers in the refrigerator, and cook it up fresh when you're ready to finish the meal.

1 tablespoon olive oil

4 scallions (white and green parts), chopped

2 to 3 cloves garlic, to your taste, minced

1¼ pounds boneless lean sirloin steak, cut into thin strips

1 teaspoon dried oregano

1 medium red or green bell pepper, seeded and thinly sliced into strips

One 14-ounce can artichoke hearts, drained and cut in half

½ cup pitted Greek olives (such as kalamata), drained

2 tablespoons drained capers

2 tablespoons marsala wine

1 tablespoon cornstarch

⅔ cup reduced-sodium beef broth

BEEF STROGANOFF WITH EGG NOODLES

Total Time: 15 to 17 minutes
PREP TIME: 5 MINUTES
ACTIVE COOKING TIME: 5–7 MINUTES
WALK-AWAY TIME: 5 MINUTES

SERVES 4

A meal that you would expect to take eons takes just minutes when you use a few shortcuts! Buy lean steak and cut it into cubes (or buy it already cut up), chopped garlic, and canned beef broth and you've got one delicious, super-fast meal! Serve this with a fresh green salad with cherry tomatoes dressed with a light vinaigrette.

• •

Cook the egg noodles according to the package directions. Drain and set aside.

Meanwhile, heat the oil in a large skillet over medium-high heat. Add the garlic and cook, stirring, for 1 minute. Add the steak and cook until browned all over, stirring frequently, 3 to 5 minutes. Add the flour and thyme and stir to coat the beef. Add the broth and Worcestershire and bring to a simmer. Partially cover the pan and simmer until the beef is cooked through, about 5 minutes. Add the noodles and cook 1 minute to heat through. Remove from the heat, stir in the sour cream and parsley, and serve.

- 12 ounces egg noodles or yolk-free egg noodles
- 2 teaspoons olive oil
- 3 to 4 cloves garlic, to taste, minced
- 1¼ pounds lean beef steak, cut into 1-inch cubes
- 1 tablespoon all-purpose flour
- 1 teaspoon dried thyme
- 1½ cups reduced-sodium beef broth
- 1 tablespoon Worcestershire sauce
- 1 cup low-fat sour cream
- 2 tablespoons chopped fresh parsley

TIME SAVER tip:

Buy cut beef cubes instead of cutting steak yourself. Do the same with vegetables: stop by the salad bar and load up on cleaned and chopped vegetables instead of doing the work at home.

QUICK FIX IT YOUR WAY:

You can turn this into a Meal Kit. Cook the egg noodles and beef mixture up to 3 days in advance and refrigerate, in separate plastic bags or containers. Reheat both together in a large saucepan or in the microwave for 3 to 4 minutes on HIGH.

PICANTE ROAST BEEF WITH TOMATOES, LIME, AND GREEN CHILES

Total Time: 21 to 26 minutes
PREP TIME: 10 MINUTES
ACTIVE COOKING TIME: 6–11 MINUTES
WALK-AWAY TIME: 5 MINUTES

SERVES 4

The dictionary says *picante* means: 1. Prepared in such a way as to be spicy; 2. Having a sauce typically containing tomatoes, onions, peppers, and vinegar. Couldn't have said it better myself (except that I use lime juice instead of vinegar). When shopping, buy deli roast beef and have it sliced thick (about ½ inch) so you can cut it into strips. I like to serve this with Adobo Rice and Pink Beans (page 225). Start the rice before the roast beef and everything will come together at the same time.

• •

Heat the oil in a large skillet over medium heat. Add the onion and garlic and cook, stirring, until softened, about 3 minutes. Add the roast beef strips and cook until browned on all sides, 3 to 5 minutes, stirring frequently. Add the tomatoes, chiles, lime juice, and cumin and stir to combine. Bring to a simmer and cook for 5 minutes to heat through.

Remove from the heat, stir in the cilantro, season to taste with salt and pepper, and serve.

2 teaspoons olive oil

½ cup chopped onion

2 to 3 cloves garlic, to taste, minced

12 ounces thickly sliced roast beef (from the deli), cut into thin strips

One 14-ounce can diced tomatoes

One 4-ounce can diced green chiles

3 tablespoons fresh lime juice

1 teaspoon ground cumin

2 tablespoons chopped fresh cilantro

Salt and freshly ground black pepper

GOOD HEALTH note:

Green chiles are crammed with the antioxidant vitamin C and capsaicin, a chemical compound that, when applied topically in a cream, can give temporary relief from the muscle and joint aches and pains associated with arthritis, backache, strains, and sprains.

BARBECUED BEEF WITH PEARL ONIONS AND CARROTS

Total Time: 17 minutes
PREP TIME: 5 MINUTES
ACTIVE COOKING TIME: 2 MINUTES
WALK-AWAY TIME: 10 MINUTES

SERVES 4

I love barbecue sauce. I put it on everything from broccoli to sweet potatoes to deli-sliced turkey. The only thing I don't do is shampoo my hair with it. Although bottled sauce is convenient, my home-made version is incredible and you can use it on any meat you want. When you simmer beef in it, the meat and vegetables devour the sauce. Serve with quick-cooking rice, pasta, or couscous on the side to soak up the barbecue sauce. You could also serve the beef and sauce on kaiser rolls, as you would Sloppy Joe sandwiches, and serve the vegetables on the side.

• •

Combine all the ingredients in a large saucepan and set over medium heat. Bring to a simmer and simmer until the sauce thickens and the carrots are tender, about 10 minutes, then serve.

1 cup frozen pearl onions (frozen or thawed)

1 cup baby carrots

1 pound thinly sliced roast beef (from the deli)

One 15-ounce can tomato sauce

¼ cup firmly packed brown sugar

2 tablespoons red wine vinegar

1 teaspoon Worcestershire sauce

2 teaspoons chili powder

1 teaspoon ground cumin

1 teaspoon garlic powder

Pinch of cayenne pepper

CURRIED LAMB CHOPS WITH CUCUMBER RELISH

Total Time: 21 minutes
PREP TIME: 10 MINUTES
ACTIVE COOKING TIME: 11 MINUTES

SERVES 4

For some people, the taste of lamb is too strong. I completely understand because I'm one of those people. But here's the good news: This dish blasts the lamb with so much flavor that even the die-hard lamb-phobe will love it! First the chops are infused with a rich curry sauce, then they're topped with a refreshing relish of cucumber, red onion, and parsley. In this dish, if you want a traditional pairing of flavors, substitute mint for the parsley in the relish. I like to serve this with Swiss Chard with Garlic and Pine Nuts (page 213) or Caramelized Cocktail Onions with Red Peppers (page 220) because both are ready when the lamb is!

• •

Heat the oil in a large skillet over medium-high heat. Add the shallots and garlic and cook until softened, about 3 minutes. Add the curry powder and cumin and cook, stirring, for 1 minute, until fragrant.

Push the shallots and garlic aside to allow room for the lamb chops. Season both sides of the chops with salt and pepper, place them in the hot pan, and cook until golden brown, about 2 minutes per side. Add the broth, bring to a simmer, and simmer until the lamb is browned on the outside and slightly pink on the inside, about 3 minutes.

Meanwhile, in a medium bowl, combine the cucumber, onion, parsley, and vinegar. Season to taste with salt and pepper. Serve the lamb chops with the relish spooned over the top.

1 tablespoon olive oil

½ cup chopped shallots

2 cloves garlic, minced

2 teaspoons curry powder

1 teaspoon ground cumin

8 lamb loin chops, trimmed of fat if necessary

Salt and freshly ground black pepper

½ cup reduced-sodium chicken broth

1 cup peeled, seeded, and finely diced cucumber

¼ cup finely slivered red onion

1 tablespoon chopped fresh parsley

2 teaspoons red wine vinegar

TIME SAVER tip:

Instead of chopping shallots for the lamb and red onion for the relish, use red onion in both parts of the dish. Use an English cucumber (usually sold wrapped in plastic) and you don't have to peel or seed it before chopping.

CHICKEN FINGERS WITH SPICY AVOCADO SAUCE

Total Time: 30 minutes
PREP TIME: 10 MINUTES
WALK-AWAY TIME: 20 MINUTES

SERVES 4

Chicken fingers aren't just for kids! Who doesn't love to eat with their hands? This makes a great meal and it's also perfect party food. The chicken is breaded with a crunchy herb-and-spice coating and baked until golden brown (no deep-fryer required). Then, the tender little fingers are served with a creamy avocado sauce that boasts jalapeños, lime juice, and fresh cilantro. If you don't like spicy foods, simply eliminate the jalapeños and hot sauce.

For a complete meal, serve with Quick Fix Mashed Potatoes (page 218) and Sliced Tomatoes with Tarragon and Honey-Balsamic Vinaigrette (page 200).

● ●

Preheat the oven to 400°F. Coat a large baking sheet with cooking spray.

In a shallow dish, combine the bread crumbs, garlic powder, onion powder, oregano, thyme, paprika, salt, and pepper. Add the chicken strips and turn to coat evenly, tapping off any excess. Transfer to the prepared baking sheet and spray the top of them with cooking spray. Bake until golden brown and cooked through, about 20 minutes.

Meanwhile, using the back of a spoon, mash the avocados and sour cream together in a medium bowl. Fold in the jalapeños, lime juice, cilantro, and hot sauce, then season to taste with salt and pepper. Serve the chicken fingers with the avocado sauce on the side for dipping.

TIME SAVER tip:

Instead of cutting chicken breasts, buy chicken tenders, which are already the right size and shape. They may cost a little more, but sometimes convenience is worth the extra money.

Cooking spray

2/3 cup dry unseasoned bread crumbs

1 teaspoon garlic powder

1 teaspoon onion powder

1 teaspoon dried oregano

1 teaspoon dried thyme

1/2 teaspoon paprika

1/2 teaspoon salt

1/2 teaspoon freshly ground black pepper

1 1/4 pounds boneless, skinless chicken breasts, cut into thin strips

2 ripe avocados, pitted and peeled

2 tablespoons low-fat sour cream

2 tablespoons minced pickled jalapeños

1 tablespoon fresh lime juice

1 tablespoon chopped fresh cilantro

1/2 teaspoon hot sauce, or more to taste

QUICK FIX IT YOUR WAY:

Make a double batch of the chicken and use the leftovers in Chicken Taco Salad with Cilantro-Ranch Dressing (page 109) or Strawberry-Chicken Salad with Mixed Greens and Walnuts (page 110).

PAN-SEARED CHICKEN WITH CILANTRO PESTO

Total Time: 11 to 16 minutes
PREP TIME: 5–10 MINUTES
ACTIVE COOKING TIME: 6 MINUTES

SERVES 4

Pan-searing meat and fish in a seasoned olive oil not only adds incredible flavor, it eliminates extra ingredients you may not have handy! I love garlic-flavored olive oil and, in this dish, I use it for both pan-searing the chicken and creating a garlicky cilantro pesto. You can certainly buy pesto already prepared, but when you create your own, you can use different herbs, like cilantro, parsley, and sage. Pesto perfect! I like to serve this chicken with cooked egg noodles tossed in chive-spiked butter.

● ●

Heat 1 tablespoon of the oil in a large skillet over medium-high heat. Season both sides of the chicken with salt and pepper. Place the chicken in the hot pan and cook until golden brown and just cooked through, about 3 minutes per side.

Meanwhile, place the pine nuts in a small dry skillet and set over medium heat. Toast the nuts until golden brown, about 3 minutes, shaking the pan frequently to prevent burning. Transfer the pine nuts to a blender or food processor and add cilantro, sour cream, the remaining 1 tablespoon oil, the garlic, and ½ teaspoon salt. Process until smooth, adding water as necessary to create a thick paste. Serve the chicken with the pesto spooned over the top.

- 2 tablespoons garlic-flavored or regular olive oil, divided
- 4 boneless, skinless chicken breast halves
- Salt and freshly ground black pepper
- 3 tablespoons pine nuts
- 1 cup packed fresh cilantro leaves
- ¼ cup low-fat sour cream
- 3 cloves garlic, peeled

STORAGE SAVVY:

Prep ahead for future meals and double the amount of pesto. It will keep in a tightly covered container in the fridge up to 4 days or in the freezer up to 3 months; thaw completely in the refrigerator or microwave for 2 to 3 minutes on LOW before using.

QUICK FIX IT YOUR WAY:

Cook two extra chicken breast halves and use the leftovers in Chicken and Wild Mushroom Quesadillas (page 105), Thai Chicken Salad with Peanuts and Lime (page 106) or Chicken Reubens with Swiss and Kraut (page 102).

CHICKEN PICCATA
WITH OLIVES

Total Time: 19 to 21 minutes
PREP TIME: **10 MINUTES**
ACTIVE COOKING TIME: **4–6 MINUTES**
WALK-AWAY TIME: **5 MINUTES**

SERVES 4

Traditional chicken piccata has always been a Quick Fix meal. Chicken pieces are pounded thin, coated with flour, pan-seared in olive oil, and then simmered in broth, wine, and capers. Since the chicken is thin, it cooks through in just minutes. My variation gives the flavors a jolt with garlic-and-herb seasoning, pimiento-stuffed olives, lemon juice, and honey. If you already have those ingredients in your Quick Fix pantry, you can enjoy this meal any night of the week.

Serve this up with rice or angel hair pasta tossed with olive oil and grated Parmesan cheese and a nice mixed green salad.

• •

4 boneless, skinless chicken breast halves

¼ cup all-purpose flour

1 teaspoon salt-free garlic-and-herb seasoning

½ teaspoon salt

1 tablespoon olive oil

1 cup reduced-sodium chicken broth

½ cup sliced pimiento-stuffed green olives, drained

¼ cup fresh lemon juice

1 tablespoon honey

Place the chicken in a zip-top plastic bag and pound with a meat mallet, rolling pin, or the bottom of a heavy skillet until about ½-inch thick. Add the flour, garlic-and-herb seasoning, and salt to the bag, seal, and shake to coat the chicken evenly.

Heat the oil in a large skillet over medium-high heat for 2 to 3 minutes, until hot. Remove the chicken from the bag and shake off any excess flour. Add the chicken to the hot skillet and cook until golden brown, 2 to 3 minutes per side. Add the broth, olives, lemon juice, and honey, bring to a simmer, and simmer until the sauce thickens and the chicken is cooked through, about 5 minutes.

QUICK FIX IT YOUR WAY:

For families that eat at different times, prepare individual plates (such as a chicken dinner with vegetables and a potato), cover with plastic wrap, and refrigerate until ready to reheat in the microwave.

CHICKEN CURRY WITH SHALLOTS AND RAISINS

Total Time: 22 minutes
PREP TIME: 10 MINUTES
ACTIVE COOKING TIME: 7 MINUTES
WALK-AWAY TIME: 5 MINUTES

SERVES 4

I like meals that slam your palate from all angles. To do that, you need to combine the flavors of sweet, sour, salty, and whatever else you can think of. In this dazzler, chicken breasts are simmered with raisins, tangy vinegar, cumin, and curry. This is a super-satisfying meal the whole family (and guests) will love. Typically, I serve this over quick-cooking rice or couscous with steamed spinach or broccoli on the side. It's also terrific with Coconut Rice (page 227). Start the rice before you start the chicken and everything will come together at the same time.

• •

Heat the oil in a large saucepan or Dutch oven over medium heat. Add the chicken and cook, stirring, until golden brown all over, about 2 minutes. Add the shallots and cook, stirring, for 2 minutes. Add the curry powder, cumin, garlic powder, ginger, salt, and pepper and cook, stirring, until fragrant, about 1 minute. Add the broth, raisins, and vinegar, bring to a simmer, then partially cover the pan and simmer until the chicken is cooked through, about 5 minutes. Remove from the heat, stir in the cilantro, and serve.

1 tablespoon peanut oil

1¼ pounds boneless, skinless chicken breasts, cut into 2-inch cubes

½ cup thinly sliced shallots

1 teaspoon curry powder

1 teaspoon ground cumin

1 teaspoon garlic powder

¼ teaspoon ground ginger

½ teaspoon salt

¼ teaspoon freshly ground black pepper

1 cup reduced-sodium chicken broth

½ cup raisins

2 tablespoons cider vinegar or red wine vinegar

¼ cup chopped fresh cilantro

STORAGE SAVVY:

Double this recipe and freeze leftovers in freezer bags or plastic containers for up to 3 months. Thaw and reheat in the microwave about 2 to 3 minutes on HIGH.

PONZU CHICKEN AND VEGETABLE KEBABS

Total Time: 18 to 20 minutes
PREP TIME: 10 MINUTES
ACTIVE COOKING TIME: 8–10 MINUTES

SERVES 4

I like to marinate chicken, steak, and shrimp in ponzu sauce, a Japanese dipping sauce made with soy sauce, lemon juice, rice vinegar, and bonito flakes (bonito is a type of tuna). Ponzu sauce is sold with other Asian sauces (near the soy sauce). I often serve this dish with rice noodles or rice on the side. If you don't have a stove-top grill pan, get one! Until then, you can broil the kebabs under the broiler. You can also serve this dish with Coconut Rice (page 227)—start the rice first and it will be ready when the kebabs are finished.

• •

Coat a large stove-top grill pan or skillet with cooking spray and set over medium-high heat to preheat for about 5 minutes.

Alternate pieces of chicken, squash, bell pepper, mushrooms, and onion on the skewers.

In a shallow dish, whisk together the ponzu sauce and black bean sauce. Add the skewers and turn to coat. Place the kebabs on the hot pan and cook until the chicken is cooked through and the vegetables are tender, 8 to 10 minutes, turning frequently.

TIME SAVER tip:

You can assemble the skewers and soak them in the ponzu marinade up to 2 days in the refrigerator.

Cooking spray

1¼ pounds boneless, skinless chicken breasts, cut into 2-inch cubes

1 medium yellow squash, cut into 2-inch chunks

1 medium green bell pepper, seeded and cut into 2-inch squares

24 small button or cremini mushrooms, stems trimmed

1 small red onion, cut into 1-inch chunks

Wooden or metal skewers

½ cup ponzu sauce

1 tablespoon Chinese black bean sauce

COCONUT-LIME CHICKEN WITH CHILES

Total Time: 22 minutes
PREP TIME: 10 MINUTES
ACTIVE COOKING TIME: 12 MINUTES

SERVES 4

A blast for your palate! Imagine this: piquant garlic, rich curry, distinct coconut, the kick of green chiles, and fresh lime, all in one dish. The sauce is so amazing, it's almost perfect by itself, drizzled over leftover rice; try it with shrimp, too. I like to serve this over jasmine rice with steamed snow peas on the side. Let no drop of sauce go asunder.

• •

Heat the oil in a large skillet over medium heat. Add the garlic and cook, stirring, for 1 minute. Add the chicken and cook until golden brown on all sides, about 5 minutes, stirring frequently. Add the curry and cook, stirring, for 1 minute, until it's fragrant. Add the coconut milk, chiles, and lime juice and zest, bring to a simmer, and simmer until the chicken is just cooked through, about 5 minutes. Season to taste with salt and pepper. Remove from the heat, stir in the scallions and cilantro, and serve.

2 teaspoons peanut oil

3 cloves garlic, minced

1¼ pounds boneless, skinless chicken breasts, cut into 1-inch cubes

1 teaspoon curry powder

One 14-ounce can light or regular coconut milk

One 4-ounce can diced green chiles, drained if necessary

1 tablespoon fresh lime juice

1 teaspoon finely grated lime zest

Salt and freshly ground black pepper

¼ cup chopped scallions (white and green parts)

2 tablespoons chopped fresh cilantro

GOOD HEALTH note:

Fourteen ounces of regular coconut milk contains 840 calories and 70 grams of fat (49 grams of saturated fat). The same amount of light coconut milk has 315 calories and 28 grams of fat (21 grams of saturated fat).

STUFFED SPAGHETTI SQUASH WITH TOMATOES, OLIVES, AND CHICKEN

Total Time: 20 minutes
PREP TIME: 10 MINUTES
ACTIVE COOKING TIME: 10 MINUTES

SERVES 4

I adore spaghetti squash. In fact, I've been known to steam and eat the whole thing! It's like spaghetti (in shape and texture) but slightly sweet and definitely wonderful. It also makes a fabulous base for this mildly salty chicken mixture.

● ●

Arrange the spaghetti squash halves, flesh side down, in the bottom of a shallow microwave-safe dish. Cover with plastic wrap and microwave on HIGH until the flesh is tender, about 5 minutes.

Meanwhile, heat the oil in large skillet over medium heat. Add the chicken and cook until browned on all sides, 3 to 5 minutes. Add the tomatoes, olives, basil, and oregano, bring to a simmer, and simmer until the chicken is cooked through, about another 5 minutes.

Preheat the broiler.

Flip the spaghetti squash over and, using a fork, pull the strands from it, creating spaghetti-like pieces. Season the flesh with salt and pepper. Make a slight "hole" in the center of each squash half to make room for the chicken filling, then spoon the filling into the squash halves. Sprinkle the top of each with the feta. Transfer the stuffed squash to a baking sheet or roasting pan and place under the broiler. Broil until the cheese is golden brown, about 2 minutes, then serve.

2 medium spaghetti squash, cut in half lengthwise

2 teaspoons olive oil

3/4 pound boneless, skinless chicken breasts, cut into 1/2-inch dice

One 14-ounce can diced tomatoes

1/2 cup pimiento-stuffed green olives, drained and chopped

1/4 cup chopped fresh basil

1 teaspoon dried oregano

Salt and freshly ground black pepper

1/4 cup crumbled feta cheese

QUICK FIX IT YOUR WAY:

Turn this into a Meal Kit. Cook the squash up to 3 days in advance, wrap in plastic, and refrigerate until ready to stuff. Make the chicken filling up to 3 days in advance and store in a plastic bag in the refrigerator. Come mealtime, reheat the squash in the microwave (about 1 minute on HIGH), reheat the chicken filling in the microwave (about 1 minute on HIGH), then stuff the squash with the chicken filling and broil as directed.

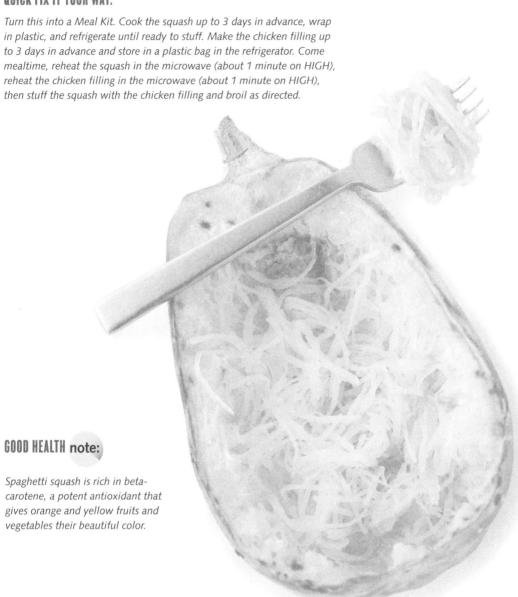

GOOD HEALTH note:

Spaghetti squash is rich in beta-carotene, a potent antioxidant that gives orange and yellow fruits and vegetables their beautiful color.

MOROCCAN CHICKEN WITH TOMATOES AND ZUCCHINI

Total Time: 17 minutes
PREP TIME: 5 MINUTES
ACTIVE COOKING TIME: 12 MINUTES

SERVES 4

The interesting balance of Moroccan flavors in this dish comes from pungent, slightly grassy cumin, cardamom (which contributes its warm, lemony-ginger flavor), cinnamon, and fresh tomatoes. It's a beautiful combination.

I usually serve this with couscous or quick-cooking rice. For something different, try serving the dish over quinoa (pronounced keen-wa), a South American grain that starts brown, but cooks up slightly translucent in just 10 minutes (cook it while the chicken cooks). Season the quinoa with a little salt and pepper and you've got a complete meal. Quinoa is sold in the grain aisle next to the rice.

• •

Heat the oil in a large skillet over medium-high heat. Add the garlic and cook, stirring, for 1 minute. Add the chicken and cook until golden brown on all sides, about 5 minutes, stirring frequently. Add the cumin, cardamom, and cinnamon and cook, stirring, until the spices are fragrant, about 1 minute. Add the tomatoes and zucchini and bring to a simmer. Partially cover the pan and simmer until the chicken is just cooked through, about 5 minutes. Season to taste with salt and pepper and serve.

2 teaspoons olive oil

2 cloves garlic, minced

1¼ pounds boneless, skinless chicken breasts, cut into 2-inch chunks

1 teaspoon ground cumin

1 teaspoon ground cardamom

¼ teaspoon ground cinnamon

One 14-ounce can diced tomatoes

1 medium zucchini, diced

Salt and freshly ground black pepper

QUICK FIX IT YOUR WAY:

To turn this into a Meal Kit, store the uncooked prepped chicken in one bag and the tomatoes, zucchini, and seasonings in another. Everything will be ready to go when you are.

BACON-WRAPPED TURKEY BURGERS WITH BLUE CHEESE SAUCE

Total Time: 15 minutes
PREP TIME: 5 MINUTES
ACTIVE COOKING TIME: 10 MINUTES

SERVES 4

Since ground turkey breast is super-lean, it partners well with fattier foods. Smoky bacon adds incredible flavor, as does the creamy blue cheese sauce. Since the flavors are so intense, I like to serve these burgers on whole wheat or whole grain buns with White Bean–Green Pepper Salad with Mandarin Oranges and Chives (page 199) or Sautéed Bell Peppers with Scallions and Cilantro (page 206) on the side. You can also add your favorite toppings, such as fried onions, lettuce, and sliced tomatoes.

• •

Coat a stove-top griddle or large skillet with cooking spray and set over medium-high heat.

In a large bowl, combine the turkey and poultry seasoning until thoroughly mixed, then shape into 4 patties, each about 1 inch thick. Wrap two slices of bacon around each burger, covering the outer edge (secure with a wooden toothpick if necessary). Place the burgers on the hot griddle and cook until cooked through, about 5 minutes per side.

Meanwhile, in a small bowl, combine the sour cream, blue cheese, and chives. Place burgers on buns and top with the blue cheese sauce.

Cooking spray

1¼ pounds ground turkey breast

1½ teaspoons poultry seasoning

8 slices regular bacon or turkey bacon

¼ cup low-fat sour cream

¼ cup crumbled blue cheese

1 teaspoon chopped fresh chives

4 hamburger buns, preferably whole wheat

QUICK FIX IT YOUR WAY:

You can turn this into a Meal Kit. Wrap the burgers in bacon, cover tightly with plastic wrap, and refrigerate up to 3 days or freeze up to 3 months in freezer bags; thaw completely in the refrigerator or microwave for 3 to 4 minutes on LOW before cooking. The blue cheese sauce will keep in the fridge up to 3 days.

Or, you can make a double batch of burgers and use the leftovers in Greek Pita Pockets with Yogurt-Cucumber Sauce (page 97) later in the week.

GOOD HEALTH note:

One slice of pork bacon contains 42 calories and 3.2 grams of fat. One slice of turkey bacon has 24 calories and 1.7 grams of fat.

TERIYAKI TURKEY BREAST WITH PINEAPPLE AND PICKLED ONIONS

Total Time: 19 minutes
PREP TIME: 10 MINUTES
ACTIVE COOKING TIME: 9 MINUTES

SERVES 4

I love turkey breast. In this dish, you create a jazzed-up teriyaki sauce by adding a few simple ingredients to the bottled variety. You're going to love this one and I suggest you double the recipe or buy a larger turkey breast and save leftovers. You can enjoy the same meal again or slip the turkey slices between two pieces of hearty bread for a sensational sandwich (just add sliced tomato and lettuce). Or dice 2 cups of the leftover turkey and use it instead of pork in the Pork Tortilla Soup (page 79). I serve this with rice noodles on the side.

● ●

Heat the oil in a large skillet over medium-high heat. Season the turkey all over with salt and pepper and place in the hot pan. Sear until golden brown, about 2 minutes per side. Add the pineapple with juice, onions, teriyaki, and honey and bring to a simmer. Partially cover the pan and simmer until the turkey is just cooked through, about 5 minutes.

Arrange the turkey on individual plates (or a serving platter) and spoon the sauce over the top. Sprinkle with the cilantro just before serving.

2 teaspoons olive oil

One 1-pound boneless, skinless turkey breast, cut crosswise into ½-inch-thick slices

Salt and freshly ground black pepper

One 8-ounce can crushed pineapple in juice

½ cup pickled onions, drained

⅓ cup teriyaki sauce

2 tablespoons honey

2 tablespoons chopped fresh cilantro

GOOD HEALTH note:

Turkey is low in fat, high in protein, and a good source of iron, zinc, phosphorus, potassium, and B vitamins. One serving (about 3½ ounces) is the size of a deck of cards.

HERB-CRUSTED FLOUNDER
IN ROASTED GARLIC SAUCE

Total Time: 20 to 22 minutes

PREP TIME: 10 MINUTES

ACTIVE COOKING TIME: 10–12 MINUTES

SERVES 4

Let's face it, flounder isn't the tastiest fish in the sea. The fact is, it's downright bland. But never fear, the seasoning is here. First, I use spicy mustard to get a coating to stick. Then, my coating is a flavorful combo of fresh and dried herbs and spices. Once that's all baked into the crust, I serve the fish with the most incredible roasted garlic sauce you've ever laid your palate on. Good-bye, bland. For a complete meal, while the fish bakes and the garlic sauce simmers, whip up Green Beans with Pearl Onions and Parsley (page 212).

● ●

Preheat the oven to 450°F.

Cut off the pointy end of the garlic head to reveal the cloves. Wrap the head in aluminum foil and bake until the cloves are soft and buttery, 10 to 15 minutes. Set aside until cool enough to handle (keep the oven at 450°F).

Meanwhile, season both sides of the flounder fillets with salt and pepper. Brush the mustard all over both sides of the fish. Set aside.

In a shallow dish, combine the flour, parsley, garlic and onion powders, oregano, and ¼ teaspoon each of salt and pepper. Add the mustard-coated fish and turn to coat evenly.

1 head garlic

Four 6-ounce flounder or halibut fillets

Salt and freshly ground black pepper

1 tablespoon spicy brown mustard

¼ cup all-purpose flour

1 tablespoon chopped fresh parsley

1 teaspoon garlic powder

½ teaspoon onion powder

½ teaspoon dried oregano

Cooking spray

1 cup reduced-sodium vegetable or chicken broth, divided

2 teaspoons cornstarch

STORAGE SAVVY:

Since you're taking the time to roast the garlic, roast several heads at one time and save leftovers for future recipes. Squeeze leftover garlic cloves from the skins and store in a plastic container in the refrigerator for up to 7 days or freeze for up to 3 months; thaw completely in the refrigerator or microwave for 1 to 2 minutes on LOW before using.

Cover a large baking sheet with aluminum foil. Place the fish fillets on the sheet and spray them with cooking spray. Bake until the fish is fork-tender and the crust is golden brown, 10 to 12 minutes.

Meanwhile, squeeze the garlic cloves from the head and place in a small saucepan. Add ¾ cup of the broth and bring to a boil, stirring with a wire whisk to break up the garlic. Dissolve the cornstarch in the remaining ¼ cup broth and add to the simmering liquid. Cook 1 to 2 minutes, until the mixture thickens to the consistency of gravy. Serve the fish with the roasted garlic sauce spooned over the top.

QUICK FIX IT YOUR WAY:

Cook two additional flounder fillets and use the leftovers in Fish and Corn Chowder (page 67) or Artichoke Salad with Capers and Red Lettuce (page 65) for meals in moments later in the week.

GOOD HEALTH note:

Garlic is a nutrient power-house, containing sulfur compounds that lower cholesterol and blood pressure and reduce the risk of cancer.

CORNMEAL-CRUSTED FLOUNDER WITH SPICY PINK BEANS

Total Time: 11 to 16 minutes
PREP TIME: 5–10 MINUTES
ACTIVE COOKING TIME: 6 MINUTES

SERVES 4

Cornmeal is the ideal crust for fish because it cooks up golden and crunchy—a perfect partner for seafood's tender flesh. Another perfect partner? Pink beans spruced up with the smoky hot flavor of chipotle chiles and then cooled off with sour cream and cilantro. Put the beans with the fish and you've got one sensational meal! I like to serve a fresh green salad on the side, drizzled with a lemon vinaigrette.

• •

Season both sides of the flounder with salt and pepper. In a shallow dish, combine the cornmeal and lemon-and-herb seasoning. Add the fillets and turn to coat evenly, tapping off any excess.

Heat the oil in a large skillet over medium-high heat. Add the flounder and cook until fork-tender, about 3 minutes per side.

Meanwhile, in a small saucepan, combine the beans, chipotle and sauce, and garlic powder. Set the pan over medium heat and cook until the beans are hot, stirring frequently. Remove from the heat and stir in the sour cream and cilantro. Serve the beans alongside the flounder.

Four 6-ounce flounder fillets

Salt and freshly ground black pepper

½ cup yellow cornmeal

1 teaspoon salt-free lemon-and-herb seasoning

1 tablespoon olive oil

One 15-ounce can pink beans, drained

1 teaspoon minced canned chipotle chiles in adobo with ½ teaspoon sauce from the can

½ teaspoon garlic powder

¼ cup low-fat sour cream

2 tablespoons chopped fresh cilantro

TIME SAVER tip:

Lemon-and-herb seasoning, sold in the spice aisle, is a tasty combination of onion, sugar, oregano, basil, sherry wine solids, and lemon juice solids. With several ingredients in one bottle, it saves you time and money.

MOROCCAN-STYLE TILAPIA WITH MANGO-RAISIN RELISH

Total Time: 16 to 20 minutes
PREP TIME: 10 MINUTES
ACTIVE COOKING TIME: 6–10 MINUTES

SERVES 4

What's so Moroccan about this fish dish? Rich, earthy cumin and lemony coriander. Both create a wonderfully flavorful crust as the fillets sear in olive oil. The addition of ripe mango and fresh cilantro takes an otherwise bland fish over the top in both flavor and color. Serve this with Swiss Chard with Garlic and Pine Nuts (page 213)—it's ready when the fish is if you start the two dishes at the same time—or serve with steamed green beans (steam them in the microwave). If you can't find tilapia, substitute flounder, halibut, or any other white-fleshed fish.

● ●

1 tablespoon olive oil

Four 6-ounce tilapia fillets

Salt and freshly ground black pepper

1 teaspoon ground cumin

1 teaspoon ground coriander

1½ cups peeled, pitted, and diced ripe mango

½ cup dark raisins

2 teaspoons fresh lemon juice

2 tablespoons chopped fresh cilantro

Heat the oil in a large skillet over medium heat. Season both sides of the fillets with salt and pepper, then rub all over with the cumin and coriander. Place the tilapia in the hot pan and cook until fork-tender, 3 to 5 minutes per side.

Meanwhile, in a medium bowl, combine the mango, raisins, lemon juice, and cilantro. Season to taste with salt and pepper. Top the tilapia fillets with the mango-raisin mixture just before serving.

PREP POINTER:

Choose a mango that yields slightly to gentle pressure from your fingers. All mangos have a large, flat seed inside and the skin is not edible. To remove the seed and flesh, hold the mango upright (stem end up) and slice down along the flat side of the seed. Once you cut away both sides of the fruit, cut the flesh into cubes by slicing down almost to the skin, making hash marks across the flesh (leaving the flesh still attached to the skin). Fold back the skin and the scored flesh will pop out or it can be easily removed with your fingers or a paring knife.

BROILED TILAPIA WITH HORSERADISH AND HERB-SPIKED MAYO

Total Time: 16 minutes
PREP TIME: 10 MINUTES
ACTIVE COOKING TIME: 6 MINUTES

SERVES 4

Tilapia isn't the most flavorful fish in the sea, but when you season it well, broil it until golden brown, and then add a zesty, spiked mayonnaise, you really send the flavors through the roof. You can do the same thing with any white-fleshed fish, such as flounder, halibut, and snapper. Feel free to switch up the herbs—use what you already have in your fridge or what you can pluck from your garden! I like to serve this dish with Parmesan-Crusted Cauliflower (page 209) and a quick-cooking pasta, such as orzo, drizzled with sun-dried tomato–flavored olive oil.

• •

Preheat the broiler. Coat a large baking sheet with cooking spray.

Finely grate 1 teaspoon of zest from the lemon and set aside. Squeeze the juice from the lemon over both sides of the fish. Season both sides of the fish with salt and pepper to taste and the garlic powder. Place the fish on the prepared baking sheet and broil until fork-tender, about 3 minutes per side.

Meanwhile, in a medium bowl, combine the mayonnaise, lemon zest, horseradish, chives, and parsley. Serve the fish with the mayonnaise mixture spooned over the top.

Cooking spray

1 lemon

Four 6-ounce tilapia fillets

Salt and freshly ground black pepper

½ teaspoon garlic powder

⅓ cup light mayonnaise

2 teaspoons prepared horseradish, or more to taste

2 tablespoons chopped fresh chives

2 tablespoons chopped fresh parsley

STORAGE SAVVY:

You can make the mayonnaise mixture up to 3 days in advance and refrigerate until ready to serve.

TUNA STEAKS WITH TOMATOES, MUSHROOMS, AND THYME

Total Time: 19 to 21 minutes
PREP TIME: 5 MINUTES
ACTIVE COOKING TIME: 9–11 MINUTES
WALK-AWAY TIME: 5 MINUTES

SERVES 4

If you're not a tuna fan, any fish "steak" will work in this dish (salmon, swordfish). The savory combination of mushrooms, thyme, tomatoes, and sweet wine pairs perfectly with practically any type of fish. In fact, fish fillets will work, too, just shorten the simmering time from 5 minutes to 2 minutes. Serve with couscous or pasta tossed with olive oil and minced garlic.

● ●

Heat 1 tablespoon of the oil in a large skillet over medium-high heat. Season both sides of the tuna steaks with salt and pepper and place in the hot skillet. Cook until golden brown, about 2 minutes per side. Remove from the heat and set aside.

Heat the remaining 1 tablespoon oil in the same skillet over medium heat. Add the shallots and cook, stirring, until softened, about 2 minutes. Add the mushrooms and cook until they release their juice, 3 to 5 minutes. Stir in the thyme, then add the tomatoes and vermouth and bring to a simmer. Return the tuna steaks to the pan and simmer until fork-tender, about 5 minutes.

2 tablespoons olive oil, divided

Four 6-ounce tuna steaks

Salt and freshly ground black pepper

¼ cup chopped shallots

1 cup sliced button or cremini mushrooms (or any other type of mushroom you like)

1 teaspoon dried thyme

One 14-ounce can diced tomatoes

¼ cup vermouth or dry white wine

QUICK FIX IT YOUR WAY:

You can turn this into a Meal Kit. Make the tomato-based sauce up to 3 days in advance. Refrigerate until ready to reheat in a large skillet or in the microwave for 2 to 3 minutes on HIGH. Sear the tuna just before adding it to the simmering sauce.

GRILLED TUNA STEAKS WITH TANGERINE-ROASTED RED PEPPER SALSA

Total Time: 11 to 20 minutes
PREP TIME: 5–10 MINUTES
ACTIVE COOKING TIME: 6–10 MINUTES

SERVES 4

You'll love this gorgeous salsa with the bold colors of orange tangerines, red peppers, and green cilantro. Your mouth will enjoy it even more since sweet, smoky, and sharp flavors party together on grilled fish. Feel free to spoon it over chicken or beef, or serve it up with cheese and crackers! I like this with Rice Pilaf with Tomatoes and Olives (page 229) or couscous on the side. Start the rice pilaf before making the tuna so everything is ready at the same time (or make the rice up to 3 days in advance and refrigerate until ready to reheat in the microwave).

● ●

Coat a stove-top grill pan or outdoor grill with cooking spray and preheat to medium-high.

Season the tuna steaks all over with salt and pepper and place in the pan or on the grill. Cook until well seared and cooked to your desired degree of doneness, 3 to 5 minutes per side.

Meanwhile, in a medium bowl, combine the tangerine, peppers, onion, cilantro, lime juice, cumin, and garlic powder, tossing to combine. Season to taste with salt and pepper.

Serve the tuna with the salsa spooned over the top.

Cooking spray

Four 6-ounce tuna steaks (preferably sushi-quality)

Salt and freshly ground black pepper

1½ cups tangerine sections (fresh or canned), chopped

½ cup diced roasted red peppers (from water-packed jar)

2 tablespoons minced red onion

2 tablespoons chopped fresh cilantro

1 tablespoon fresh lime juice

½ teaspoon ground cumin

¼ teaspoon garlic powder

QUICK FIX IT YOUR WAY:

Cook two extra tuna steaks and use the leftovers in Stuffed Red Bell Peppers (page 66).

TUNA NICOISE WITH EGG NOODLES, SUN-DRIED TOMATOES, AND OLIVES

Total Time: 20 minutes
PREP TIME: 10 MINUTES
ACTIVE COOKING TIME: 10 MINUTES

SERVES 4

This meal uses fresh tuna steaks in a unique twist on the classic niçoise salad. I love the combination of tuna, pasta, fresh lemon, sun-dried tomatoes, and olives. No doubt, you'll love this, too. If you're not a tuna fan, substitute salmon, cooked shrimp, or cooked chicken.

• •

Cook the egg noodles according to the package directions, adding the green beans for the last 30 seconds of cooking. Drain and transfer to a large bowl.

Meanwhile, preheat the broiler.

Season both sides of the tuna steaks with salt and pepper. Place them on an aluminum foil–lined baking sheet and broil until fork-tender, about 5 minutes per side.

In a small bowl, whisk together the broth, oil, lemon juice, mustard, thyme, and ½ teaspoon each salt and pepper. Add this to the noodles and green beans and toss to combine.

Using a fork, pull the tuna apart into 2-inch chunks and fold into the pasta along with the tomatoes, olives, and parsley. Sprinkle the Romano over the top just before serving.

QUICK FIX IT YOUR WAY:

You can turn this into a Meal Kit. Cook the egg noodles and tuna up to 3 days in advance and store the egg noodles and tuna in separate zip-top plastic bags or containers in the refrigerator. When ready to serve, pull the tuna apart, make the dressing, and mix everything together as directed. Reheat the mixture (once combined) in the microwave for 3 to 4 minutes on HIGH before topping with the Romano cheese.

12 ounces egg or yolk-free egg noodles

1 cup frozen green beans

1¼ pounds tuna steaks

Salt and freshly ground black pepper

½ cup reduced-sodium chicken or vegetable broth

2 tablespoons olive oil

2 tablespoons fresh lemon juice

2 teaspoons Dijon mustard

½ teaspoon dried thyme

½ cup sliced oil-packed sun-dried tomatoes, drained

½ cup pitted niçoise olives, drained and cut in half lengthwise

2 tablespoons chopped fresh parsley

¼ cup shredded or grated Romano cheese

TIME SAVER tip:

Purchase already cooked tuna or substitute cans or packets of chunk white tuna in water (some supermarkets also sell tuna "steaks" in packets, already cooked).

TARRAGON ROASTED SALMON WITH SWEET-N-HOT MUSTARD SAUCE

Total Time: 20 to 25 minutes
PREP TIME: 10 MINUTES
WALK-AWAY TIME: 10–15 MINUTES

SERVES 4

The slight licorice flavor of tarragon works incredibly well with both salmon and mustard. It's hard to believe so much flavor can come from so few ingredients. Not a salmon fan? No big deal, use chicken or pork loin chops instead. I like to serve this dish with Pan-Seared Portobello Mushrooms with Balsamic Vinegar (page 224) and quick-cooking rice, both of which can be made while the salmon cooks.

• •

Preheat the oven to 400°F. Coat a shallow baking dish with cooking spray. Place the salmon in the dish and set aside.

In a small bowl, whisk together the Dijon, honey, and dry mustard until well blended. Remove 2 tablespoons of the mustard sauce and use it to brush all over the salmon fillets (reserve the remaining mustard sauce). Season the tops of the salmon fillets with the tarragon, salt, and pepper. Roast until the fish is fork-tender, 10 to 15 minutes. Serve the salmon with the reserved sauce spooned over the top.

Cooking spray

Four 6-ounce salmon fillets

¼ cup Dijon mustard

2 tablespoons honey

1 teaspoon dry mustard

4 teaspoons dried tarragon

Salt and freshly ground black pepper

QUICK FIX IT YOUR WAY:

Cook two extra salmon fillets and use them in Asian Salmon Cakes with Sesame-Wasabi Cream (page 69).

SWEET MUSTARD-GLAZED SALMON FILLETS

Total Time: 15 to 20 minutes
PREP TIME: 5–10 MINUTES
WALK-AWAY TIME: 10–15 MINUTES

SERVES 4

There's no question mustard, especially mildly spicy Dijon, is awesome with fish. Adding a little sweetness (in the form of brown sugar) really takes this fish flying. If you don't like salmon, substitute any type of fish fillet. I like to serve this with egg noodles (tossed with a little olive oil) and cob corn or succotash (both frozen and microwaved). You also have time (while the salmon bakes) to whip up Sautéed Leeks with Prosciutto and Goat Cheese (page 222) or Soy-Sesame Green Beans with Ginger (page 211) for a stellar meal for guests.

● ●

Preheat the oven to 400°F.

In a shallow baking dish, whisk together the lemon juice, mustard, brown sugar, and cumin. Season both sides of the fillets with salt and pepper, place in the dish, and turn to coat the salmon with the mixture. Bake until the fish is fork-tender, 10 to 15 minutes.

2 tablespoons fresh lemon juice

2 tablespoons Dijon mustard

2 tablespoons brown sugar

1 teaspoon ground cumin

Four 6-ounce salmon fillets

Salt and freshly ground black pepper

TIME SAVER tip:

To cook the fish in the microwave, cover the dish with plastic and microwave on HIGH for 5 minutes, rotating the dish halfway through cooking, until the fish is fork-tender.

CURRIED SHRIMP WITH CILANTRO, LIME, AND GARLIC

Total Time: 11 minutes
PREP TIME: 5 MINUTES
ACTIVE COOKING TIME: 6 MINUTES

SERVES 4

Think outside the "continent box" with this winner. Southwest meets India when you combine Indian curry with the bold flavors of lime juice, cilantro, and sour cream. Don't be afraid to experiment with international ingredients to create a literal "melting pot" on your stove. I love to serve this over quick-cooking white or brown rice with green peas on the side.

● ●

Heat the oil in a large skillet over medium heat. Add the shallots and garlic and cook, stirring, until softened, about 2 minutes. Add the curry powder and cook, stirring, until fragrant, about 1 minute. Add the broth and bring to a simmer. Add the shrimp and lime juice and simmer until the shrimp are bright pink and cooked through, about 3 minutes. Remove from the heat and stir in the sour cream and cilantro. Season to taste with salt and pepper and serve.

"DON'T BE AFRAID TO EXPERIMENT with international ingredients."

2 teaspoons olive oil

3 medium shallots, minced

2 to 3 cloves garlic, to taste, minced

1½ teaspoons curry powder

1 cup reduced-sodium vegetable or chicken broth

1¼ pounds large shrimp, peeled and deveined

2 tablespoons fresh lime juice

½ cup low-fat sour cream

¼ cup chopped fresh cilantro

Salt and freshly ground black pepper

GOOD HEALTH note:

Why use low-fat sour cream? Per ½ cup, it has 84 fewer calories and 10 less grams of fat.

PINEAPPLE-SHRIMP SKEWERS
WITH RUM SAUCE

Total Time: 10 to 15 minutes
PREP TIME: 5–10 MINUTES
ACTIVE COOKING TIME: 5 MINUTES

SERVES 4

Skewers are incredibly fun to put together and these colorful creations boast juicy pineapple, tender shrimp, and red onion. Plus, slightly sweet, salty hoisin sauce not only adds flavor to the skewers, it's a superb partner for the rum sauce. I serve these skewers over rice or Asian noodles to catch all the delicious sauce. Serve with another brilliant side dish that's ready in the same amount of time as the skewers: Lemon-Curry Rice with Golden Raisins (page 228). You can also make the rice in advance (up to 3 days) and reheat it in the microwave for 1 to 2 minutes on HIGH.

● ●

Coat a large stove-top grill pan, griddle, or skillet with cooking spray and set over medium-high heat.

Fill your skewers, alternating pieces of shrimp, pineapple, and onion. Brush the shrimp, pineapple, and onion with the hoisin. Place the skewers in the hot pan and cook until the shrimp are bright pink and just cooked through, about 5 minutes, turning frequently.

Meanwhile, in a small saucepan, whisk together the broth, rum, and cornstarch. Set the pan over medium heat, bring to a simmer, and simmer until the sauce thickens, about 3 minutes, stirring frequently. Drizzle the rum sauce over the skewers just before serving or serve it as a dipping sauce on the side.

PREP POINTER:

It really isn't that hard to peel, core, and cut a fresh pineapple into chunks. Using a large chef's knife, trim off the top and bottom of the pineapple. Now that you have a flat end, stand the pineapple up and cut down through the center to create two halves. Cut each half into two wedges and remove the coarse core. Use a paring knife to cut slices into each wedge, stopping at the skin. Finally, move your knife parallel to the skin to release the fruit.

Cooking spray

Metal or wooden skewers

1¼ pounds large shrimp, peeled and deveined

1 cup cubed pineapple (fresh or canned in juice)

1 large red onion, cut into 2-inch chunks

2 tablespoons hoisin sauce

¾ cup reduced-sodium chicken or vegetable broth

¼ cup dark rum

2 teaspoons cornstarch

EGGPLANT-MOZZARELLA MELTS

Total Time: 24 to 29 minutes
PREP TIME: 10–15 MINUTES
ACTIVE COOKING TIME: 4 MINUTES
WALK-AWAY TIME: 10 MINUTES

SERVES 4

Think of this as my Quick Fix version of eggplant Parmesan, without the red sauce. I like to serve it with my favorite store-bought pasta sauce on the side for dunking but I also sometimes have pasta on the side (angel hair or cappellini) and a nice Caesar salad!

● ●

Preheat the oven to 400°F. Coat a large baking sheet with cooking spray.

Combine the flour, salt, and pepper in a shallow dish. Whisk together the milk, egg, and garlic powder in a separate shallow dish. Place the bread crumbs on a large plate. Dip the eggplant slices one at a time into the flour mixture and turn to coat both sides. Transfer to the milk mixture and turn to coat both sides. Transfer to the bread crumbs and turn to coat both sides. Set the slices on a platter.

Heat the oil in a large skillet over medium-high heat. Add the eggplant slices several at a time and cook until golden brown, about 2 minutes per side. Transfer the slices to paper towels to drain while you finish cooking the remaining slices.

Transfer the eggplant to the prepared baking pan, arranging them in a single layer, and evenly sprinkle the mozzarella and Parmesan over the eggplant. Bake until the cheese is golden and bubbly, about 10 minutes. Let rest a few minutes before serving.

Cooking spray

½ cup all-purpose flour

½ teaspoon salt

¼ teaspoon freshly ground black pepper

1 cup low-fat milk

1 large egg

½ teaspoon garlic powder

1 cup seasoned dry bread crumbs

1 large eggplant, peeled and cut crosswise into ¼-inch-thick slices

1 tablespoon olive oil

1 cup shredded part-skim mozzarella cheese

2 tablespoons grated Parmesan cheese, preferably freshly grated

STORAGE SAVVY:

You can assemble the eggplant in the baking pan, cover with plastic wrap, and refrigerate up to 3 days or freeze up to 3 months; thaw completely in the refrigerator or microwave for 4 to 5 minutes on LOW before baking.

POLENTA PARMESAN

Total Time: 26 to 41 minutes
PREP TIME: 10 MINUTES
ACTIVE COOKING TIME: 6–16 MINUTES
WALK-AWAY TIME: 10–15 MINUTES

SERVES 4

If you've ever wondered what to do with those super-convenient cooked polenta tubes at the grocery store (typically in the rice aisle or with other Italian ingredients), here's your answer. This makes a complete meal when served with Warm Spinach Salad with Pancetta and Gorgonzola (page 196) or any crisp green salad. It also makes an excellent first course (or side dish) with grilled chicken or fish.

● ●

Preheat the oven to 400°F. Coat a large baking sheet with cooking spray.

Heat the oil in a large skillet over medium-high heat. Add the polenta slices a few at time and cook until golden brown, 1 to 2 minutes per side. Transfer them to the prepared baking sheet, arranging them in a single layer.

Spoon the sauce over the polenta and then sprinkle with the basil. Top with the mozzarella and then the Parmesan. Sprinkle the oregano over everything. Bake until the cheese is golden and bubbly, 10 to 15 minutes.

Cooking spray

2 teaspoons olive oil

One 16-ounce tube prepared polenta, plain or seasoned, cut crosswise into 1-inch-thick rounds

1 cup prepared pasta sauce

¼ cup chopped fresh basil

1 cup shredded part-skim mozzarella cheese

¼ cup grated Parmesan cheese, preferably freshly grated

1 tablespoon dried oregano

5

Salads, veggies, and grains

SIMPLE SIDES:

to complete your meal

"IN THE TIME IT TAKES TO REHEAT DINNER, YOU CAN WHIP UP A SIDE DISH that will knock everybody's SOCKS OFF."

Let's face it, on busy weeknights, side dishes are the least of your worries. Just getting the main course on the table can seem like a monumental task, so why bother with sides that go beyond instant rice and canned green beans? Because a few nights a week, you can whip up a side dish that will knock everybody's socks off. Sure, there's always the option of steaming a box of spinach or opening a bag of lettuce mix, and I use those items on a regular basis. In fact, my freezer is always crammed with frozen vegetables and my refrigerator drawers are brimming with prepped vegetables, such as broccoli and cauliflower florets, peeled baby carrots, and cut-up carrots and celery. I take the help when I can get it.

When I'm ready to try something beyond steamed green beans, I can pull off a unique side dish with the ingredients that are already in my pantry, refrigerator, and freezer. These are my Quick Fix side dishes and I know you'll adore them. In fact, in the time it takes to reheat dinner, you can easily whip up a sensational side. You'll feel great (and proud) serving dinner and side dishes that are fresh and bursting with color, flavor, and nutrients.

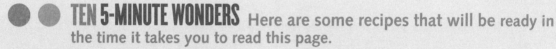

TEN 5-MINUTE WONDERS Here are some recipes that will be ready in the time it takes you to read this page.

1. Toss together sliced green seedless grapes, walnuts, and honey; serve inside radicchio leaves.

2. Stir together drained canned sliced beets and a little horseradish, arrange over watercress or baby spinach leaves, and top with crumbled feta, goat, or blue cheese.

3. Steam chopped broccoli rabe or broccoli florets in the microwave for 3 to 4 minutes, drain, and toss with bottled duck sauce or sweet-and-sour sauce (sold near the soy sauce).

4. Spoon prepared olive tapenade into endive leaves.

5. Steam cauliflower florets in the microwave for 3 to 4 minutes, drain, and toss with a little honey mustard and chopped fresh dill.

6. Steam Brussels sprouts in the microwave for 3 to 4 minutes, drain, and toss with a little orange marmalade.

7. Steam snap peas in the microwave for 3 minutes, drain, and toss with fresh lime juice and chopped salted dry-roasted peanuts.

8. Steam peas and carrots (or peas and corn) in the microwave for 3 minutes, drain, and toss with some low-fat mayonnaise and chili powder, ground cumin, and cayenne pepper to taste.

9. Combine chopped fennel bulb, sliced black olives, and enough bottled Italian dressing to coat.

10. Toss together drained oil-packed artichoke hearts and sliced plum (Roma) tomatoes with a little of the herb-seasoned oil from the artichoke jar.

QUICK BRUSCHETTA WITH TOMATOES AND OLIVES

Total Time: 10 minutes
PREP TIME: 5 MINUTES
ACTIVE COOKING TIME: 5 MINUTES

SERVES 4

Bruschetta is an Italian treat that features toasted bread slices rubbed with olive oil and garlic, then topped with tomatoes, basil, salt, and pepper. In my version, I jazz things up by adding salty Greek olives and parsley.

• •

Preheat the oven to 400°F. Arrange the bread slices on a large baking sheet. Top each slice with minced garlic, then bake until golden brown, about 5 minutes (no need to turn them).

Meanwhile, in a medium bowl, combine the tomatoes, olives, parsley, and oil, then season to taste with salt and pepper. Spoon the mixture onto the bread slices and serve.

GOOD HEALTH note:

Frozen and canned vegetables are picked and either flash-frozen or canned at their nutritional peak, meaning all the nutrients are locked in (sometimes that's not the case with fresh produce that's been sitting around too long in the produce department). That said, don't hesitate to use these convenient and inexpensive products to shave time off your prep. Just be careful about the amount of sodium in the canned varieties and opt for reduced-sodium brands or those with no salt added if they're available.

1 baguette, sliced crosswise into ½-inch-thick slices

3 to 4 cloves garlic, to taste, minced

1½ cups finely diced ripe tomatoes

⅓ cup diced pitted Greek olives (such as kalamata)

1 tablespoon chopped fresh parsley

1 teaspoon olive oil

Salt and freshly ground black pepper

QUICK FIX IT YOUR WAY:

To put this together even faster, substitute melba toast squares for the baguette and skip the toasting step.

LETTUCE WEDGES WITH THOUSAND ISLAND DRESSING

Total Time: 5 minutes
PREP TIME: 5 MINUTES

½ cup low-fat mayonnaise

2 tablespoons ketchup

1 to 2 tablespoons relish (start with 1 tablespoon and add more as desired)

¼ teaspoon freshly ground black pepper

1 head iceberg lettuce, cored and quartered into four wedges

SERVES 4

This recipe conjures up memories of childhood and salads with my dad. We both always ordered "the wedge" at restaurants! Sometimes we got blue cheese dressing, other times Thousand Island. Create your own dressing and you can enjoy this fantastic salad with pantry staples. This goes nicely with grilled steak, chicken, and fish.

● ●

In a small bowl, combine the mayonnaise, ketchup, relish, and pepper. Arrange a wedge on each salad plate and spoon the dressing over the lettuce just before serving.

QUICK FIX IT YOUR WAY:

Here's another quick salad idea—top mixed lettuce greens with sliced pears or sliced fresh figs and shaved Parmesan cheese (use a vegetable peeler to shave it). Drizzle with a mixture of sherry vinegar, olive oil, and honey (equal parts of each).

MIXED GREENS WITH STRAWBERRY-PECAN DRESSING

Total Time: 5 minutes
PREP TIME: 5 MINUTES

SERVES 4

Sure, you can top salad greens with bottled dressing. But, I'm sure you have fruit preserves in your fridge that you love. Why not take that favorite beyond toast and whisk in a little oil, vinegar, and Dijon mustard for a truly wonderful dressing? The added crunch of pecans is the icing on the cake. In place of strawberry preserves, use raspberry, apricot, or whatever you have.

• •

In a small bowl, whisk together the preserves, oil, vinegar, and mustard. Season to taste with salt and pepper.

Arrange the lettuce on salad plates, then top with the pecans and dressing just before serving.

⅓ cup strawberry preserves

3 tablespoons olive oil

1 tablespoon red wine vinegar

1 teaspoon Dijon mustard

Salt and freshly ground black pepper

6 cups mixed lettuce greens

½ cup chopped pecans

QUICK FIX IT YOUR WAY:

Here's another quick Mexican-style salad: jazz up thawed frozen rice (stored on prep day) with a handful of salad bar items, such as pickled green beans, sliced chili peppers, black olives, diced celery, peas, corn, and shredded cheese. Fold in a light, cream-style dressing such as ranch and a little chili powder and serve.

PREP POINTER:

Some preserves are thicker than others; if necessary, thin your dressing with a little water.

For added "nutty" flavor, toast the nuts in a small dry skillet over medium heat until golden, 3 to 5 minutes, shaking the pan frequently to prevent burning.

WARM SPINACH SALAD WITH PANCETTA AND GORGONZOLA

Total Time: 12 to 16 minutes
PREP TIME: 5 MINUTES
ACTIVE COOKING TIME: 7–11 MINUTES

SERVES 4

I adore warm spinach. This spinach is made wonderfully warm when it's tossed with a pancetta-infused dressing that also boasts red onion and red wine vinegar. The whole thing is topped off with creamy blue cheese crumbles.

• •

Place a large skillet over medium-high heat. Add the pancetta and cook, stirring, until browned, 3 to 5 minutes. If necessary, drain most of the fat from the pan, leaving about 2 teaspoons (keep the pancetta in the pan). Add the onion to the pan and cook until softened, 3 to 5 minutes. Add the broth, vinegar, salt, and pepper, bring to a simmer, and let simmer 1 minute to heat through.

Place the spinach in a large bowl. Pour the warm pancetta dressing over the spinach and toss to coat. Transfer the spinach to a serving platter and top with the Gorgonzola just before serving.

VARIATIONS:

Traditional spinach salad typically has mushrooms, so feel free to add sliced mushrooms just before pouring the warm dressing over the greens. Fresh pears (cored and sliced) are also excellent on this salad. Add them just before you add the Gorgonzola.

½ cup diced pancetta or bacon

½ cup thinly sliced red onion

⅔ cup reduced-sodium chicken broth

1 tablespoon red wine vinegar

½ teaspoon salt

¼ teaspoon freshly ground black pepper

6 cups spinach leaves, rinsed well and dried

¼ cup crumbled Gorgonzola or any blue cheese

PREP POINTER:

To dry spinach leaves, try a salad spinner or arrange the rinsed leaves on paper towels and blot with additional paper towels.

BABY SPINACH, FENNEL, AND GRAPEFRUIT SALAD WITH SHALLOT VINAIGRETTE

Total Time: 10 minutes
PREP TIME: 10 MINUTES

4 cups baby spinach leaves

1 fennel bulb, trimmed of any stalks or fronds and thinly sliced

1 cup grapefruit sections

½ cup reduced-sodium vegetable or chicken broth

¼ cup finely minced shallots

2 tablespoons chopped fresh parsley

2 tablespoons olive oil

1 tablespoon red wine vinegar

2 teaspoons Dijon mustard

Salt and freshly ground black pepper

SERVES 4

Who would have guessed that earthy spinach, licorice-like fennel, and tart grapefruit would play so nicely together? The fact is, they love each other's company, especially as they bask in the shallot vinaigrette!

● ●

Place the spinach, fennel, and grapefruit in a large salad bowl.

In a small bowl, whisk together the broth, shallots, parsley, oil, vinegar, and Dijon. Season to taste with salt and pepper. Pour the vinaigrette over the salad just before serving.

TIME SAVER tip:

Buy grapefruit already sectioned. It's sold in jars in the refrigerated section of the produce aisle. Also, make the dressing in a container or jar with a lid and, instead of whisking, just seal the container and shake until blended.

INGREDIENT note:

A native to the Mediterranean region, fennel is a beautiful vegetable that boasts green feathery leaves growing out of a round, white bulb. Greeks have long used fennel stalks and leaves for adding a licorice-like flavoring. The Romans not only added fennel stalks to salads, they used both the stalks and seeds for medicinal purposes. Today, many use fennel as a digestive aid. Low in calories, fennel is also a good source of vitamin C.

WILTED BABY SPINACH WITH HONEY-MAPLE VINAIGRETTE

Total Time: 5 minutes
PREP TIME: 5 MINUTES

SERVES 4

This is a simple salad that's brimming with flavor thanks to the sugary combination of maple syrup and honey. Vinegar, Dijon, and thyme cut the sweetness slightly while lending their own wonderful flavors. Plus, the warm vinaigrette gently wilts the tender baby spinach leaves. It's an excellent side salad for roasted meats and baked pasta dishes.

• •

In a small microwave-safe bowl, whisk together the honey, maple syrup, oil, vinegar, thyme, and mustard. Season to taste with salt and pepper. Cover with plastic wrap and microwave on HIGH 30 seconds, until warm.

Arrange the spinach leaves on a serving platter, drizzle the dressing over the top, and serve.

¼ cup honey

2 tablespoons maple syrup

2 tablespoons olive oil

2 tablespoons white wine vinegar

1 tablespoon chopped fresh thyme or 1 teaspoon dried

1 teaspoon Dijon mustard

Salt and freshly ground black pepper

6 cups baby spinach leaves

PREP POINTER:

No microwave? No problem. Simply warm the vinaigrette in a small saucepan over medium-low heat.

WHITE BEAN–GREEN PEPPER SALAD WITH MANDARIN ORANGES AND CHIVES

Total Time: 10 minutes
PREP TIME: **10 MINUTES**

Two 15-ounce cans white beans, rinsed and drained

1 large green bell pepper, seeded and chopped

2 tablespoons chopped fresh chives

One 11-ounce can mandarin oranges in light syrup

2 tablespoons olive oil

1 tablespoon white wine vinegar

2 teaspoons Dijon mustard

Salt and freshly ground black pepper

SERVES 4

I love every bean variety known to man and in every way possible—in soups, stews, chilis, dips, and salads. Beans are not only filling, they take on the flavors of other ingredients, making one big happy family in every recipe they're used in. This dish pairs white beans (cannellini) with green pepper, mandarin oranges, and oniony chives. The dressing utilizes the liquid from the mandarin orange can and livens it up with vinegar and Dijon. This is fantastic paired with chicken and fish.

• •

Combine the beans, bell pepper, and chives in a large bowl. Strain the mandarin oranges, reserving the liquid from the can, and add the oranges to the bean mixture.

Transfer the reserved mandarin orange liquid to a small bowl. Whisk in the oil, vinegar, and mustard, pour over the bean mixture, and stir to combine. Season to taste with salt and pepper.

STORAGE SAVVY:

You can make this dish up to 3 days in advance and refrigerate until ready to serve. Serve chilled or at room temperature.

SLICED TOMATOES WITH TARRAGON AND HONEY-BALSAMIC VINAIGRETTE

Total Time: 5 minutes
PREP TIME: 5 MINUTES

SERVES 4

This simple side is fantastic with rich main courses such as cheesy pasta, meat and potato-type dishes, and roasted chicken and fish. It's light and fresh and gorgeous. For more color and flavor, garnish the plate with fresh basil leaves.

● ●

Place the tomatoes on a serving platter. Set aside.

In a small bowl, whisk together the vinegar, oil, honey, mustard, and tarragon. Season to taste with salt and pepper, then spoon the vinaigrette over the tomatoes just before serving.

2 to 3 ripe beefsteak tomatoes, cut into ¼-inch-thick slices

2 tablespoons balsamic vinegar

2 tablespoons olive oil

2 tablespoons honey

1 teaspoon Dijon mustard

1 teaspoon dried tarragon

Salt and freshly ground black pepper

BOCCONCINI WITH TOMATOES, BASIL, AND GARLIC OLIVE OIL

Total Time: 10 minutes
PREP TIME: **10 MINUTES**

SERVES 4

Bocconcini (those adorable little mozzarella balls) with fresh tomatoes make quite an impressive side dish, not to mention an incredibly delicious one. I drizzle garlic-flavored olive oil over them both but if you don't have any handy, don't sweat it. Simply add ¼ teaspoon garlic powder to 1 tablespoon of regular olive oil. This is one gorgeous presentation and easy to assemble, making it perfect for entertaining.

• •

Arrange the tomato slices on a serving platter, slightly overlapping them. Arrange the bocconcini on top. Season the cheese and tomatoes with the oregano and salt and pepper to taste. Tear the basil leaves over the top. Drizzle the olive oil over everything just before serving.

INGREDIENT note:

Although you might be tempted, never refrigerate fresh tomatoes. Chilling them also "chills" their flavor, meaning the taste is practically nonexistent.

2 ripe beefsteak tomatoes, thinly sliced

12 ounces bocconcini, or regular-size ball of fresh mozzarella cheese, cut into 2-inch cubes

1 teaspoon dried oregano

Salt and freshly ground black pepper

½ cup packed fresh basil leaves

1 tablespoon garlic-flavored olive oil, or any flavored olive oil

PREP POINTER:

Don't tear or chop basil until you're ready to serve because the leaves (at the torn or cut area) will turn black.

TWO-CABBAGE ASIAN SLAW WITH SESAME SEEDS

Total Time: 10 minutes
PREP TIME: 7 MINUTES
ACTIVE COOKING TIME: 3 MINUTES

SERVES 4

Let's face it, regular coleslaw can be downright monotonous. Since cabbage and carrots are both nutritious, I found a way to wake up this popular salad and make it worthy of any main dish. It's also fun for picnics.

● ●

Place the sesame seeds in a small, dry skillet, set over medium heat, and toast until the seeds are golden, 3 minutes, shaking the pan frequently to prevent burning. Remove from the heat and set aside.

In a large bowl, combine both cabbages, the carrots, and cilantro. Set aside.

In a small bowl, whisk together the mayonnaise, rice wine, sesame oil, and red pepper. Add to the cabbage mixture and toss to combine (at this point, add more mayonnaise if you like a creamier slaw). Fold in the toasted sesame seeds and season to taste with salt and black pepper.

STORAGE SAVVY:

This slaw is even better when made ahead and allowed to marinate in the refrigerator for a while (the cabbage softens and melds into the flavorful dressing). Feel free to make the slaw up to 2 days in advance.

1 tablespoon sesame seeds

1½ cups shredded red cabbage

1½ cups shredded green cabbage

1 cup shredded carrots

2 tablespoons chopped fresh cilantro

½ cup light mayonnaise, or more if desired

2 tablespoons rice wine, mirin, or white wine vinegar

1 tablespoon toasted sesame oil

½ teaspoon crushed red pepper, or more to taste

Salt and freshly ground black pepper

TIME SAVER tip:

Buy shredded cabbage from the produce section of the grocery store.

VARIATION:

Substitute one 10-ounce bag of broccoli slaw mix (sold in the produce aisle next to the regular coleslaw mix and shredded carrots) for the cabbage.

"WAKE UP THIS POPULAR SALAD AND MAKE IT WORTHY OF ANY MAIN DISH. It's also FUN FOR PICNICS."

SAUTÉED CABBAGE WITH APPLES AND CINNAMON

Total Time: 13 to 15 minutes
PREP TIME: 5 MINUTES
ACTIVE COOKING TIME: 8–10 MINUTES

SERVES 4

If you don't think beyond "slaw" when cooking with cabbage, take note. In this dish, red cabbage is simmered with fresh apples, vinegar, sugar, and a hint of cinnamon. It's perfect for nights when you're looking to liven up a dinner plate with color and is delicious with chicken, duck, beef, pork, and veal.

● ●

Heat the oil in a large skillet over medium heat. Add the cabbage and apple and cook, stirring, until the cabbage wilts and the apple is tender, 5 to 7 minutes. Add the vinegar, sugar, and cinnamon and simmer until the liquid is absorbed, about 3 minutes. Season to taste with salt and pepper and serve.

1 tablespoon olive oil

4 cups shredded red cabbage

1 Granny Smith apple, cored and diced (and peeled if desired)

2 tablespoons red wine vinegar

2 tablespoons sugar

½ teaspoon ground cinnamon

Salt and freshly ground black pepper

STORAGE SAVVY:

You can make this dish up to 3 days in advance and refrigerate until ready to serve. Reheat in a saucepan or microwave for 3 minutes on HIGH.

GOOD HEALTH note:

Cabbage is rich in phytonutrients, plant compounds that block cancer-causing substances and help eliminate harmful toxins from the body.

SHREDDED CARROTS AND CURRANTS WITH ROSEMARY DRESSING

SERVES 4

This colorful side dish is the ideal partner for grilled sandwiches and burgers. The sweetness of the carrots and currants pairs perfectly with flavorful vinegar and floral rosemary. Feel free to add any extra herbs you have handy, and you can substitute raisins for the currants if you like.

• •

In a medium bowl, combine the carrots, currants, and rosemary.

In a small bowl, whisk together the broth, oil, vinegar, and mustard. Add this to the carrot mixture and toss to combine. Season to taste with salt and pepper.

3 cups shredded carrots

½ cup dried currants

2 tablespoons chopped fresh rosemary

½ cup reduced-sodium vegetable or chicken broth

2 tablespoons olive oil

1 tablespoon sherry vinegar

2 teaspoons Dijon mustard

Salt and freshly ground black pepper

QUICK FIX IT YOUR WAY:

Here's another shredded carrot idea—toss shredded carrots with a little toasted sesame oil, soy sauce, and chopped fresh cilantro and scallions for an Asian-inspired side dish.

STORAGE SAVVY:

You can make this dish up to 3 days in advance and refrigerate until ready to serve.

GOOD HEALTH note:

Carrots are brimming with beta-carotene, an amazing antioxidant and disease-fighter that protects the body from damaging free radicals that can increase the risk of heart disease and cancer.

SAUTÉED BELL PEPPERS WITH SCALLIONS AND CILANTRO

SERVES 4

This recipe capitalizes on the brilliant coloring of bell peppers, combining red, green, and yellow peppers in one dish. To give this recipe a bit of a Thai twist, I also add green onions, soy sauce, and cilantro. The result tastes phenomenal and is embarrassingly easy. This is super with chicken, turkey, beef, pork, veal, and seafood and is also terrific alongside an omelet or stuffed into a burrito.

• •

Heat the oil in a large skillet over medium-high heat. Add the scallions and cook, stirring, until softened, about 2 minutes. Add the bell peppers and soy sauce and cook until softened, 3 to 5 minutes, stirring frequently. Remove from the heat, stir in the cilantro, and season to taste with salt and pepper.

2 teaspoons olive oil

4 scallions (white and green parts), cut into 2-inch lengths

1 large red bell pepper, seeded and sliced into strips

1 large green bell pepper, seeded and sliced into strips

1 large yellow or orange bell pepper, seeded and sliced into strips

1 tablespoon reduced-sodium soy sauce

2 tablespoons chopped fresh cilantro

Salt and freshly ground black pepper

STORAGE SAVVY:

You can make this dish up to 3 days in advance and refrigerate until ready to reheat in the microwave for 3 minutes on HIGH. You can also make a double batch and freeze half for future meals. Thaw in the microwave for 2 minutes on LOW, then reheat for 2 minutes on HIGH.

TIME SAVER **tip:**

Buy frozen sliced bell peppers and use them instead of fresh (sometimes they're sold with onions included, and that's OK too!).

QUICK FIX IT YOUR WAY:

You can turn this into a Meal Kit. Slice the peppers and chop the scallions and store together in a zip-top plastic bag up to 1 week in the refrigerator and up to 3 months in the freezer; thaw in the microwave for 2 to 3 minutes on LOW before proceeding with the recipe.

BALSAMIC ROASTED ASPARAGUS

Total Time: 15 minutes
PREP TIME: 5 MINUTES
WALK-AWAY TIME: 10 MINUTES

SERVES 4

If you've never tried roasting asparagus, now's the time to preheat your oven. Roasting brings out the sweetness of the asparagus and caramelizes the exterior. This is excellent with chicken, beef, pork, fish, pasta, and even egg dishes such as quiche, eggs Benedict, and omelets.

● ●

Preheat the oven to 450°F. Coat a large baking sheet with cooking spray.

Arrange the asparagus on the sheet and spray them with the cooking spray. Brush the vinegar all over the asparagus and season with salt and pepper. Roast until crisp-tender and golden brown, about 10 minutes.

GOOD HEALTH note:

Asparagus beats all other vegetables when it comes to folate, providing 60% of the RDA in one 5.3-ounce serving. Asparagus is also a good source of potassium and fiber.

Cooking spray

1 large bunch asparagus, woody bottoms trimmed

2 tablespoons balsamic vinegar

Salt and freshly ground black pepper

PREP POINTER:

To remove the woody ends from asparagus, hold each stalk by the ends and bend until it snaps where it wants to. To save time, do that with one stalk and then use that stalk as a guide to line up the remaining stalks—slice the ends with a sharp knife.

"ROASTING BRINGS OUT THE SWEETNESS
of asparagus."

BRUSSELS SPROUTS
WITH BACON AND SHALLOTS

Total Time: 14 minutes
PREP TIME: 5 MINUTES
ACTIVE COOKING TIME: 4 MINUTES
WALK-AWAY TIME: 5 MINUTES

SERVES 4

Maybe the reason many people don't include Brussels sprouts on their regular menu is because they've never tried the little nuggets with bacon! Use regular bacon, turkey bacon, soy bacon—it doesn't matter. What matters is that the vegetable adores the smoky flavor and so will you!

• •

Heat the oil in a large skillet over medium-high heat. Add the bacon and cook, stirring, until golden brown, about 3 minutes. Add the shallots and cook, stirring, for 1 minute. Add the Brussels sprouts and broth and bring to a simmer. Reduce the heat to low, partially cover the pan, and let simmer until the sprouts are crisp-tender, about 5 minutes. Season to taste with salt and pepper.

2 teaspoons olive oil

4 slices regular bacon or turkey bacon, diced

¼ cup minced shallots

One 10-ounce package frozen Brussels sprouts, thawed

½ cup reduced-sodium chicken or vegetable broth

Salt and freshly ground black pepper

STORAGE SAVVY:

You can make this dish up to 3 days in advance and refrigerate until ready to reheat in the microwave.

PARMESAN-CRUSTED CAULIFLOWER

Total Time: 15 minutes
PREP TIME: 5 MINUTES
WALK-AWAY TIME: 10 MINUTES

SERVES 4

How can something so white taste so wonderful? It's called Parmesan cheese! We go through tons of the stuff in my house and vegetables are no exception. In this dish, I parboil the cauliflower first to get a jump-start on the cooking time. Not a cauliflower fan? This coating works with virtually all vegetables.

● ●

Preheat the oven to 400°F. Coat a large baking sheet with cooking spray.

Bring a medium pot of water to a boil. Add the cauliflower and cook for 1 minute. Drain and transfer the cauliflower to the prepared baking sheet. Spray the cauliflower with cooking spray, then sprinkle with the Parmesan and season with pepper. Bake until the cheese is golden brown, about 10 minutes.

Olive oil cooking spray

6 cups cauliflower florets

½ cup grated Parmesan cheese, preferably freshly grated

Freshly ground black pepper

GOOD HEALTH note:

Cauliflower is low in carbohydrates (2.6 grams in ½ cup), low in calories (14 calories per ½ cup), high in vitamin C, and a good source of heart-healthy folate.

"HOW CAN SOMETHING SO WHITE
taste so wonderful?"

BROCCOLI PUREE
WITH PARMESAN

Total Time: 13 minutes
PREP TIME: 5 MINUTES
ACTIVE COOKING TIME: 8 MINUTES

SERVES 4

Think of this as a combination of mashed potatoes and broccoli. The vegetables soften in garlic-infused water, then get mashed together with milk and Parmesan cheese—just fabulous. You can use cauliflower instead of broccoli.

● ●

Place the potato and garlic cloves in a medium saucepan and pour in enough water to cover by 2 inches. Bring to a boil and boil for 6 minutes. Add the broccoli and boil until the potato is fork-tender, about another 2 minutes. Drain and return the vegetables and garlic to the pan.

Add the milk and Parmesan and mash with a potato masher until smooth (or lumpy, however you like it!), adding more milk if necessary to create a smooth consistency. Season to taste with salt and pepper.

1 large Idaho potato, peeled and cut into 2-inch chunks

2 to 3 cloves garlic, to taste, peeled

4 cups broccoli florets (sold in bags in the produce aisle, near the bagged lettuce mixes and shredded coleslaw mix)

¼ cup low-fat milk, or more as needed

¼ cup grated Parmesan cheese, preferably freshly grated

Salt and freshly ground black pepper

GOOD HEALTH note:

Like its cruciferous cousins, broccoli contains disease-fighting phytochemicals that protect against cancer.

STORAGE SAVVY:

You can make this dish up to 3 days in advance and refrigerate until ready to reheat in the microwave for 3 minutes on HIGH. You can also double the batch and freeze half for future meals (up to 3 months). Store the puree in a plastic container and thaw and reheat in the microwave.

SOY-SESAME GREEN BEANS WITH GINGER

Total Time: 10 minutes
PREP TIME: 5 MINUTES
ACTIVE COOKING TIME: 5 MINUTES

SERVES 4

Yes, I know. You can steam green beans in the microwave and be finished with your side dish in 60 seconds. But how exciting is that? Reserve that solution for when you're *really* behind schedule. In this simple dish, the green gems are livened up with sesame, garlic, soy, and ginger for an Asian-inspired winner. You can give most any vegetables this treatment with delicious results.

● ●

Heat the oil in a large skillet over medium-high heat. Add the garlic and ginger and cook, stirring, for 1 minute. Add the green beans and sesame seeds and cook until the seeds are golden brown, about 2 minutes, stirring frequently. Add the broth and soy sauce and cook until the green beans are crisp-tender, about another 2 minutes. Season to taste with salt and pepper.

2 teaspoons toasted sesame oil

2 cloves garlic, minced

1 tablespoon peeled and minced fresh ginger

2 cups fresh or one 10-ounce package frozen green beans (no need to thaw)

1 tablespoon sesame seeds

½ cup reduced-sodium vegetable or chicken broth

2 tablespoons reduced-sodium soy sauce

Salt and freshly ground black pepper

GOOD HEALTH note:

Green beans are low in calories (just 44 calories per cup) and an excellent source of fiber and vitamins A, C, and K (important for maintaining strong bones).

GREEN BEANS WITH PEARL ONIONS AND PARSLEY

Total Time: 13 to 18 minutes
PREP TIME: 5 MINUTES
ACTIVE COOKING TIME: 8–13 MINUTES

SERVES 4

I often make a version of this dish for Thanksgiving (with peas and dill) to serve alongside the bird. It's colorful and refreshing and frozen pearl onions are a Quick Fix cook's true pal. Why? Because they're already peeled and blanched, all the prep work is done. I add pearl onions to soups, stews, stir-fries, sautéed combinations of meat and vegetables, and in this case, vegetable side dishes. Notice that the onions are sautéed in olive oil with a little sugar. The sugar not only caramelizes the onions, creating a golden brown exterior, it brings out the natural sweetness of these tender little things. Green beans and pimientos make excellent additions and the whole dish is livened up with the fresh taste of parsley.

● ●

Heat the oil in a large skillet over medium heat. Add the onions and sugar and cook, stirring, until the onions are golden brown and caramelized, about 5 minutes for thawed onions and 7 to 10 minutes for frozen. Add the green beans, pimientos, and vinegar and cook, stirring, until the beans are crisp-tender, about 3 minutes. Remove from the heat, stir in the parsley, season to taste with salt and pepper, and serve.

2 teaspoons olive oil

2 cups frozen pearl onions (no need to thaw)

1 tablespoon sugar

2 cups fresh or one 10-ounce package frozen green beans (no need to thaw)

One 4-ounce jar diced pimientos, drained

1 tablespoon balsamic vinegar

2 tablespoons chopped fresh parsley

Salt and freshly ground black pepper

QUICK FIX IT YOUR WAY:

For a superfast green bean side dish with similar flavors, steam the beans in the microwave (place in a shallow dish with about 2 tablespoons water, cover with plastic wrap, and cook on HIGH for 2 to 3 minutes, until crisp-tender), drain away excess water, and toss with bottled (and drained) pearl onions and prepared sundried tomato pesto.

SWISS CHARD WITH GARLIC AND PINE NUTS

Total Time: 10 minutes
PREP TIME: 5 MINUTES
ACTIVE COOKING TIME: 5 MINUTES

SERVES 4

Some types of Swiss chard are deep green and others boast incredible hues of red. Any shade of Swiss chard will do here. In this dish, I've added ginger (for a surprise on your palate) and crunchy toasted pine nuts. If you can't find Swiss chard or want to change things, substitute fresh spinach, mustard greens, bok choy, or kale.

● ●

Place the pine nuts in a large, dry skillet, set over medium heat, and toast until golden brown, 2 to 3 minutes, shaking the pan frequently; watch them carefully—they can go from toasty to burned in the time it takes to answer the phone. Remove the nuts from the pan and set aside.

Heat the oil in the same skillet over medium heat. Add the garlic and ginger and cook, stirring, for 1 minute. Add the Swiss chard and soy sauce, cover, and steam until the leaves wilt, about 1 minute. Season to taste with salt and pepper. Top with the pine nuts just before serving.

¼ cup pine nuts

2 teaspoons olive oil

3 cloves garlic, minced

1 tablespoon peeled and minced fresh ginger

8 cups chopped Swiss chard leaves (cut away all thick stems)

2 tablespoons reduced-sodium soy sauce

Salt and freshly ground black pepper

QUICK FIX IT YOUR WAY:

Since Swiss chard is packed with disease-fighting antioxidants, here's another quick idea—sauté the chopped leaves in garlic-flavored olive oil until tender, then toss in diced Niçoise olives just before serving; season to taste with salt and pepper.

TERIYAKI BOK CHOY
WITH CASHEWS

Total Time: 10 minutes
PREP TIME: 5 MINUTES
ACTIVE COOKING TIME: 5 MINUTES

SERVES 4

This Asian-inspired dish is terrific with any main course. Tangy teriyaki sauce livens up bok choy and the cashews add an amazing crunch. It's fast and elegant and perfect for a weeknight meal or fancy dinner party!

• •

Heat the oil in a large skillet over medium heat. Add the bok choy and cook, stirring, for 3 minutes. Add the teriyaki sauce and red pepper and cook, stirring, until the bok choy stalks are tender-crisp and the leaves are wilted, about another 2 minutes. Season to taste with salt and pepper.

Arrange the bok choy on plates and top with the cashews just before serving.

1 tablespoon toasted sesame oil

1 bunch bok choy, heavy bottoms trimmed off, cut crosswise into ½-inch-thick slices

1 tablespoon reduced-sodium teriyaki sauce

½ teaspoon crushed red pepper

Salt and freshly ground black pepper

½ cup dry-roasted cashews

INGREDIENT **note:**

Bok choy is a Chinese cabbage, but hardly resembles the round heads of cabbage we're familiar with, or even long-leaved Napa cabbage—in both shape and flavor. Bok choy has bold green leaves, a light, sweet flavor, and the stalks are refreshingly crisp. Nutritionally, bok choy is low in calories and high in calcium and vitamins A and C.

GARLIC-SPIKED BROCCOLI RABE WITH DRIED MANGO

Total Time: 9 minutes
PREP TIME: 5 MINUTES
ACTIVE COOKING TIME: 4 MINUTES

SERVES 4

My husband loves broccoli rabe but sometimes I find it a little bitter. The answer? I created a dish we both enjoy by adding dried mango—the sweetness of the mango pairs perfectly with the mildly bitter broccoli rabe. You can also substitute cranberries or raisins for the mango.

● ●

Heat the oil in a large skillet over medium heat. Add the garlic and cook, stirring, for 1 minute. Add the broccoli rabe and mango and cook, stirring, until the broccoli rabe leaves wilt, about 3 minutes. Season to taste with salt and pepper and serve.

2 teaspoons olive oil

3 cloves garlic, minced

6 cups chopped broccoli rabe

½ cup diced dried mango or golden raisins

Salt and freshly ground black pepper

TIME SAVER tip:

You can make this dish in the microwave instead of in a skillet; combine all the ingredients in a microwave-safe dish, cover with plastic and microwave on HIGH for 3 minutes, until the broccoli rabe is tender.

CREAMED SPINACH MY WAY

Total Time: 10 minutes
PREP TIME: 5 MINUTES
ACTIVE COOKING TIME: 5 MINUTES

SERVES 4

I grew up on creamed spinach and I love the stuff—creamy and smooth, with a subtle hint of onions and garlic. This version is amazing *and* fast and excellent with steak, chicken, and seafood.

• •

In a blender, combine the spinach, milk, onion, and garlic powder and process until smooth (you can also puree the mixture directly in a medium saucepan using a handheld blender).

Transfer the mixture to a medium saucepan and set over medium heat. Bring to a simmer and cook until the liquid reduces and the mixture thickens, about 5 minutes, stirring frequently. Season to taste with salt and pepper and serve.

"I GREW UP ON CREAMED SPINACH
and I love the stuff."

One 10-ounce package frozen chopped spinach, thawed and drained

One 12-ounce can evaporated fat-free milk or low-fat milk

1 teaspoon dehydrated minced onion (also sold as onion flakes in the spice aisle)

½ teaspoon garlic powder

Salt and freshly ground black pepper

STORAGE SAVVY:

Double this recipe and freeze leftovers for future meals. Thaw in the microwave for 2 to 3 minutes on LOW, then reheat for 2 to 3 minutes on HIGH.

GOOD HEALTH note:

Spinach is on the top ten list of the highest sources of carotenoids, antioxidants that help prevent disease. Spinach is also high in iron, magnesium, lutein, folate, and vitamins A, C, and E.

MASHED ACORN SQUASH
WITH SUNFLOWER SEEDS

Total Time: 10 to 12 minutes
PREP TIME: 5 MINUTES
WALK-AWAY TIME: 5-7 MINUTES

SERVES 4

Acorn squash is succulent and wonderful and deserves a place on your regular menu. You can quickly steam it in the microwave and enjoy the flesh right from the skin with a spoon. Add a little olive oil, salt, and black pepper and you're good to go! In this recipe, the flesh is mashed with sour cream, smoky cumin, and garlic, then topped with crunchy dry-roasted sunflower seeds. Wow!

● ●

Place the acorn squash halves in a microwave-safe dish and cover with plastic wrap. Microwave on HIGH until the flesh is tender, 5 to 7 minutes.

Using a spoon or an ice cream scoop, remove the flesh from the squash and transfer to a large bowl. Add the sour cream, cumin, and garlic powder and mash together with a fork until blended and smooth, adding more sour cream as necessary to create a nice consistency. Season to taste with salt and pepper.

Spoon the squash onto plates and top with sunflower seeds just before serving.

PREP POINTER:

No microwave? No problem. Simply steam the squash in a colander over simmering water for about 10 minutes, until the flesh is tender.

2 acorn squash, cut in half and seeded

⅓ cup low-fat sour cream, or more as needed

1 teaspoon ground cumin

½ teaspoon garlic powder

Salt and freshly ground black pepper

¼ cup shelled dry-roasted sunflower seeds

VARIATION:

You can top the smooth squash puree with any crunchy topping—pumpkin seeds, sesame seeds, or chopped hazelnuts, cashews, or pistachio nuts.

STORAGE SAVVY:

You can make the squash puree up to 3 days in advance and refrigerate until ready to serve. Reheat in the microwave for 3 minutes on HIGH and top with sunflower seeds just before serving.

QUICK FIX MASHED POTATOES

Total Time: 13 minutes
PREP TIME: 5 MINUTES
WALK-AWAY TIME: 8 MINUTES

SERVES 4

A cookbook just isn't complete without a recipe for mashed pota-toes. In the Quick Fix kitchen, prepping ahead is the key to week-night, homemade (not boxed!) mashed spuds.

• •

Place the potatoes in a large saucepan and pour in enough water to cover. Set the pan over high heat, bring to a boil, and boil until the potatoes are fork-tender, about 8 minutes. Drain and return the potatoes to the pan. Add the sour cream and seasoning and mash until smooth (or lumpy, depending on how you like it), adding more sour cream for a creamier consistency. Season to taste with salt and pepper and serve.

STORAGE SAVVY:

The mashed potatoes can be made up to 3 days in advance and refrigerated until ready to serve. Reheat in the microwave until hot (about 3 minutes on HIGH).

4 medium Idaho potatoes, peeled and cut into 1-inch cubes

⅓ cup low-fat sour cream, or more to taste

1 teaspoon salt-free garlic-and-herb seasoning

Salt and freshly ground black pepper

QUICK FIX IT YOUR WAY:

You can turn this into a Meal Kit. Boil the potatoes in advance, cool, transfer to a plastic bag or container, and refrigerate up to 1 week. Reheat the potatoes in the microwave until hot, about 2 to 3 minutes on HIGH, then mash with the sour cream and seasonings as instructed.

RED POTATOES WITH CAPERS, TOMATOES, AND ONION

Total Time: 18 minutes

PREP TIME: 10 MINUTES

ACTIVE COOKING TIME: 8 MINUTES

SERVES 4

Have you noticed that red potatoes run the gamut in terms of size these days? Some spuds are golf ball-size while others rival a large Idaho. Don't fret—buy what looks the freshest (or what you can buy in bulk).

This is an excellent side for roasted meat dishes (chicken, pork, veal, beef) and is also tasty alongside eggs.

● ●

Place the potatoes in a large saucepan and pour in enough water to cover by about 2 inches. Set the pan over high heat, bring to a boil, and boil until the potatoes are fork-tender, about 8 minutes.

Drain and transfer the potatoes to a large bowl. While they are still warm, add the capers, tomato, onion, oil, vinegar, and thyme and toss to combine. Season to taste with salt and pepper.

STORAGE SAVVY:

You can make this dish up to 3 days in advance and refrigerate until ready to serve. Serve chilled, at room temperature, or warm (reheat in the microwave for 2 to 3 minutes on HIGH).

- 6 small or 4 medium red potatoes, cut in half (or quartered if slightly bigger)
- ½ cup drained capers
- ½ cup diced ripe tomato
- ¼ cup minced red onion
- 1½ tablespoons olive oil
- 1 tablespoon red wine vinegar
- 1 tablespoon chopped fresh thyme or 1 teaspoon dried
- Salt and freshly ground black pepper

TIME SAVER tip:

Cut larger potatoes into 2-inch pieces to speed up your cooking time and to make them more bite-size.

CARAMELIZED COCKTAIL ONIONS WITH RED PEPPERS

Total Time: 10 minutes
PREP TIME: 3 MINUTES
ACTIVE COOKING TIME: 7 MINUTES

SERVES 4

It's my nature to find an alternate use for all foods. Cocktail onions aren't just for martinis in my house (although they're welcome there, too!). I love to caramelize the little gems in sugar, then toss them with roasted red peppers and tangy balsamic vinegar to create an amazing side dish in minutes that's excellent with fish, pork, and chicken dishes and over mixed greens.

• •

Heat the oil in a large skillet over medium heat. Add the onions and sugar and cook, stirring frequently, until golden brown on all sides, about 5 minutes. Add the red peppers and vinegar and cook for 2 minutes to heat through. Season to taste with salt and pepper.

1 tablespoon olive oil

2 cups cocktail onions (sold near the pickles), drained

2 tablespoons sugar

1 cup chopped roasted red peppers (from water-packed jar)

2 teaspoons balsamic vinegar

Salt and freshly ground black pepper

STORAGE SAVVY:

Double this recipe and store leftovers in freezer bags for up to 3 months. Thaw in the microwave for 2 to 3 minutes on LOW, then reheat for 2 to 3 minutes on HIGH.

GOOD HEALTH note:

Roasted red peppers are chock full of vitamin C; one red pepper has 10 times the beta-carotene of one green bell pepper.

SAUTÉED LEEKS WITH PROSCIUTTO AND GOAT CHEESE

Total Time: 11 to 15 minutes
PREP TIME: 5–7 MINUTES
ACTIVE COOKING TIME: 6–8 MINUTES

SERVES 4

The ingredient list may look simple, but this is one stellar side dish. Salty prosciutto and goat cheese partner with mild, tender leeks—an incredible taste sensation for your mouth. In fact, add some broth and toss this mixture over cooked pasta for a complete meal! When serving it as a side dish, it pairs nicely with chicken, turkey, and pork tenderloin. If you can't find prosciutto, substitute regular bacon, turkey bacon, or lean ham.

• •

Heat the oil in a large skillet over medium heat. Add the prosciutto and cook, stirring, for 3 minutes. Add the leeks and cook, stirring, until softened, 3 to 5 minutes. Season to taste with salt and pepper. Sprinkle the goat cheese over the leeks just before serving.

- 2 teaspoons olive oil
- ½ cup diced prosciutto
- 4 leeks (white part only), rinsed well and chopped
- Salt and freshly ground black pepper
- ½ cup crumbled goat cheese

PREP POINTER:

To clean leeks, slice off the green tops. Halve the white portion lengthwise and immerse the separate layers in a large bowl of cold water, allowing the dirt and grit to fall to the bottom of the bowl. Dry on paper towels before using.

GOOD HEALTH note:

Leeks, like their onion cousins, are rich in cancer-fighting sulfur compounds.

SAUTÉED WILD MUSHROOMS

Total Time: 12 to 14 minutes

PREP TIME: 5 MINUTES

ACTIVE COOKING TIME: 7–9 MINUTES

SERVES 4

Now that wild mushrooms are widely available in every grocery store, you can enjoy a variety of different flavors in one dish. Grab a bunch on your next shopping trip and you'll be glad you did. This is awesome with steak, chicken, and veal. If you end up with leftovers, add them to omelets, stir-fries, gravies, and soft tacos.

• ●

Heat the oil in a large skillet over medium-high heat. Add the onion and garlic and cook until softened, about 2 minutes. Add the mushrooms and cook until they are tender and releasing juice, 3 to 5 minutes, stirring frequently. Add the thyme and stir to coat. Add the sherry and soy sauce and simmer for 2 minutes to heat through.

Remove from the heat and stir in the parsley. Season to taste with salt and pepper.

"THIS IS AWESOME WITH STEAK, CHICKEN, and veal."

2 teaspoons olive oil

½ red onion, sliced into half-moons

2 cloves garlic, minced

4 cups sliced mushrooms (any combination of cremini, portobello, shiitake, oyster, button, and porcini)

1 teaspoon dried thyme

¼ cup sherry wine

1½ tablespoons reduced-sodium soy sauce

2 tablespoons chopped fresh parsley

Salt and freshly ground black pepper

STORAGE SAVVY:

You can make this dish up to 3 days in advance and refrigerate until ready to reheat in the microwave for 3 minutes on HIGH.

GOOD HEALTH note:

Low in calories, mushrooms are rich in two cancer-fighters—selenium and lentinan.

PAN-SEARED PORTOBELLO MUSHROOMS WITH BALSAMIC VINEGAR

Total Time: 12 minutes
PREP TIME: 5 MINUTES
ACTIVE COOKING TIME: 7 MINUTES

SERVES 4

Searing mushrooms in a hot pan not only softens them, it brings out more of their distinct earthy flavor. I love portobello mushrooms with balsamic vinegar; the better the quality of the vinegar, the more delicious the dish. Add fresh thyme and parsley and you've got a winner in minutes! You can also cook the mushrooms on a stove-top grill pan or outdoor grill.

• •

Heat the oil in a large skillet over medium-high heat. Season both sides of the mushrooms with salt and pepper. Rub the thyme on the inside of the mushrooms (the stem side). Place the mushrooms in the skillet and cook until golden brown and tender, about 3 minutes per side. Add the vinegar and cook 1 minute to heat through.

Transfer the mushrooms to a serving platter or individual plates and top with parsley just before serving.

2 teaspoons olive oil

4 large portobello mushrooms, stems removed (remove the black gills from the inside of caps if desired)

Salt and freshly ground black pepper

1 tablespoon chopped fresh thyme or 1 teaspoon dried

2 tablespoons balsamic vinegar, preferably aged balsamic

2 tablespoons chopped fresh parsley

ADOBO RICE AND PINK BEANS

Total Time: 10 to 12 minutes
PREP TIME: 2 MINUTES
WALK-AWAY TIME: 8–10 MINUTES

SERVES 4

Why do I call this adobo? Because it contains the wonderful Mexican-inspired flavors of chili powder, cumin, and garlic, classic ingredients in tomato-based adobo sauce. The combination of rice and beans is super satisfying and a great source of protein. Serve this at any meal that features grilled or roasted meat, fish, or poultry.

• •

Bring the water to a boil in a medium saucepan over medium-high heat. Add the rice, beans, chiles, chili powder, cumin, garlic powder, and onion powder and stir to combine. Cover, reduce the heat to low, and cook until the liquid is absorbed, 8 to 10 minutes.

Remove from the heat and fluff with a fork. Season to taste with salt and pepper and serve.

2¼ cups water

2 cups quick-cooking brown rice

One 15-ounce can pink beans, rinsed and drained

One 4-ounce can diced green chiles, drained if necessary

1 teaspoon chili powder

1 teaspoon ground cumin

½ teaspoon garlic powder

½ teaspoon onion powder

Salt and freshly ground black pepper

STORAGE SAVVY:

Prep ahead for another night and double this recipe. Store the cooled rice and beans in plastic bags or containers in the refrigerator for up to 1 week or freeze up to 3 months. Thaw the mixture in the refrigerator or microwave for 3 to 4 minutes on LOW. Reheat in the microwave for 3 to 4 minutes on HIGH before serving.

QUICK FIX IT YOUR WAY:

Make this dish with leftover frozen rice. Thaw the rice in the microwave for 3 minutes on LOW, then add the pink beans and remaining ingredients. Heat everything together in the microwave for 3 minutes on HIGH and serve.

COCONUT RICE

Total Time: 10 minutes
PREP TIME: 5 MINUTES
WALK-AWAY TIME: 5 MINUTES

SERVES 4

In the time it takes to make regular quick-cooking rice, you can add a few ingredients to make an ordinary side dish an extraordinary one. Throw this together the next time you make rice for a stir-fry!

● ●

Combine the coconut milk and broth in a medium saucepan and bring to a boil. Add the rice, cover, and remove from the heat. Let stand until the liquid is absorbed, about 5 minutes. Fluff with a fork, stir in the cilantro, and season to taste with salt and pepper.

One 14-ounce can light or regular coconut milk

½ cup reduced-sodium chicken broth or water

2¼ cups quick-cooking white rice

¼ cup chopped fresh cilantro

Salt and freshly ground black pepper

STORAGE SAVVY:

Double the batch and freeze leftovers (in freezer bags) for up to 3 months. Thaw in the microwave for 2 to 3 minutes on LOW, then reheat for 3 minutes on HIGH before serving.

VARIATION:

For added coconut flavor, add 2 tablespoons shredded coconut just before serving. You can also toast the coconut on a baking sheet in a 350°F oven until golden brown, about 5 minutes.

LEMON-CURRY RICE
WITH GOLDEN RAISINS

Total Time: 10 minutes
PREP TIME: 5 MINUTES
WALK-AWAY TIME: 5 MINUTES

SERVES 4

It takes just a few ingredients to turn a simple side dish into a memorable one. This Indian-inspired recipe is rich with the flavors of curry and raisins and excellent with grilled shrimp, steak, and chicken or as a bed for meat and vegetable stews.

• •

Combine the broth, curry powder, and cumin in a medium saucepan and bring to a boil. Add the rice and lemon zest, cover, and remove from the heat. Let stand until the liquid is absorbed, about 5 minutes. Fluff with a fork, stir in the raisins, and season to taste with salt and pepper.

2 cups reduced-sodium vegetable or chicken broth

1 teaspoon curry powder

1 teaspoon ground cumin

2 cups quick-cooking white rice

1 teaspoon finely grated lemon zest

½ cup golden raisins

Salt and freshly ground black pepper

GOOD HEALTH note:

Raisins are an antioxidant powerhouse, stimulating the body to burn up its own cholesterol.

TIME SAVER tip:

Save time and cook the whole dish in the microwave for 4 minutes on HIGH instead of on the stove.

RICE PILAF WITH TOMATOES AND OLIVES

Total Time: 10 to 12 minutes
PREP TIME: 5–7 MINUTES
ACTIVE COOKING TIME: 5 MINUTES

SERVES 4

Sure, you could buy a rice pilaf "kit" at the grocery store. But then who controls the ingredients? I like to spruce up quick-cooking rice with my own ideas! In this case, I add diced tomatoes and oil-cured olives for a sensational Italian twist. No tomatoes or olives? Add roasted red peppers and capers. For added flavor, cook the rice in chicken or vegetable broth instead of water.

● ●

Cook the rice according to the package directions.

Meanwhile, heat the oil in a large skillet over medium heat. Add the onion and garlic and cook, stirring, until softened, about 2 minutes. Add the oregano and cook, stirring, until fragrant, about 1 minute. Add the tomatoes and olives and cook until the liquid reduces, about 1 minute. Add the rice and cook 1 minute to heat through, stirring frequently. Remove from the heat and stir in the parsley. Season to taste with salt and pepper.

2 cups quick-cooking white rice

2 teaspoons olive oil

¼ cup chopped onion

2 cloves garlic, minced

1 teaspoon dried oregano

One 14-ounce can petite-cut diced tomatoes, drained

¼ cup diced oil-cured black olives

2 tablespoons chopped fresh parsley

Salt and freshly ground black pepper

STORAGE SAVVY:

You can make the pilaf up to 3 days in advance and refrigerate until ready to serve. Reheat in the microwave for 3 minutes on HIGH. You can also double the recipe and freeze for up to 3 months; thaw in the refrigerator or microwave for a few minutes on LOW and then reheat for 1 to 2 minutes on HIGH.

QUICK FIX IT YOUR WAY:

Save leftover rice from Chinese take-out and freeze it in plastic bags. Thaw the rice in the microwave for 2 to 3 minutes on LOW and turn it into this pilaf (simply combine everything together and heat in the microwave until hot).

CURRIED COUSCOUS
WITH PEAS AND CARROTS

Total Time: 7 minutes
PREP TIME: 2 MINUTES
WALK-AWAY TIME: 5 MINUTES

SERVES 4

Couscous and Quick Fix go hand in hand. What's better than a tender grain that's ready in 5 minutes? How about one jazzed up with curry and the bright color and flavor of peas and carrots? Plus, there's no need to thaw the frozen vegetables—use whatever fresh or frozen vegetables you have on hand.

● ●

Combine the broth and curry in a small saucepan and bring to a boil. Add the couscous and peas and carrots and stir to combine. Remove from the heat, cover, and let stand until the liquid is absorbed, about 5 minutes.

Fluff the couscous with a fork and fold in the cilantro. Season to taste with salt and pepper and serve.

"WHAT'S BETTER THAN A TENDER GRAIN that's ready in 5 minutes?"

- 1¼ cups reduced-sodium chicken broth or water
- 1 teaspoon curry powder
- 1 cup couscous
- 1½ cups mixed frozen peas and carrots
- 2 tablespoons chopped fresh cilantro
- Salt and freshly ground black pepper

STORAGE SAVVY:

The next time you make couscous, make a double batch and freeze leftovers for up to 3 months. When ready to make this side dish, thaw the couscous in the microwave for about 2 minutes on LOW, then reheat it with the peas and carrots. Add the cilantro just before serving.

ORZO SALAD WITH GIARDINIERA AND SUN-DRIED TOMATO VINAIGRETTE

Total Time: 10 to 15 minutes
PREP TIME: 10–15 MINUTES

1½ cups orzo or any small pasta

1 cup chopped oil-packed sun-dried tomatoes

½ cup reduced-sodium chicken or vegetable broth

1 tablespoon red wine vinegar

2 cloves garlic, chopped

1 teaspoon dried oregano

2 cups giardiniera garden vegetable mix, drained

¼ cup chopped fresh basil

Salt and freshly ground black pepper

SERVES 4

Giardiniera is an Italian mix of garden vegetables, sold in bottles in the pickle aisle. I love to use it not only for its magnificent flavor and color, but its convenience—not having to slice up all those vegetables individually cuts down on prep time dramatically. There's also a "hot" version, if you're so inclined.

• •

Cook the pasta according to the package directions. Drain and transfer to a large bowl.

Meanwhile, in a blender or food processor, combine the tomatoes, broth, vinegar, garlic, and oregano and process until smooth. Add this to the pasta and toss to combine. Stir in the giardiniera and basil and toss to combine. Season to taste with salt and pepper. Serve warm, at room temperature, or chilled.

QUICK FIX IT YOUR WAY:

If you've got rice or leftover pasta sitting in your freezer, pull it out, thaw it in the microwave for a few minutes on LOW, and use it in this salad. This amazing side dish will be ready in less than 5 minutes.

STORAGE SAVVY:

You can make this up to 3 days in advance and refrigerate until ready to serve. For room temperature salad, pull it out of the refrigerator 30 minutes before serving. For a warm salad, reheat it in the microwave for 2 to 3 minutes on HIGH.

PARMESAN-HERB-DUSTED POLENTA ROUNDS

Total Time: 13 to 15 minutes
PREP TIME: 5 MINUTES
WALK-AWAY TIME: 8-10 MINUTES

SERVES 6 TO 8

Precooked polenta is a must-have for the Quick Cook. It's sold in tubes near the rice and grain products in the grocery store. Sometimes you can find it in the refrigerated section of the produce aisle. This recipe calls for plain polenta, but feel free to try one of the seasoned varieties. To quickly turn this into a main dish, top the polenta with a thick stew or chili. I sometimes serve these with my Chicken Cacciatore with Wild Mushrooms (page 112) so they can help mop up the fabulous sauce!

• •

Preheat the oven to 450°F. Coat a large baking sheet with cooking spray.

Arrange the polenta rounds on the sheet and spray them with cooking spray. Season with salt and pepper.

In a small bowl, combine the Parmesan and parsley and sprinkle this mixture evenly over the polenta rounds. Bake until golden brown, 8 to 10 minutes.

Olive oil cooking spray

One 16-ounce tube prepared polenta, sliced crosswise into ½-inch-thick rounds

Salt and freshly ground black pepper

½ cup grated Parmesan cheese, preferably freshly grated

2 tablespoons chopped fresh parsley

GOOD HEALTH note:

Polenta is made from yellow cornmeal, which is an excellent source of iron and a good source of calcium.

6

There's always time for DESSERT:
Sweets in a hurry

"QUICK FIX DESSERTS TO THE RESCUE! RECIPES YOUR PALATE WILL SAVOR."

Ever feel like skipping dinner and going straight to dessert? I do most every night. But since dessert recipes typically take time to prepare, sweets during the week often mean store-bought cookies, ice cream, and leftover Halloween candy. I don't know about you, but when I'm reaching for sweets, a cookie shaped like SpongeBob SquarePants isn't going to cut it. Of course, cookies and candy don't offer much in the way of nutrition. They're yummy, but a dessert with fruit would be just as satisfying (if not more so) and offer some valuable nutrients. Quick Fix desserts to the rescue! I've developed dessert recipes that your palate will savor while your body feasts on powerful vitamins, minerals, and antioxidants.

CHARRED PEACHES WITH LEMON SORBET AND GRANOLA

Total Time: 10 minutes
PREP TIME: 5 MINUTES
ACTIVE COOKING TIME: 5 MINUTES

SERVES 4

Can't find good peaches? Not a problem, nectarines and plums work, too! Pick a fruit and start broiling! If you're grilling, throw your fruit right on the grill after you're finished cooking the main course.

● ●

Preheat the broiler.

In a small bowl, whisk together the maple syrup, vanilla, and cinnamon. Place the peach halves, flesh side up, on a baking sheet. Brush the maple mixture over the flesh and broil until golden brown and the syrup is bubbly, about 5 minutes.

Transfer the peaches to individual dessert dishes. Spoon the sorbet over each peach half, sprinkle the granola over the top, and serve.

2 tablespoons maple syrup

1 teaspoon vanilla extract

¼ teaspoon ground cinnamon

2 peaches or nectarines, cut in half and pitted

1 cup lemon sorbet

1 cup low-fat granola (with or without raisins)

CHOCOLATE-DUNKED BANANAS WITH PEANUTS

Total Time: 20 minutes
PREP TIME: **10 MINUTES**
WALK-AWAY TIME: **10 MINUTES**

SERVES 4

My mom always had frozen chocolate-covered bananas in the freezer. Frozen bananas (with or without the chocolate) make a nice snack anytime, so make a big batch and keep them in the freezer. Kids love the fact that there's a stick inside—it's more like a Popsicle® or ice cream treat!

● ●

Place the chocolate morsels in a large, microwave-safe bowl and cover the bowl with plastic wrap. Microwave on HIGH for 3 to 5 minutes, until the chocolate is melted, stirring every 2 minutes.

Insert a Popsicle stick into one end of each banana and dunk the bananas in the melted chocolate, turning to coat all sides (if necessary, use a pastry brush to brush the chocolate onto the banana). Sprinkle the peanuts evenly over each banana.

Place the bananas on wax paper set on a plate and refrigerate until the chocolate hardens, about 10 minutes (or speed things up by placing the bananas in the freezer!)

1 cup semisweet chocolate morsels

4 medium-size firm bananas, peeled and ends trimmed

4 Popsicle sticks (sold in the baking or ice cream section of the grocery store)

1 cup chopped salted dry-roasted peanuts

STORAGE SAVVY:

Store the bananas in the freezer, where they'll keep for up to 3 months. Wrap them in plastic wrap, then store in freezer bags. Or line them up in a plastic container. Eat the bananas frozen or set them out at room temperature for about 30 minutes before serving to soften a bit.

BROWN SUGAR–GLAZED PINEAPPLE WITH TOASTED COCONUT

Total Time: 15 minutes
PREP TIME: 5 MINUTES
WALK-AWAY TIME: 10 MINUTES

SERVES 4

There are few things better than a perfectly ripe pineapple. The problem is, sometimes it's hard to find a perfect one. This recipe is ideal whether you've found the pot-of-gold pineapple or not. Brushed with brown sugar and then topped with coconut, it's an excellent way to end a meal. It's also amazing with a scoop of vanilla ice cream.

• •

Preheat the oven to 375°F. Coat a large baking sheet with cooking spray.

Arrange the pineapple slices on the sheet. In a small bowl, whisk together the brown sugar and water until the sugar dissolves. Brush the mixture all over the pineapple rings. Sprinkle the coconut over the tops. Bake until the coconut is golden brown and the pineapple tender, about 10 minutes. Serve warm.

Cooking spray

12 pineapple rings (fresh or canned in juice)

¼ cup firmly packed light brown sugar

2 teaspoons hot water

½ cup sweetened shredded coconut

TIME SAVER tip:

Buy pineapple already cored and peeled from the refrigerated section of the produce aisle. Cut the pineapple crosswise into 1-inch-thick slices if it's not already sliced.

MANDARIN NAPOLEONS WITH SUGARED WONTON WRAPPERS

Total Time: 15 to 20 minutes
PREP TIME: 10–15 MINUTES
WALK-AWAY TIME: 5 MINUTES

SERVES 4

Don't limit wonton wrappers to savory dishes. In this dish, I sweeten them with sugar and then toast until golden brown. They make the perfect, sturdy layers for mandarin orange–filled Napoleons.

● ●

Preheat the oven to 400°F. Coat a large baking sheet with cooking spray.

Arrange the wonton wrappers on the sheet and spray them with cooking spray. Sprinkle them evenly with the granulated sugar, then bake until golden brown, about 5 minutes.

Remove from the oven and arrange four of the wontons on a serving platter or individual dessert dishes. Top each one with 2 tablespoons of the whipped topping and then one-eighth of the mandarin sections. Top each with a second wonton wrapper. Repeat the layers (whipped topping, mandarin oranges, wonton wrapper). Sift the confectioners' sugar over the top layer and serve.

Cooking spray

12 wonton wrappers (see Dollar Saver Tip on page 73)

2 tablespoons granulated sugar

1 cup whipped nondairy dessert topping or whipped cream

One 11-ounce can mandarin oranges in light syrup, drained

1 tablespoon confectioners' sugar

QUICK FIX IT YOUR WAY:

The sugared wonton wrappers can be prepared up to 1 week in advance. Store them in airtight containers or plastic bags at room temperature. Assemble the dessert no more than 1 hour before serving. When assembling ahead, refrigerate until ready to serve.

APRICOT PUFF-PASTRY TWISTS

Total Time: 20 minutes
PREP TIME: **10 MINUTES**
WALK-AWAY TIME: **10 MINUTES**

SERVES 4 TO 6 (ABOUT 3 TWISTS PER SERVING)

Next time you make your way down the freezer aisle, grab a box of puff pastry. You won't believe how simple it can be to whip up a sensational and impressive dessert with just two ingredients. Use any filling you want, not just apricot preserves (orange marmalade, raspberry preserves, apple butter, and Nutella® would all be fantastic).

• •

Preheat the oven to 400°F.

Using a rolling pin, roll out the puff pastry into a rectangle about 14 x 17 inches. Spread the preserves over one-half of the dough to within ¼ inch of the edges. Fold the dough in half over the preserves, like a book. Pop the "book" in the freezer for a few minutes for easy cutting.

Using a sharp knife or pizza wheel, cut the dough crosswise into ½-inch-thick ribbons. Take each ribbon by the ends and twist into a corkscrew. Arrange the corkscrews on a large baking sheet and press down the ends against the sheet (this prevents them from untwisting during baking). Bake until puffed up and golden brown, about 10 minutes. These twists are super warm or cold.

1 sheet frozen puff pastry, thawed according to package directions

½ cup apricot preserves

STORAGE SAVVY:

Be prepared for drop-in guests: make a big batch for leftovers. Store them in plastic bags at room temperature for up to 1 week or in freezer bags in the freezer for up to 3 months. Thaw at room temperature before serving. If desired, you can recrisp them in a preheated 350°F oven for 10 minutes.

GOOD HEALTH note:

Apricots are one of the best food sources of vitamin A, a powerful antioxidant that's essential for healthy skin and good vision.

PEACH-CHERRY GALETTE

Total Time: 30 minutes
PREP TIME: 10 MINUTES
WALK-AWAY TIME: 20 MINUTES

SERVES 4 TO 6

Galette is a fancy word for a pie cooked without a pie pan. It's simply a flat crust of pastry covered with toppings. Think of it as a dessert pizza that makes your life much easier. You simply top a pre-made pie crust with ingredients, fold over the edges, and bake until golden. It's simple and sensational. The cooking time may appear long for a dessert (in a Quick Fix world), but you can assemble the galette in advance and bake it while you're enjoying dinner.

• •

Preheat the oven to 375°F.

Unroll the pie crust on a large baking sheet. Place the peach slices in the center of the crust, leaving a 2-inch border around the edge. Sprinkle the cherries over the peaches, then top with the sugar and cinnamon. Pull up the sides of the crust slightly and roll over toward the center, covering the filling by 1 to 2 inches. Bake until the crust is golden brown, about 20 minutes. Serve warm or at room temperature.

One 9-inch refrigerated pie crust

3 large ripe peaches, peeled, pitted, and thinly sliced or an equal amount of frozen, thawed sliced peaches

⅓ cup dried sweet cherries (sold in the produce aisle)

2 tablespoons sugar

½ teaspoon ground cinnamon

VARIATIONS:

If you can't find dried cherries, substitute dried blueberries or dried sweetened cranberries. You can also substitute canned sliced peaches for fresh if desired (you will need about 2 cups).

PLUM PIZZA WITH RICOTTA, APRICOT PRESERVES, AND PINE NUTS

Total Time: 20 to 22 minutes
PREP TIME: 10 MINUTES
WALK-AWAY TIME: 10–12 MINUTES

SERVES 4 TO 6

This dessert pizza layers together sweetened ricotta cheese, fresh plum slices, apricot preserves, and toasted pine nuts. It's an excellent choice for entertaining.

● ●

Preheat the oven to 375°F.

Unroll the pie crust on a large baking sheet.

In a small bowl, combine the ricotta and confectioners' sugar, then spread all over the pie crust to within ¼ inch of the edge. Top with the plum slices, making slightly overlapping rows. Warm the apricot preserves in the microwave on HIGH for 30 seconds, then brush over the plum slices. Sprinkle the pine nuts over the top. Bake until the crust and pine nuts are golden brown, 10 to 12 minutes. Serve warm or at room temperature.

One 9-inch refrigerated pie crust

½ cup part-skim ricotta cheese

2 tablespoons confectioners' sugar

4 ripe plums, pitted and thinly sliced

⅔ cup apricot preserves

¼ cup pine nuts

GOOD HEALTH note:

Plums are an excellent source of vitamins A and C, calcium, magnesium, iron, potassium, and fiber. As is true of all nuts, pine nuts are a good source of heart-friendly unsaturated fats.

VARIATION:

Can't find ripe plums? Substitute canned peaches or pears or fresh nectarines and slice as directed. You will need an 11- to 15-ounce can or 2 to 3 nectarines.

TOASTED ANGEL FOOD CAKE WITH FUDGE-RASPBERRY SAUCE

Total Time: 10 minutes
PREP TIME: 3 MINUTES
ACTIVE COOKING TIME: 7 MINUTES

Cooking spray

½ prepared angel food cake, cut into 1-inch cubes

1 cup store-bought chocolate fudge sauce

1 cup frozen raspberries (not in syrup; don't bother to thaw)

SERVES 4

Angel food cake is amazing—so light and airy! Even better? You can buy it premade from the grocery store. I like to cut the cake into cubes and toast it to bring out even more sweetness. I also worship chocolate, so drizzling it over the cake is right up my alley!

● ●

Preheat the oven to 400°F. Coat a large baking sheet with cooking spray.

Arrange the angel food cake cubes on the sheet and bake until golden brown, 5 to 7 minutes.

Meanwhile, combine the fudge sauce and raspberries in a small saucepan and set over medium heat. Bring to a simmer and cook until the raspberries break down and the sauce thickens, about 5 minutes.

Place the angel food cake cubes on dessert plates, cover with the chocolate sauce, and serve.

POUND CAKE WITH ALMOND CREAM AND TOASTED ALMONDS

Total Time: 8 to 10 minutes
PREP TIME: 5–7 MINUTES
ACTIVE COOKING TIME: 3 MINUTES

SERVES 4

Pound cake is one of those decadent desserts we'd probably all enjoy more often if we didn't have to make it ourselves. The good news is, delicious pound cakes are available at the grocery store. Add a few ingredients and you can turn a simple slice of butter, flour, and sugar into an amazing layer of cake, almond- and vanilla-spiked whipped topping, and crunchy toasted almonds.

• •

Place the almonds in a small dry skillet over medium heat and toast until golden brown, about 3 minutes, shaking the pan frequently to prevent burning. Remove from the heat and set aside.

Arrange the pound cake on individual plates. Mix together the whipped topping and extracts, then spoon over the pound cake. Top with the toasted almonds just before serving.

¼ cup slivered almonds

Four 1-inch-thick slices pound cake

1 cup light whipped nondairy dessert topping

½ teaspoon almond extract

½ teaspoon vanilla extract

GOOD HEALTH note:

You can also make this dish with fat-free pound cake, sold right next to the regular pound cake!

FROZEN LIME PIE

Total Time: 35 minutes
PREP TIME: 5 MINUTES
WALK-AWAY TIME: 30 MINUTES

SERVES 6 TO 8

My grandmother made a version of this when she lived in the Florida Keys. She was lucky enough to have fresh Key lime juice on hand, so if you can get your hands on that, substitute it for regular lime juice.

• •

In a medium bowl, combine the whipped topping, condensed milk, and lime juice until blended and smooth. Spoon the mixture into the crust and smooth the surface. Freeze until firm, about 30 minutes.

One 8-ounce tub frozen nondairy whipped topping, thawed slightly

One 14-ounce can sweetened condensed milk (regular or fat-free)

½ cup fresh lime juice

One 6-ounce prepared graham cracker pie crust

QUICK FIX IT YOUR WAY:

Make the pie in advance and freeze (up to 3 months) until ready to splurge!

BANANA-RASPBERRY BREAD

Total Time: 70 to 85 minutes
PREP TIME: 10–15 MINUTES
WALK-AWAY TIME: 1 HOUR

SERVES 8

This is my husband's very favorite recipe, hands down. In fact, every time he takes a long trip overseas, I make sure there's a fresh batch of banana bread waiting for him when he gets home. At first it was just plain banana bread, but since he loves raspberries so much (he'll eat 10 pints in one sitting if you let him), I decided to weave in the berries. If you like strawberries or blueberries better, please substitute!

● ●

Preheat the oven to 350°F. Coat an 8-inch loaf pan with cooking spray.

In a medium bowl, combine the flour, sugar, baking powder, baking soda, and salt, mixing well with a fork.

In a large bowl, peel, then mash the bananas until mushy (I use a potato masher). Add the milk, egg, and vanilla and mix until well blended.

Add the dry ingredients to the banana mixture and mix until just blended. Fold in the raspberries (don't overstir, or they'll start to break up and turn the batter pink). Pour the batter into the prepared pan.

Bake until a knife or wooden toothpick inserted near the center comes out almost clean (little bits clinging to the knife or pick mean the bread's still moist), about 1 hour. Let cool in the pan, set on a wire rack, for 10 minutes. Remove the bread from the pan and let cool completely before slicing.

Cooking spray

2 cups all-purpose flour

¾ cup sugar

2 teaspoons baking powder

½ teaspoon baking soda

½ teaspoon salt

4 large overripe bananas

¼ cup nonfat or low-fat milk

1 large egg

1 teaspoon vanilla extract

1 cup fresh or frozen raspberries (not in syrup; don't bother to thaw)

STORAGE SAVVY:

This bread freezes exceptionally well. When I make it, I often make a double batch and freeze one loaf. To do that, double the recipe and pour the batter into two loaf pans. Once cool, wrap one loaf in plastic wrap, then in aluminum foil and freeze for up to 3 months. Thaw completely at room temperature before slicing.

TIME SAVER tip:

When making ahead, mix the wet ingredients and dry ingredients separately. The wet ingredients can be stored in the refrigerator up to 2 days, the dry indefinitely. When ready to bake, mix them together, fold in the raspberries, then bake as directed.

PUDDING-FILLED SPONGE CAKES WITH MIXED BERRIES

Total Time: 10 minutes
PREP TIME: **10 MINUTES**

2 cups fresh berries (any combination of blueberries, raspberries, blackberries, and/or hulled and sliced strawberries)

1 tablespoon fresh lemon juice

2 teaspoons sugar

4 mini sponge cakes

1 cup prepared vanilla pudding (sold in six-pack cups in the pudding aisle or refrigerated section of the grocery store)

Fresh mint leaves (optional)

SERVES 4

Ever wondered what to do with those mini sponge cakes found at the supermarket? They're sold in the produce department for a reason—that's the produce guy's way of saying, "Ever thought about filling these with fruit?" Spoon them full of pudding, ice cream, whipped cream, or yogurt, then top with fresh fruit. It's simple, fast, delicious, and gorgeous!

• •

In a medium bowl, combine the berries, lemon juice, and sugar and toss to combine.

Arrange the sponge cakes on a serving platter or individual plates. Fill each cake with ¼ cup of the pudding, then top with the sugar-coated berries. Garnish with fresh mint, if desired.

GOOD HEALTH note:

Blue and red fruits such as berries are loaded with antioxidants and, thanks to the seeds, they're packed with fiber. One cup of raspberries contains 8 grams of fiber, putting you well on your way to the recommended daily allotment of 25 to 30 grams.

STORAGE SAVVY:

Since sponge cakes rapidly absorb moisture from other ingredients, assemble the dessert no more than 1 hour before serving. When assembling ahead, refrigerate until ready to serve.

"LEFTOVER RICE" PUDDING WITH CINNAMON AND RAISINS

Total Time: 15 minutes
PREP TIME: 5 MINUTES
ACTIVE COOKING TIME: 10 MINUTES

SERVES 4

Rice pudding is so warm and soothing. What's not wonderful is slaving over a hot stove to get to it! This Quick Fix version is the perfect recipe for leftover cooked rice. In fact, it's so delicious, it's worth making extra rice just for the dessert.

• •

In a medium saucepan, stir together the milk and cream cheese until blended and smooth. Add the remaining ingredients and set over medium heat. Bring to a simmer, then continue to simmer until the liquid reduces and the mixture thickens, about 10 minutes, stirring frequently. Serve the pudding warm, at room temperature, or chilled—every way is delicious!

"RICE PUDDING IS SO WARM
and soothing."

- ⅔ cup low-fat milk
- ½ of an 8-ounce package reduced-fat cream cheese
- 2 cups leftover cooked rice (regular or quick-cooking)
- ½ cup dark raisins
- ¼ cup sugar
- 1 teaspoon ground cinnamon
- 1 teaspoon vanilla extract

QUICK FIX IT YOUR WAY:

Store leftover rice in freezer bags or plastic containers in the freezer for up to 3 months so you can make this dessert any time. There's no need to thaw the rice before cooking.

MIXED PUDDING PARFAITS WITH BANANA CHIPS AND CHOCOLATE CURLS

Total Time: 10 minutes
PREP TIME: 10 MINUTES

4 cups pudding, any combination of vanilla, chocolate, banana, and/or butterscotch

½ cup banana chips

1 semisweet chocolate bar

SERVES 4

Pick your favorite pudding flavors and layer them into a glass. Sure, it seems ridiculously easy, but it truly makes an amazing presentation. Topping the pudding with crunchy banana chips and decorative chocolate curls doesn't hurt either!

● ●

Spoon the pudding into four tall parfait glasses, alternating flavors and colors. Top with the banana chips. Using a vegetable peeler, scrape the chocolate bar, making chocolate curls. Sprinkle the curls over the parfaits and serve.

VARIATION:

For an instant "gross" dessert or treat for kids (especially around Halloween), spoon chocolate pudding into small bowls and then insert gummy worms into the pudding, just under the surface. Top the pudding with crushed chocolate cookies to make dirt. Serve with a spoon and let the fun begin!

QUICK FIX IT YOUR WAY:

You can assemble this dessert up to 1 day before serving. Cover glasses with plastic wrap and refrigerate until ready to serve.

CHERRY PARFAITS
WITH CANDIED NUTS

Total Time: 10 minutes
PREP TIME: 10 MINUTES

SERVES 4

I use cherry pie filling for this dessert because, quite frankly, I never use the stuff to make a pie! But it's so wonderful and convenient that I felt compelled to find a use for it! Parfaits aren't just easy, they're fun to look at. If you're looking for an arts-and-craft project for your kids, look no further: they love layering the colors into tall glasses. You can also substitute blueberry or apple pie filling, canned pumpkin, or regular pudding.

• •

Spoon 2 tablespoons of the pie filling into each of four tall glasses. Top each with 2 tablespoons frozen yogurt. Repeat with the remaining pie filling, then the remaining yogurt. Spoon whipped topping evenly among the glasses, then sprinkle with the nuts.

1 cup canned cherry pie filling (look for it in the baking section of the supermarket)

1 cup vanilla frozen yogurt or light ice cream, softened slightly

1 cup nondairy whipped topping or whipped cream

½ cup candied nuts (pecans, walnuts, peanuts)

QUICK FIX IT YOUR WAY:

You can assemble this dessert (everything but the nuts on top) up to 3 days in advance and store upright in the freezer (cover the tops of the glasses with plastic wrap, then aluminum foil). Pull the glasses from the freezer a few minutes before serving, then top with the nuts.

GOOD HEALTH note:

Frozen yogurt and light ice cream dish up about 120 to 140 calories and 4 grams of fat per ½ cup serving. The same amount of regular ice cream has 184 calories and 12 grams of fat.

CHOCOLATE FROZEN YOGURT WITH CHUNKY ROCKY ROAD SAUCE

Total Time: 5 minutes
PREP TIME: 5 MINUTES

SERVES 4

You probably already have these ingredients in your pantry. I'm not trying to reinvent the wheel, just dessert, and sometimes that means taking what you have and mixing it all together! The sauce is also phenomenal spooned over sliced bananas.

• •

In a medium microwave-safe bowl, combine the chocolate syrup and peanut butter. Cover with plastic wrap and microwave on HIGH for 30 seconds, until warm. Stir in the marshmallows and raisins.

Spoon the frozen yogurt into individual dessert bowls, then spoon the rocky road sauce over the top and serve.

½ cup chocolate syrup or chocolate fudge sauce

¼ cup chunky peanut butter

¼ cup mini marshmallows

¼ cup yogurt-covered raisins

2 cups chocolate frozen yogurt or chocolate ice cream

FROZEN YOGURT WITH CINNAMON-SPIKED BLUEBERRY SAUCE

Total Time: 10 minutes
PREP TIME: 5 MINUTES
ACTIVE COOKING TIME: 5 MINUTES

SERVES 4

Use this sauce recipe as a base for all future sauce creations. You can make it with any berry variety or diced fruit, such as peaches, nectarines, plums, pears, and even citrus. Using confectioners' sugar does double duty; it adds sweetness while helping to thicken the sauce. Garnish with fresh mint sprigs when you want to impress someone.

• •

One 10-ounce bag frozen blueberries

1 tablespoon confectioners' sugar

1 teaspoon ground cinnamon

2 cups vanilla frozen yogurt

Combine the blueberries, confectioners' sugar, and cinnamon in a medium saucepan, set over medium heat, bring to a simmer, and simmer until the sauce thickens, about 5 minutes.

Spoon the frozen yogurt into dessert bowls and top with the blueberry sauce.

STORAGE SAVVY:

This sauce can be made up to 3 days in advance and refrigerated until ready to use. Reheat the sauce in the microwave for 2 minutes on HIGH. You can also make a double batch and freeze leftovers in freezer bags or plastic containers. Thaw and reheat in the microwave or in a medium-size saucepan over medium heat.

PEANUT BUTTER AND JELLY SWIRLED ICE CREAM WITH VANILLA WAFER COOKIES

SERVES 4

Peanut butter and jelly infused into ice cream? Yup, and it's a slam dunk! Use your favorite preserves (raspberry, blackberry, orange marmalade) instead of grape, if desired.

• •

Combine the ice cream, jelly, and peanut butter in a large bowl. Gently stir to combine, leaving streaks of jelly and peanut butter throughout the ice cream. Spoon into dessert bowls and garnish with wafer cookies.

2 cups low-fat vanilla ice cream, softened

¼ cup grape jelly or jam or strawberry preserves

¼ cup smooth peanut butter

8 vanilla wafer cookies

PREP POINTER:

Soften the ice cream in the microwave on 50% power for 15 to 30 seconds.

GOOD HEALTH note:

Opt for light or low-fat ice cream and, per ½ cup serving, dodge about 75 calories, 9 grams of fat, and 6 grams of artery-jamming saturated fat.

ROOT BEER FLOATS
WITH CHOCOLATE-STUFFED
PEANUT BUTTER COOKIES

Total Time: 30 to 45 minutes
PREP TIME: 20–30 MINUTES
COOLING TIME FOR
COOKIES: 10–15 MINUTES

SERVES 4

I grew up drinking root beer floats. I can still remember standing at the counter (way above my head) and watching as the ice cream clunked into a tall glass, followed quickly by root beer and a tall straw! For fun (and your enjoyment), I've added an amazing cookie to serve alongside, ready in just minutes thanks to refrigerated cookie dough. Feel free to substitute sugar cookie dough or chocolate chip cookie dough if desired.

● ●

Prepare the cookies according to package directions. Cool.

Spread icing on one cookie (1 to 2 teaspoons per cookie), then top with a second cookie to make a sandwich.

To make root beer floats, spoon ½ cup ice cream into four tall glasses. Pour root beer over the ice cream and serve with cookie sandwiches on the side.

1 package refrigerated peanut butter cookie dough

1 container chocolate icing

2 cups ice cream (any flavor), slightly softened

4 cups root beer

QUICK FIX IT YOUR WAY:

Bake the cookies in advance and assemble them when you're ready to indulge.

SHERBET-STUFFED ORANGES WITH CARAMEL-PECAN SAUCE

Total Time: 10 minutes
PREP TIME: **10 MINUTES**

SERVES 4

Why bother stuffing oranges with sherbet? Because you can! The outcome is amazing.

• •

In a small saucepan, combine the caramel sauce and pecans, set over medium heat, bring to a simmer, and let simmer for 5 minutes.

Meanwhile, using a spoon, remove the orange sections from the orange halves, leaving about ¼ inch of flesh with the skin and allowing room for the sherbet. Reserve the orange sections.

Spoon the sherbet into the hollowed-out orange halves. Place them on dessert dishes, arrange the orange sections alongside, and serve drizzled with the caramel-pecan sauce.

¾ cup store-bought caramel sauce

¼ cup chopped pecans

4 navel oranges, cut in half

2 cups orange or rainbow sherbet

QUICK FIX IT YOUR WAY:

You can assemble the oranges and freeze them up to 1 week before serving. Spoon the warm caramel-pecan sauce over the oranges just before serving.

INDEX